INTERNATIONAL SOCIALISM ★

A quarterly journal of socialist theory

Autumn 1994
Contents

Editorial

Chris Harman	*The prophet and the proletariat*	3
Kieran Allen	*What is changing in Ireland?*	65
Mike Haynes	*The wrong road on Russia*	105
Rob Ferguson	*Hero and villain?*	115
Jane Elderton	*Suffragette style*	123
Chris Nineham	*Two faces of modernism*	133
Mike Hobart, Dave Harker and Matt Kelly	*Three replies to 'Jazz—a people's music?'*	141
Charlie Kimber	*Bookwatch: South Africa —the struggle continues*	159

Issue 64 of INTERNATIONAL SOCIALISM, quarterly journal of the Socialist Workers Party (Britain)

Published September 1994
Copyright © International Socialism
Distribution/subscriptions: International Socialism,
PO Box 82, London E3.
American distribution: B de Boer, 113 East Center St, Nutley, New Jersey 07110.
Subscriptions and back copies: PO Box 16085, Chicago Illinois 60616
Editorial and production: 071-538 5821/071-538 0538
Sales and subscriptions: 071-538 5821
American sales: 312 666 7337

ISBN 1898877009

Printed by BPCC Wheatons Ltd, Exeter, England
Typeset by East End Offset, London E3

Cover design by Ian Goodyer

For details of back copies see the end pages of this book

Subscription rates for one year (four issues) are:

Britain and overseas (surface):	individual	£14.00 ($30)
	institutional	£25.00
Air speeded supplement:	North America	nil
	Europe/South America	£2.00
	elsewhere	£4.00

Note to contributors

The deadline for articles intended for issue 66 of *International Socialism* is 1 December 1994

All contributions should be double-spaced with wide margins. Please submit two copies. If you write your contribution using a computer, please also supply a disk, together with details of the computer and programme used.

A quarterly journal of socialist theory

ISLAMIC FUNDAMENTALISM is rapidly emerging as the ideology that Western politicians and media pundits most like to hate. The kind of abuse once reserved for 'Communism' is now directed at the Islamic movements which threaten to destabilise key areas of Western influence in the Middle East and beyond. But the campaign against Islamism has found allies on the left among those fearful that it threatens an irrationalist, even fascist, backlash.

Chris Harman charts a careful course through the contradictions of Islamism, revealing its class roots and arguing that when the Islamists are in opposition the socialist attitude should be 'with the state never, with Islamism sometimes'. He goes on to show in which circumstances Islamism plays a reactionary role and in which circumstances the Islamists challenge the establishment.

IRISH SOCIETY is at a fateful juncture, both North and South of the border. Kieran Allen looks at the break up of traditional institutions and the rise of the class struggle in the South and at the impasse which faces the British, the Unionists and the Republicans in the North. He claims that socialists are better placed than at any time in the last 25 years.

RUSSIAN HISTORY and the contemporary crisis of Russian society are the subject of two of this issue's book reviews—Rob Ferguson looks at Donny Gluckstein's life of Bukharin and Mike Haynes reviews *What About the Workers?*, an attempt to give a socialist perspective on the transition to the market. Other reviews look at Sylvia Pankhurst's life and *Bookwatch* examines South Africa's history of struggle.

CULTURAL DEBATE has been sparked by two recent articles. Charlie Hore's 'Jazz—a People's Music?', published in *International Socialism 61*, has prompted three replies while Gareth Jenkins's review of a history of the 20th century novel in *International Socialism 62* has drawn a defence of modernism from Chris Nineham.

Editor: John Rees. Assistant Editors: Alex Callinicos, Sue Clegg, Chris Harman, John Molyneux, Lindsey German, Ann Rogers, Colin Sparks, Mike Gonzalez, Peter Morgan, Ruth Brown, Mike Haynes and Rob Hoveman.

The prophet and the proletariat

CHRIS HARMAN

The politics of the Middle East and beyond have been dominated by Islamist movements at least since the Iranian revolution of 1978-9. Variously described in the West as 'Islamic fundamentalism', 'Islamicism', 'integrism', 'political Islam' and 'Islamic revivalism', these movements stand for the 'regeneration' of society through a return to the original teachings of the prophet Mohammed. They have become a major force in Iran and the Sudan (where they still hold power), Egypt, Algeria and Tajikistan (where they are involved in bitter armed struggles against the state), Afghanistan (where rival Islamist movements have been waging war with each other since the collapse of the pro-Russian government), the occupied West Bank of the Jordan (where their militancy is challenging the old PLO hegemony over the Palestinian resistance), Pakistan (where they make up a significant portion of the opposition) and most recently Turkey (where the Welfare Party has taken control of Istanbul, Ankara and many other municipalities).

The rise of these movements has been an enormous shock to the liberal intelligentsia and has produced a wave of panic among people who believed that 'modernisation', coming on top of the victory of the anti-colonial struggles of the 1950s and 1960s, would inevitably lead to more enlightened and less repressive societies.[1]

Instead they witness the growth of forces which seem to look back to a more restricted society which forces women into purdah, uses terror to crush free thought and threatens the most barbaric punishments on those who defy its edicts. In countries like Egypt and Algeria the liberals are now lining up with the state, which has persecuted and imprisoned them in the past, in the war it is waging against Islamist parties.

But it has not only been liberals who have been thrown into disarray by the rise of Islamism. So too has the left. It has not known how to react to what it sees as an obscurantist doctrine, backed by traditionally reactionary forces, enjoying success among some of the poorest groups in society. Two opposed approaches have resulted.

The first has been to see Islamism as Reaction Incarnate, as a form of fascism. This was, for example, the position taken soon after the Iranian revolution by the then left wing academic Fred Halliday, who referred to the Iranian regime as 'Islam with a fascist face'.[2] It is an approach which much of the Iranian left came to adopt after the consolidation of the Khomeini regime in 1981-2. And it is accepted by much of the left in Egypt and Algeria today. Thus, for example, one Algerian revolutionary Marxist group has argued that the principles, ideology and political action of the Islamist FIS 'are similar to those of the National Front in France', and that it is 'a fascist current'.[3]

Such an analysis easily leads to the practical conclusion of building political alliances to stop the fascists at all costs. Thus Halliday concluded that the left in Iran made the mistake of not allying with the 'liberal bourgeoisie' in 1979-81 in opposition to 'the reactionary ideas and policies of Khomeini'.[4] In Egypt today the left, influenced by the mainstream communist tradition, effectively supports the state in its war against the Islamists.

The opposite approach has been to see the Islamist movements as 'progressive', 'anti-imperialist' movements of the oppressed. This was the position taken by the great bulk of the Iranian left in the first phase of the 1979 revolution, when the Soviet influenced Tudeh Party, the majority of the Fedayeen guerrilla organisation and the left Islamist People's Mojahedin all characterised the forces behind Khomeini as 'the progressive petty bourgeoisie'. The conclusion of this approach was that Khomeini deserved virtually uncritical support.[5] A quarter of a century before this the Egyptian Communists briefly took the same position towards the Muslim Brotherhood, calling on them to join in 'a common struggle against the "fascist dictatorship" of Nasser and his "Anglo-American props"'.[6]

I want to argue that both positions are wrong. They fail to locate the class character of modern Islamism or to see its relationship to capital, the state and imperialism.

Islam, religion and ideology

The confusion often starts with a confusion about the power of religion itself. Religious people see it as a historical force in its own right, whether for good or for evil. So too do most bourgeois anti-clerical and free thinkers. For them, fighting the influence of religious institutions and obscurantists ideas is in itself the way to human liberation.

But although religious institutions and ideas clearly play a role in history, this does not happen in separation from the rest of material reality. Religious institutions, with their layers of priests and teachers, arise in a certain society and interact with that society. They can only maintain themselves as society changes if they find some way of changing their own base of support. So, for instance, one of the world's major religious institutions, the Roman Catholic Church, originated in the late ancient world and survived by adapting itself first to feudal society for 1,000 years and then, with much effort, to the capitalist society that replaced feudalism, changing much of the content of its own teaching in the process. People have always been capable of giving different interpretations to the religious ideas they hold, depending on their own material situation, their relations with other people and the conflicts they get involved in. History is full of examples of people who profess nearly identical religious beliefs ending up on opposite sides in great social conflicts. This happened with the social convulsions which swept Europe during the great crisis of feudalism in the 16th and 17th century, when Luther, Calvin, Munzer and many other 'religious' leaders provided their followers with a new world view through a reinterpretation of biblical texts.

Islam is no different to any other religion in these respects. It arose in one context, among a trading community in the towns of 7th century Arabia, in the midst of a society still mainly organised on a tribal basis. It flourished within the succession of great empires carved out by some of those who accepted its doctrines. It persists today as the official ideology of numerous capitalist states (Saudi Arabia, Sudan, Pakistan, Iran etc), as well as the inspiration of many oppositional movements.

It has been able to survive in such different societies because it has been able to adapt to differing class interests. It has obtained the finance to build its mosques and employ its preachers in turn from the traders of Arabia, the bureaucrats, landowners and merchants of the great empires, and the industrialists of modern capitalism. But at the same time it has gained the allegiance of the mass of people by putting across a message offering consolation to the poor and oppressed. At every point its message has balanced between promising a degree of protection to the oppressed and providing the exploiting classes with protection against any revolutionary overthrow.

So Islam stresses that the rich have to pay a 2.5 percent Islamic tax (the *zakat*) for the relief of the poor, that rulers have to govern in a just way, that husbands must not mistreat their wives. But it also treats the expropriation of the rich by the poor as theft, insists disobedience to a 'just' government is a crime to be punished with all the vigour of the law and provides women with fewer rights than men within marriage, over inheritance, or over the children in the event of divorce. It appeals to the wealthy and the poor alike by offering regulation of oppression, both as a bulwark against still harsher oppression and as a bulwark against revolution. It is, like Christianity, Hinduism or Buddhism, both the heart of the heartless world and the opium of the people.

But no set of ideas can have such an appeal to different classes, especially when society is shaken by social convulsions, unless it is full of ambiguities. It has to be open to differing interpretations, even if these set its adherents at each other's throats.

This has been true of Islam virtually from its inception. After Mohammed's death in 632 AD, just two years after Islam had conquered Mecca, dissension broke out between the followers of Abu Bakr, who became the first Caliph (successor to Mohammed as leader of Islam), and Ali, husband of the prophet's daughter Fatima. Ali claimed that some of Abu Bakr's rulings were oppressive. Dissension grew until rival Muslim armies fought each other at the battle of the Camel resulting in 10,000 deaths. It was out of this dissension that the separation of the Sunni and Shia versions of Islam arose. This was but the first of many splits. Groups repeatedly arose who insisted that the oppressed were suffering at the hands of the godless and demanded a return to the original 'pure' Islam of the prophet's time. As Akbar S Ahmed says:

> *Throughout Islamic history, Muslim leaders would preach a move to the ideal... They gave expression to often vague ethnic, social or political movements... The basis was laid for the entire schismatic gamut in Islamic thought from the Shia, with its offshoots like the Ismailis, to more temporary movements... Muslim history is replete with Mahdis leading revolts against established authority and often dying for their efforts... Leaders have often been poor peasants and from deprived ethnic groups. Using Islamic idiom has reinforced their sense of deprivation and consolidated the movement.*[7]

But even mainstream Islam is not, in its popular forms at least, a homogenous set of beliefs. The spread of the religion to cover the whole region from the Atlantic coast of north west Africa to the Bay of Bengal involved the incorporation into Islamic society of peoples who fitted into Islam many of their old religious practices, even if these contradicted some of Islam's original tenets. So popular Islam often includes cults of local saints or of holy relics even though orthodox Islam regards such practices as sacrilegious idolatry. And *Sufi* brotherhoods flourish which, while not constituting a formal rival to mainstream Islam, put an emphasis on mystical and magical experience which many fundamentalists find objectionable.[8]

In such a situation, any call for a return to the practices of the prophet's time is not in reality about conserving the past but about reshaping people's behaviour into something quite new.

This has been true of Islamic revivalism over the last century. It arose as an attempt to come to terms with the material conquest and cultural transformation of Asia and North Africa by capitalist Europe. The revivalists argued this had only been possible because the original Islamic values had been corrupted by the worldly pursuits of the great medieval empires. Regeneration was only possible by reviving the founding spirit of Islam as expressed by the first four Caliphs (or, for Shiites, by Ali). It was in this spirit that Khomeini, for instance, could denounce virtually the whole history of Islam for the last 1,300 years:

> *Unfortunately, true Islam lasted for only a brief period after its inception. First the **Umayyids*** [the first Arab dynasty after Ali] *and then the **Abbasids*** [who conquered them in 750 AD] *inflicted all kinds of damage on Islam. Later the monarchs ruling Iran continued in the same path; they completely distorted Islam and established something quite different in its place.*[9]

So, although Islamism can be presented by both defenders and opponents as a traditionalist doctrine, based on a rejection of the modern world, in reality things are more complicated than this. The aspiration to recreate a mythical past involves not leaving existing society intact, but recasting it. What is more, the recasting cannot aim to produce a carbon copy of 7th century Islam, since the Islamists do not reject every feature of existing society. By and large they accept modern industry, modern technology and much of the science on which it is based—indeed, they argue that Islam, as a more rational and less superstitious doctrine than Christianity, is more in tune with modern science. And so the 'revivalists' are, in fact, trying to bring about something which has never existed before, which fuses ancient traditions and the forms of modern social life.

This means it is wrong simply to refer to all Islamists as 'reactionary', or to equate 'Islamic fundamentalism' as a whole with the sort of Christian fundamentalism which is the bastion of the right wing of the Republican Party in the US. Figures like Khomeini, the heads of the rival Mujahedin groups in Afghanistan or the leaders of the Algerian FIS may use traditionalist themes and appeal to the nostalgia of disappearing social groups, but they also appeal to radical currents produced as society is transformed by capitalism. Olivier Roy, referring to the Afghan Islamists, argues that:

> *Fundamentalism is quite different (to traditionalism): for fundamentalism it is of paramount importance to get back to the scriptures, clearing away the obfuscation of tradition. It always seeks a return to a former state; it is characterised by the practice of re-reading texts and a search for origins. The enemy is not modernity but tradition, or rather, in the context of Islam, of everything which is not the Tradition of the Prophet. This is true reform...*[10]

Traditionalist Islam is an ideology which seeks to perpetuate a social order which is being undermined by the development of capitalism—or at least, as with the version promoted by the ruling family in Saudi Arabia, to hark back to this order in order to conceal the transformation of an old ruling class into modern capitalists. Islamism is an ideology which, although it appeals to some of the same themes, seeks to transform society, not to conserve it in the old way. For this reason, even the term 'fundamentalism' is not really appropriate. As Abrahamian has observed:

> *The label 'fundamentalism' implies religious inflexibility, intellectual purity, political traditionalism, even social conservatism and the centrality of scriptural-doctrinal principles. 'Fundamentalism' implies rejection of the modern world.*[11]

But, in fact, movements like that of Khomeini in Iran have been based on 'ideological adaptability and intellectual flexibility, with political protests against the established order, and with socio-economic issues that fuel mass opposition to the status quo'.[12]

Yet there is often a blurring of the differences between Islamism and traditionalism. Precisely because the notion of social regeneration is wrapped in religious language, it is open to different interpretations. It can mean simply ending 'degenerate practices' through a return to the forms of behaviour which allegedly preceded the 'corruption' of Islam' by 'cultural imperialism'. The stress then is on female 'modesty' and the wearing of the veil, an end to 'promiscuous' mixing of the sexes in schools and workplaces, opposition to Western popular music and so on. Thus one of the most popular leaders of the Algerian FIS, Ali Belhadj, can denounce the 'violence' against Muslims that comes from 'cultural invasion':

> *We Muslims believe that the most serious form of violence we have suffered is not physical violence, for which we are ready... It is the violence which represents a challenge to the Muslim community by the imposition of diabolical legislation instead of the* **sharia**...
>
> *Is there any violence worse than that which consists in encouraging that which God has forbidden? They open wine making enterprises, the work of the demon, and they are protected by the police...*

> Can you conceive of any violence greater than that of this woman who burns the scarf in a public place, in the eyes of everyone, saying the Family Code penalises women and finding support from the effeminised, the half-men and the transexuals...
>
> It is not violence to demand that woman stays at home, in an atmosphere of chastity, reserve and humility and that she only goes out in cases of necessity defined by the legislator...to demand the segregation of sexes among school students and the absence of that stinking mixing that causes sexual violence...[13]

But regeneration can also mean challenging the state and elements of imperialism's political domination. Thus the Iranian Islamists did close down the biggest US 'listening' station in Asia and seize control of the US embassy. The Hezbollah in the southern Lebanon and Hamas in the West Bank and Gaza have played a key role in the armed struggle against Israel. The Algerian FIS did organise huge demonstrations against the US war against Iraq—even though these lost them their Saudi funding. Regeneration can even mean, in certain instances, giving support to the material struggles against exploitation of workers and peasants, as with the Iranian Mujahedin in 1979-82.

The different interpretations of regeneration naturally appeal to those from different social classes. But the religious phraseology can prevent those involved recognising their differences with one another. In the heat of the struggle individuals can mix the meanings together, so that the fight against the unveiling of women is seen as the fight against the Western oil companies and the abysmal poverty of the mass of people. Thus in Algeria in the late 1980s, Belhadj,

> made himself the voice of all those with nothing to lose... Conceiving Islam in its most pure scriptural form, he preached strict application of its commandments... Every Friday Belhadj made war against the entire world, Jews and Christians, Zionists, communists and secularists, liberals and agnostics, governments of the East and the West, Arab or Muslim heads of state, Westernised party leaders and intellectuals, were the favourite targets of his weekly preaching.[14]

Yet beneath this confusion of ideas there were real class interests at work.

The class base of Islamism

Islamism has arisen in societies traumatised by the impact of capitalism—first in the form of external conquest by imperialism and then, increasingly, by the transformation of internal social relations accompanying the rise of a local capitalist class and the formation of an independent capitalist state.

Old social classes have been replaced by new ones, although not instantaneously or in a clear cut manner. What Trotsky described as 'combined and uneven development' has occurred. Externally, colonialism has retreated, but the great imperialist powers—especially the US—continue to use their military forces as a bargaining tool to influence the production of the Middle East's single major resource, oil. Internally, state encouragement—and often ownership—has led to the development of some large scale modern industry, but large sectors of 'traditional' industry remain, based on vast numbers of small workshops where the owner works with a couple of workers, often from his own family. Land reform has turned some peasants into modern capitalist farmers—but displaced many more, leaving them with little or no land, so forcing them to eke out a livelihood from casual labour in the workshops or markets of sprawling urban slums. A massive expansion of the education system is turning out vast numbers of high school and college graduates, but these then find insufficient job opportunities in the modern sectors of the economy and place their hopes on getting into the state bureaucracy, while eking out a living with scraps of work around the informal sector—touting for custom from shopkeepers, acting as guides for tourists, selling lottery tickets, driving taxis and so on.

The crises of the world economy over the last 20 years have aggravated all these contradictions. The modern industries have found the national economy too small for them to operate efficiently, but the world economy too competitive for them to survive without state protection. The traditional industries have not generally been able to modernise without state support and they cannot compensate for the failure of modern industry to provide jobs for the burgeoning urban population. But a few sectors have managed to establish links of their own with international capital and increasingly resent the state's domination of the economy. The urban rich increasingly lap up the luxury goods available on the world market, creating growing resentment among the casual workers and the unemployed.

Islamism represents an attempt to come to terms with these contradictions by people who have been brought up to respect traditional Islamic ideas. But it does not find its support equally in all sections of society. For some sections embrace a modern secular bourgeois or nationalist ideology, while other sections gravitate towards some form of secular working class response. The Islamic revival gets sustenance from four different social groupings—each of which interprets Islam in its own way.

i) The Islamism of the old exploiters: First there are those members of the traditional privileged classes who fear losing out in the capitalist modernisation of society—particularly landowners (including clergy dependent on incomes from land belonging to religious foundations), traditional merchant capitalists, the owners of the mass of small shops and workshops. Such groups have often been the traditional sources of finance for the mosques and see Islam as a way of defending their established way of life and of making those who oversee change listen to their voices. Thus in Iran and Algeria it was this group which provided the resources to the clergy to oppose the state's land reform programme in the 1960s and 1970s.

ii) The Islamism of the new exploiters: Second, often emerging from among this first group, are some of the capitalists who have enjoyed success despite hostility from those groups linked to the state. In Egypt, for instance, the present day Muslim Brotherhood 'wormed their way into the economic fabric of Sadat's Egypt at a time when whole sections of it had been turned over to unregulated capitalism. Uthman Ahmad Uthman, the Egyptian Rockefeller, made no secret of this sympathy for the Brethren'.[15]

In Turkey the Welfare Party, which is led by a former member of the main conservative party, enjoys the support of much of middle sized capital. In Iran among the *bazaaris* who gave support to Khomeini against the Shah were substantial capitalists resentful at the way economic policies favoured those close to the crown.

iii) The Islamism of the poor: The third group are the rural poor who have suffered under the advance of capitalist farming and who have been forced into the cities as they desperately look for work. Thus in Algeria out of a total rural population of 8.2 million only 2 million gained anything from the land reform. The other 6 million were faced with the choice between increased poverty in the countryside and going to the cities to seek work.[16] But in the cities: 'The lowest group are the hard core jobless made up of displaced former peasants who have flooded the cities in search of work and social opportunity...detached from rural society without being truly integrated into urban society'.[17]

They lost the certainties associated with an old way of life—certainties which they identify with traditional Muslim culture—without gaining a secure material existence or a stable way of life: 'Clear guidelines for behaviour and belief no longer exist for millions of Algerians caught between a tradition that no longer commands their total loyalty and a modernism that cannot satisfy the psychological and spiritual needs of young people in particular'.[18]

In such a situation even Islamic agitation against land reform on behalf of the old landowners in the 1970s could appeal to the peasants and ex-peasants. For the land reform could be a symbol of a transformation of the countryside that had destroyed a secure, if impoverished, way of life. 'To the landed proprietors and the peasants without land, the Islamists held out the same prospect: the Koran stigmatised the expropriation of things belonging to others; it recommended to the rich and those who ruled according to the *Sunna* to be generous to others'.[19]

The appeal of Islamism grew through the 1980s as economic crisis increased the contrast between the impoverished masses and the elite of about 1 percent of the population who run the state and the economy. Their wealth and their Westernised lifestyles ill fitted their claim to be the heirs of the liberation struggle against the French. It was very easy for the ex-peasants to identify the 'non-Islamic' behaviour of this elite as the cause of their own misery.

In Iran likewise the capitalist transformation of agriculture embodied in the Shah's land reform of the 1960s benefitted a minority of the toilers, while leaving the rest no better off and sometimes worse off. It increased the antagonism of the rural and recently urbanised poor against the state—an antagonism which did no harm to Islamic forces which had opposed the land reform. So when, for instance, in 1962 the Shah used the forces of the state against Islamic figures, this turned them into a focus for the discontent of very large numbers of people.

In Egypt the 'opening up' of the economy to the world market through agreements with the World Bank and the IMF from the mid-1970s onwards substantially worsened the situation of the mass of peasants and ex-peasants, creating enormous pools of bitterness. And in Afghanistan the land reforms which were imposed after the PDPA (Communist Party) coup of 1978 led to a series of spontaneous risings from all sections of the rural population:

> *The reforms put an end to the traditional ways of working based on mutual self interest without introducing any alternative. The landowners who had been dispossessed of their land were careful not to distribute any seed to their sharecroppers; people who traditionally had been willing to provide loans now refused to do so. There were plans for the creation of a bank for agricultural development and for setting up an office to oversee the distribution of seed and fodder, but none of this had been done when the reforms actually took place... So it was the very act of announcing the reforms that cut the peasant off from his seed supplies... The reform destroyed not just the economic structure but the whole social framework of production... It is not surprising, therefore, that instead of setting 98 percent of the people against 2 percent of the exploiting classes, these reforms led to a general revolt of 75*

percent of the rural areas. [And] *when the new system was seen not to be working* [even] *the peasants who had initially welcomed reform felt they would be better off going back to the old system.*[20]

But it is not only hostility to the state that makes ex-peasants receptive to the message of the Islamists. The mosques provide a social focus for people lost in a new and strange city, the Islamic charities the rudiments of welfare services (clinics, schooling, etc) which are lacking from the state. So in Algeria the growth of the cities in the 1970s and 1980s was accompanied by a massive increase in the number of mosques: 'Everything happened as if the paralysis in education and Arabisation, the absence of structures of culture and leisure, the lack of space for public liberty, the shortage of homes, made thousands of adults, youth and children disposed for the mosques'.[21]

In this way, funds which came from those with diametrically opposed interests to the mass of people—from the old landowning class, the new rich or the Saudi government—could provide both a material and a cultural haven for the poor. 'In the mosque, everyone—new or old bourgeois, fundamentalist, worker in an enterprise—saw the possibility of the elaboration or realisation of his own strategy, dreams and hopes'.[22]

This did not obliterate the class divisions within the mosque. In Algeria, for example, there were innumerable rows in mosque committees between people whose different social background made them see the building of the mosques in different ways—for instance, over when they should refuse to accept donations for the mosque because they came from sinful (*haram*) sources. 'It is rare in fact for a religious committee to accomplish its mandate, fixed in principle at two years, with the harmony and agreement recommended by the cult of the unity of the divine which the *muezzins* chant without cease.'[23] But the rows remained cloaked in a religious guise—and have not stopped the proliferation of the mosques and the growth in the influence of Islamism.

iv) The Islamism of the new middle class: However, neither the 'traditional' exploiting classes nor the impoverished masses provide the vital element which sustains revivalist, political Islam—the cadre of activists who propagate its doctrines and risk injury, imprisonment and death in confrontation with their enemies.

The traditional exploiting classes are by their very nature conservative. They are prepared to donate money so that others can fight—especially in defence of their material interests. They did so when faced with the land reform in Algeria in the early 1970s; when the Baathist regime in Syria encroached upon the interests of the urban merchants and traders in the spring of 1980s[24]; and when the merchants and small businessmen of the Iranian bazaars felt themselves under attack from the Shah in 1976-78 and threatened by the left in 1979-81. But they are wary of putting their own businesses, let alone their own lives, at risk. And so they can hardly be the force that has torn societies like Algeria and Egypt apart, caused a whole town, Hama, to rise in revolt in Syria, used suicide bombs against the Americans and Israelis in Lebanon—and which caused the Iranian Revolution to take a turn much more radical than any section of the Iranian bourgeoisie expected.

This force, in fact, comes from a fourth, very different stratum—from a section of the new middle class that has arisen as a result of capitalist modernisation right across the Third World.

In Iran the cadres of all three of the Islamist movements that dominated the politics of the first years of the revolution came from this background. Thus one account tells of the support for the first post-revolutionary prime minister, Bazargan:

> *As Iran's educational system expanded in the 1950s and 1960s, even wider groups of traditional middle class people gained access to the country's universities. Confronted with institutions dominated by the older, Westernised elites, these newcomers to academia felt an urgent need to justify their continued adherence to Islam to themselves. They joined the Muslim Students Associations* [run by Bazargan etc]*...upon entering professional life, the new engineers often joined the Islamic Association of Engineers, also founded by Bazargan. This association network constituted the real organised social support for Bazargan and Islamic modernism... Bazargan's and Taleqani's appeal* [depended on] *the way they gave the rising members of the traditional middle classes a sense of dignity which allowed them to affirm their identity in a society politically dominated by what they saw as a Godless, Westernised and corrupt elite.*[25]

Writing of the People's Mojahedin of Iran, Abrahamian comments that many studies of the first years of the Iranian Revolution have talked of the appeal of radical Islam to the 'oppressed', but that it was not the oppressed in general who formed the basis of the Mojahedin; rather it was that very large section of the new middle class whose parents had been part of the traditional petty bourgeoisie. He gives breakdowns of the occupations of Mojahedin arrested under the Shah and subject to repression under Khomeini to support his argument.[26]

Although the third Islamist force, the ultimately victorious Islamic Republican Party of Khomeini, is usually thought of as run by the clergy linked to the traditional *bazaari* merchant capitalists, Moaddel has shown that more than half its MPs were from the professions, teachers, government employees or students—even if a quarter came from *bazaari* families.[27] And Bayat has noted that in their struggle to defeat the workers' organisations in the factories, the regime could rely on the professional engineers who worked there.[28]

Azar Tabari notes that after the downfall of the Shah very large numbers of women in the Iranian cities opted to wear the veil and lined up with the followers of Khomeini against the left. She claims these women came from that section of the middle class that was the first generation to undergo a process of 'social integration'. Often from traditional petty bourgeois families—with fathers who were bazaar merchants, tradesmen and so on—they were forced into higher education as traditional opportunities for their families to make money declined with industrialisation. There were openings for them in professions like teaching and nursing. But 'these women had to go through the often painful and traumatic experience of first generation adjustment':

> As the young women from such families began to go to universities or work in hospitals, all these traditional concepts came under daily attack from 'alien' surroundings, where women mixed with men, wore no veils, and sometimes dressed according to the latest European fashions. Women were often torn between accepted family norms and the pressure of the new environment. They could not be veiled at work, nor could they leave home unveiled.

One widespread response to these contradictory pressures was 'a retreat into Islam', 'symbolised by deliberately veiled women demonstrators during large mobilisations'. Tabari claims this response stood in marked contrast to that of women whose families had been part of the new middle class for two or three generations, and who refused to wear the veil and identified with the liberals or the left.[29] In Afghanistan, Roy notes:

> The Islamist movement was born in the modern sectors of society and developed from a critique of the popular movements that preceded it... The Islamists are intellectuals, the products of modernist enclaves within traditional society; their social origins are what we have termed the state bourgeoisie—products of the government education system which only leads to employment in the state machine... The Islamists are products of the state educational system. Very few of them have an education in the arts. On the campus they mostly mix with the Communists, with whom they are violently opposed, rather that with the **ulama** [religious scholars] towards whom they have an ambivalent attitude. They share many beliefs in common with the **ulama**, but Islamist thought has developed from contact with the great western ideologies, which they see as holding the key to the west's technical development. For them, the problem is to develop a modern political ideology

based upon Islam, which they see as the only way to come to terms with the modern world and the best means of confronting foreign imperialism.[30]

In Algeria the most important recruitment ground for the FIS has been among Arabic speaking (as opposed to French speaking) high school and university students, and that wide section of youth that would like to be students but cannot get college places:

The FIS draws its membership from three sections of the population: the commercial middle classes, including some who are quite rich, a mass of young people who are unemployed and excluded from higher education, forming the new lumpen proletariat of the streets, and a layer of upwardly mobile Arab speaking intellectuals. These last two groups are the most numerous and important.[31]

The Islamic intellectuals have made careers for themselves through their domination of the theological and Arab language faculties of the universities, using these to gain control of many of the positions as *imams* in the mosques and teachers in the *lycees* (high schools). They form a network that ensures the recruitment of more Islamists to such positions and the inculcation of Islamist ideas into the new generation of students. This in turn has enabled them to exert influence over vast numbers of young people.

Ahmed Rouadia writes that the Islamist groups began to grow from the mid-1970s onwards, receiving support in the universities from Arab speaking students who found their lack of fluency in French kept them from getting jobs in administration, areas of advanced technology and higher management.[32] Thus, there was, for instance, a bitter conflict with the principal of Constantine university in the mid-1980s, who was accused of impugning the 'dignity of Arab language' and 'being loyal to French colonialism' for allowing French to remain the predominant language in the science and technology faculties[33]:

The qualified Arab speakers find access blocked to all the key sectors, above all in industries requiring technical knowledge and foreign languages... The Arab speakers, even if they have diplomas, cannot get a place in modern industry. For the most part they end by turning towards the mosque.[34]

The students, the recent Arab speaking graduates and, above all, the unemployed ex-students form a bridge to the very large numbers of discontented youth outside the colleges who find they cannot get college places despite years spent in an inefficient and underfunded educational system. Thus, although there are now nearly a million students in secondary education, up to four fifths of them can expect to fail the bacalauriate—the key to entry into university—and to face a life of insecurity on the margins of employment:[35]

> *Integrism* [Islamism] *gets its strength from the social frustrations which afflict a large part of the youth, those left out of account by the social and economic system. Its message is simple: If there is poverty, hardship and frustration, it is because those who have power do not base themselves on the legitimacy of* **shorah** [consultation], *but simply on force... The restoration of the Islam of the first years would make the inequalities disappear.*[36]

And through its influence over a wide layer of students, graduates and the intellectual unemployed, Islamism is able to spread out to dominate the propagation of ideas in the slums and shanty towns where the ex-peasants live. Such a movement cannot be described as a 'conservative' movement. The educated, Arab speaking youth do not turn to Islam because they want things to stay as they are, but because they believe it offers massive social change.[37]

In Egypt the Islamist movement first developed some 65 years ago, when Hassan al-Banna formed the Muslim Brotherhood. It grew in the 1930s and 1940s as disillusionment set in with the failure of the secular nationalist party, the Wafd, to challenge British domination of the country. The base of the movement consisted mainly of civil servants and students, and it was one of the major forces in the university protests of the late 1940s and early 1950s.[38] But it spread out to involve some urban labourers and peasants, with a membership estimated to have peaked at half a million. In building the movement Banna was quite willing to collaborate with certain figures close to the Egyptian monarchy, and the right wing of the Wafd looked on the Brotherhood as a counter to communist influence among workers and students.[39]

But the Brotherhood could only compete with the communists for the support of the impoverished middle classes—and via them to sections of the urban poor—because its religious language concealed a commitment to reform which went further than its right wing allies wished. Its objectives were 'ultimately incompatible with the perpetuation of the political, economic and social status quo to which the ruling groups were dedicated'. This ensured 'the liaison between the Muslim Brotherhood and the conservative rulers would be both unstable and tenuous'.[40]

The Brotherhood was virtually destroyed once a new military regime around Abdul Nasser had concentrated full power into its hands in the early 1950s. Six of the Brotherhood's leaders were hanged in December 1954 and thousands of its members thrown into concentration camps. An attempt to revive the movement in the mid-1960s led to still more executions, but then, after Nasser's death, his successors Sadat and Mubarak allowed it to lead a semi-legal existence—provided it avoided any head on confrontation with the regime. The leadership of what is sometimes called the 'Neo-Islamic Brotherhood' has been willing to accept these restraints, following a relatively 'moderate' and 'reconciliatory' approach, getting large sums of money from members who were exiled to Saudi Arabia in the 1950s and prospered from the oil boom.[41] This has enabled the Brothers to provide 'an alternative model of a Muslim state' with 'their banks, social services, educational services and...their mosques'.[42]

But it has also led them to lose influence over a new generation of radical Islamists which has arisen, as the Brotherhood itself originally did, from the universities and the impoverished section of the 'modern' middle class. These are the Islamists who were responsible for the assassination of Sadat in 1981 and who have been waging armed struggle ever since both against the state and against the secular intelligentsia:

> When we speak of the fundamentalists in Egypt, what we mean is a minority group of people who are even against the Moslem Brothers... These groups are composed mainly of youth... They are very pure people, they are prepared to sacrifice their lives, to do anything... And they are used as the spearheads of the different movements because they are able to undertake terrorist actions.[43]

The Islamist student associations which became a dominant force in Egyptian universities during Sadat's presidency 'constituted the Islamicist movement's only genuine mass organisations'.[44] They grew in reaction to conditions in the universities and to the dismal prospects facing students if they succeeded in graduating:

> The number of students rose from slightly less than 200,000 in 1970 to more than half a million in 1977... In the absence of the necessary resources, providing free high education for the greatest possible number of the country's youth has produced a system of cut rate education.[45]

Overcrowding represents a particular problem for female students, who find themselves subject to all sorts of harassment in the lecture theatres and overcrowded buses. In response to this situation,

> The *jamaa al islamiyya* [Islamic associations] *drew their considerable strength from their ability to identify* [these problems] *and to pose immediate solutions—for instance, using student unions funds to run minibuses for female students* [giving priority to those who wore the veil], *calling for separate rows in the lecture theatres for women and men, organising course*

revision groups which met in the mosques, turning out cheap editions of essential textbooks.⁴⁶

Graduating students do not escape the endemic poverty of much of Egyptian society:

> Every graduate has the right to public employment. This measure is actually the purveyor of massive disguised unemployment in the offices of a swollen administration in which employees are badly paid... He can still manage to feed himself by buying the state subsidised products, but he is unlikely to rise above the bare level of subsistence... Almost every state employee has a second or a third job... Innumerable employees who sit all morning at desks in one or other of the countless ministry offices spend the afternoon working as plumbers or taxi drivers, jobs they perform so inadequately they might as well be filled by illiterates... An illiterate peasant woman who arrives in the city to land a job as a foreigner's maid will be paid more or less double the salary of a university assistant lecturer.⁴⁷

The only way to get out of this morass for most graduates is to get a job abroad, especially in Saudi Arabia or the Gulf states. And this is not just the only way out of poverty, it is, for most people, the precondition for getting married in a society where pre-marital sexual relations are rare.

The Islamists were able to articulate these problems in religious language. As Kepel writes of one of the leaders of one of the early Islamist sects, his position does not involve 'acting as a fanatic for a bygone century... He is putting his finger—in his own way—on a crucial problem of contemporary Egyptian society'.⁴⁸

As in Algeria, once the Islamists had established a mass base in the universities, they were then in a situation to spread out into a wider milieu—the milieu of the impoverished streets of the cities where the students and ex-students mixed with a mass of other people scrabbling for a livelihood. This began to happen after the regime clamped down hard on the Islamist movement in the universities following the negotiation of the peace agreement with Israel in the late 1970s. 'Far from halting the *jamaa*, however, this harassment gave them a second wind...the message of the *jamaa* now began to spread beyond the world of students. Islamicist cadres and agitators went to preach in the poor neighbourhoods'.⁴⁹

Radical Islam as a social movement

The class base of Islamism is similar to that of classical fascism and of the Hindu fundamentalism of the BJP, Shiv Sena and RSS in India. All these movements have recruited from the white collar middle class and students, as well as from the traditional commercial and professional petty bourgeoisie. This, together with the hostility of most Islamist movements to the left, women's rights and secularism has led many socialist and liberals to designate the movements as fascist. But this is a mistake.

The petty bourgeois class base has not only been a characteristic of fascism, it has also been a feature of Jacobinism, of Third World nationalisms, of Maoist Stalinism, and Peronism. Petty bourgeois movements only become fascist when they arise at a specific point in the class struggle and play a particular role. This role is not just to mobilise the petty bourgeoisie, but to exploit the bitterness they feel at what an acute crisis of the system has done to them and so turn them into organised thugs prepared to work for capital to tear workers' organisations apart.

That is why Mussolini's and Hitler's movements were fascist while, say, Peron's movement in Argentina was not. Even though Peron borrowed some of the imagery of fascism, he took power in exceptional circumstances which allowed him to buy off workers' organisations while using state intervention to divert the profits of the large agrarian capitalists into industrial expansion. During his first six years in office an specific set of circumstances allowed real wages to rise by about 60 percent. This was the complete opposite to what would have happened under a genuinely fascist regime. Yet the liberal intelligentsia and the Argentine Communist Party were still capable of referring to the regime as 'Nazi Peronism', in much the same way that much of the left internationally refers to Islamism today.[50]

The Islamist mass movements in countries like Algeria and Egypt likewise play a different role to that of fascism. They are not primarily directed against workers' organisations and do not offer themselves to the main sectors of capital as a way of solving its problems at workers' expense. They are often involved in direct, armed confrontation with the forces of the state in a way in which fascist parties rarely have been. And, far from being direct agents of imperialism, these movements have taken up anti-imperialist slogans and some anti-imperialist actions which have embarrassed very important national and international capitalist interests (eg in Algeria over the second Gulf War, in Egypt against 'peace' with Israel, in Iran against the American presence in the aftermath of the overthrow of the Shah).

The American CIA was able to work with Pakistan intelligence and the pro-Western Middle East states to arm thousands of volunteers from right across the Middle East to fight against the Russians in Afghanistan. But now these volunteers are returning home to discover they were fighting for the US when they thought they were fighting 'for Islam', and constituting a bitter hard core of opposition to most of the governments which encouraged them to go. Even in Saudi Arabia, where the ultra-puritan Wahhabist interpretation of the Islamic *sharia* (religious law) is imposed with all the might of the state, the opposition now claims the support of 'thousands of Afghan fighters', disgusted by the hypocrisy of a royal family that is increasingly integrated into the world capitalist ruling class. And the royal family is now retaliating, further antagonising some of the very people it encouraged so much in the past, cutting off funds to the Algerian FIS for supporting Iraq in the second Gulf War and deporting a Saudi millionaire who has been financing Islamists in Egypt.

Those on the left who see the Islamists simply as 'fascists' fail to take into account the destabilising effect of the movements on capital's interests right across the Middle East, and end up siding with states that are the strongest backers both of imperialism and of local capital. This has, for instance, happened to those sections of the left influenced by the remnants of Stalinism in Egypt. It happened to much of the Iranian left during the closing stages of the first Gulf War, when American imperialism sent in its fleet to fight on the same side as Iraq against Iran. And it is in danger of happening to the secular left in Algeria, faced with a near civil war between the Islamists and the state.

But if it is wrong to see the Islamist movements as 'fascist', it is just as wrong to simply see them as 'anti-imperialist' or 'anti-state'. They do not just fight against those classes and states that exploit and dominate the mass of people. They also fight against secularism, against women who refuse to abide by Islamic notions of 'modesty', against the left and, in important cases, against ethnic or religious minorities. The Algerian Islamists established their hold on the universities in the late 1970s and early 1980s by organising 'punitive raids' against the left with the connivance of the police, and the first person killed by them was not a state official but a member of a Trotskyist organisation; another of their actions was to denounce *Hard Rock Magazine*, homosexuality, drugs and punk at the Islamic book fair in 1985; in the Algerian towns where they are strongest, they do organise attacks on women who dare to show a little of their skin; the first public demonstration of the FIS in 1989 was in response to 'feminist' and 'secularist' demonstrations against Islamist violence, of which women were the main victims.[51] Its hostility is directed not just against the state and foreign capital, but also against the more than 1 million Algerian citizens who, through no fault of their own, have been brought up with French as their first language, and the 10 percent of the population who are Berber rather than Arabic speakers.

Similarly, in Egypt, the armed Islamic groups do murder secularists and Islamists who disagree strongly with them; they do encourage communal hatred by Muslims, including pogroms, against the 10 percent of the population who happen to be Coptic Christians. In Iran the Khomeini wing of Islamism did execute some 100 people for 'sexual offences' like homosexuality and adultery in 1979-81; they did sack women from the legal system and organise gangs of thugs, the Iranian Hezbollah, to attack unveiled women and to assault left wingers; and they did kill thousands in the repression of the left Islamist People's Mujahedin. In Afghanistan the Islamist organisations which waged a long and bloody war against the Russian occupation of their country did turn their heavy weaponry on each other once the Russians had left, reducing whole areas of Kabul to rubble.

In fact, even when Islamists put the stress on 'anti-imperialism', they more often than not let imperialism off the hook. For imperialism today is not usually the direct rule of Western states over parts of the Third World, but rather a world system of independent capitalist classes ('private' and state), integrated into a single world market. Some ruling classes have greater power than others and so are able to impose their own bargaining terms through their control over access to trade, the banking system or on occasions crude force. These ruling classes stand at the top of a pinnacle of exploitation, but those just below are the ruling classes of poorer countries, rooted in the individual national economies, also gaining from the system, increasingly linking themselves into the dominant multinational networks and buying into the economies of the advanced world, even if on occasion they lash out at those above them.

The suffering of the great mass of people cannot *simply* be blamed on the great imperialist powers and their agencies like the World Bank and the IMF. It is also a result of the enthusiastic participation in exploitation of the lesser capitalists and their states. It is these who actually implement the policies that impoverish people and wreck their lives. And it is these who use the police and the prisons to crush those who try to resist.

There is an important difference here with what happened under the classic imperialism of the colonial empires, where Western colonists manned the state and directed repression. The local exploiting classes would be pulled two ways, between resisting a state when it trampled on their interests, and collaborating with it as a bulwark against those they themselves exploited. But they were not necessarily in the front line of defending the whole system of exploitation against revolt. They are today. They are part of the system, even if they sometimes quarrel with it. They are no longer its inconsistent opponents.[52]

In this situation any ideology which restricts itself to targeting foreign imperialism as the enemy evades any serious confrontation with the system. It expresses people's bitterness and frustration, but evades focusing it on real enemies. This is true of most versions of Islamism, just as it is true these days of most Third World nationalisms. They point to a real enemy, the world system, and on occasions they clash bitterly with the state. But they absolve from responsibility most of the local bourgeoisie—imperialism's most important long term partner.

A recent study of Khomeinism in Iran by Abrahamian compares it with Peronism and similar forms of 'populism':

> *Khomeini adopted radical themes... At times he sounded more radical than the Marxists. But while adopting radical themes he remained staunchly committed to the preservation of middle class property. This form of middle class radicalism made him akin to Latin American populists, especially the Peronists.*[53]

And Abrahamian goes on to say:

> *By 'populism' I mean a movement of the propertied middle class that mobilises the lower classes, especially the urban poor, with radical rhetoric directed against imperialism, foreign capitalism, and the political establishment... Populist movements promise to drastically raise the standard of living and make the country fully independent of outside powers. Even more important in attacking the status quo with radical rhetoric, they intentionally stop short of threatening the petty bourgeoisie and the whole principle of private property. Populist movements thus, inevitably, emphasise the importance, not of economic-social revolution, but of cultural, national and political reconstruction.*[54]

Such movements tend to confuse matters by moving from any real struggle against imperialism to a purely ideological struggle against what they see as its cultural effects. 'Cultural imperialism', rather than material exploitation, is identified as the source of everything that is wrong. The fight is then not directed against forces really involved in impoverishing people, but rather against those who speak 'foreign' languages, accept 'alien' religions or reject allegedly 'traditional' lifestyles. This is very convenient for certain sections of local capital who find it easy to practice the 'indigenous culture', at least in public. It is also of direct material interest to sections of the middle class who can advance their own careers by purging others from their jobs. But it limits the dangers such movements present to imperialism as a system.

Islamism, then, both mobilises popular bitterness and paralyses it; both builds up people's feelings that something must be done and directs those feelings into blind alleys; both destabilises the state and limits the real struggle against the state.

The contradictory character of Islamism follows from the class base of its core cadres. The petty bourgeoisie as a class cannot follow a consistent, independent policy of its own. This has always been true of the traditional petty bourgeoisie—the small shopkeepers, traders and self employed professionals. They have always been caught between a conservative hankering for security that looks to the past and a hope that they individually will gain from radical change. It is just as true of the impoverished new middle class—or the even more impoverished would-be new middle class of unemployed ex-students—in the less economically advanced countries today. They can hanker after an allegedly golden past. They can see their futures as tied up with general social advance through revolutionary change. Or they can blame the frustration of their aspirations on other sections of the population who have got an 'unfair' grip on middle class jobs: the religious and ethnic minorities, those with a different language, women working in an 'untraditional' way.

Which direction they turn in does not just depend on immediate material factors. It also depends on the struggles that occur on a national and international scale. Thus in the 1950s and 1960s the struggles against colonialism and imperialism did inspire much of the aspirant middle class of the Third World, and there was a general feeling that state controlled economic development represented the way forward. The secular left, or at least its Stalinist or nationalist mainstream, was seen as embodying this vision, and it exercised a degree of hegemony in the universities. At that stage even those who began with a religious orientation were attracted by what was seen as the left—by the example of the Vietnamese War against America or by the so called cultural revolution in China—and began to reject traditional religious thinking over, for instance, the women's question. This happened with the Catholic liberation theologists in Latin America and the People's Mojahedin in Iran. And even in Afghanistan the Islamist students,

> *Demonstrated against Zionism during the six-day war, against American policies in Vietnam and the privileges of the establishment. They were violently opposed to important figures on the traditionalist side, to the King and especially his cousin Daoud... They protested against foreign influences in Afghanistan, both from the Soviet Union and the West, and against the speculators during the famine of 1972, by demanding there should be curbs on personal wealth.*[55]

In the late 1970s and 1980s the mood changed. On the one hand there was the beginning of a global wave of disillusionment with the so called 'socialist' model presented by the Eastern European states as a result of the killing fields of Cambodia, the mini-war between Vietnam and China, and the move of China towards the American camp. This disillusionment grew in intensity in the later 1980s as a result of the changes in Eastern Europe and the collapse of the USSR.

It was even more intense in certain Middle Eastern countries than elsewhere in the world because the illusions had not merely been a question of foreign policy. The local regimes had claimed to be implementing nationalist versions of 'socialism', based to a greater or lesser extent on the East European model. Even those on the left who were critical of their governments tended to accept and identify with these claims. Thus in Algeria the left in the universities volunteered in the early 1970s to go to the countryside to assist in the 'land reform', even though the regime had already repressed the left student organisation and was maintaining police control over the universities. And in Egypt the Communists continued to proclaim Nasser as a socialist, even after he had thrown them into prison. So disillusionment with the regime became also, for many people, disillusionment with the left.

On the other hand, there was the emergence of certain Islamic states as a political force—the seizure of power by Gadaffi in Libya, the Saudi-led oil embargo against the West at the time of the Arab-Israeli war of 1973, and then, most dramatically, the revolutionary establishment of the Iranian Islamic Republic in 1979.

Islamism began to dominate among the very layers of students and young people who had once looked to the left: in Algeria, for instance, 'Khomeini began to be regarded by layers of young people as Mao and Guevara once had been'.[56] Support for the Islamist movements went from strength to strength as they seemed to offer immanent and radical change. The leaders of the Islamist movements were triumphant.

Yet the contradictions in Islamism did not go away, and expressed themselves forcefully in the decade that followed. Far from being an unstoppable force, Islamism has, in fact, been subject to its own internal pressures which, repeatedly, have made its followers turn on one another. Just as the history of Stalinism in the Middle East in the 1940s and 1950s was one of failure, betrayals, splits and repression, so has the history of Islamism been in the 1980s and 1990s.

The contradictions of Islamism: Egypt

The contradictory character of Islamism expresses itself in the way in which it sees 'the return to the Koran' taking place. It can see this as through a reform of the 'values' of existing society, meaning simply a return to religious practices, while leaving the main structures of society intact. Or it can be seen as meaning a revolutionary overthrow of existing society. The contradiction is to be seen in the history both of the old Islamic Brotherhood of Egypt in the 1930s, 1940s and 1950s, and in the new radical Islamist movements of the 1970s, 1980s and 1990s.

The Muslim Brotherhood grew rapidly in the 1930s and 1940s as it picked up support from those disillusioned by the compromises the bourgeois nationalist Wafd made with the British, as we have seen. It was further aided by the gyrations of the Communist left under Stalin's influence, which went so far as to support the establishment of Israel. By recruiting volunteers to fight in Palestine and against the British occupation of the Egyptian Canal Zone, the Brotherhood could seem to support the anti-imperialist struggle. But just as the Brotherhood reached its peak of support, it began to run into troubles. Its leadership based themselves on a coalition of forces—recruitment of a mass of petty bourgeois youth, links with the palace, deals with the right wing of the Wafd, plots with junior armed forces officers—which were themselves moving in different directions.

As strikes, demonstrations, assassinations, military defeat in Palestine, and guerrilla warfare in the Canal Zone tore Egyptian society apart, so the Brotherhood itself was in danger of disintegrating. Many members were indignant at the personal behaviour of the general secretary, Banna's brother in law Abadin. Banna himself condemned members of the Brotherhood who assassinated the premier Nuqrashi. After Banna's death in 1949 his successor as 'supreme guide' was dismayed to discover the existence of a secret terrorist section. The seizure of power by the military under Nasser in 1952-4 produced a fundamental divide between those who supported the coup and those who opposed it until finally rival groups within the Brotherhood ended up physically battling for control of its offices.[57] 'An all-important loss of confidence in the leadership' enabled Nasser eventually to crush what had once been a massively powerful organisation.[58]

But the loss of confidence was not an accident. It followed from the unbridgeable divisions which were bound to arise in a petty bourgeois movement as the crisis in society deepened. On the one hand, there were those who were drawn to the notion of using the crisis to force the old ruling class to do a deal with them to enforce 'Islamic values' (Banna himself dreamt of being involved with the monarchy in establishing a 'new Caliphate' and on one occasion gave backing to a government in return for it promising to clamp down on alcohol consumption and prostitution[59]); on the other, there were the radical petty bourgeois recruits wanting real social change, but only able to conceive of getting it through immediate armed struggle.

The same contradictions run right through Islamism in Egypt today. The reconstituted Muslim Brotherhood began operating semi-legally around the magazine *al-Dawa* in the late 1960s, turning its back on any notion of overthrowing the Egyptian regime. Instead it set its goal as reform of Egyptian society along Islamic lines by pressure from within. The task, as the supreme guide of the Brotherhood had put it in a book written from prison, was to be 'preachers, not judges'.[60] This meant, in practice, adopting a 'reformist Islamist' orientation, seeking an accommodation with the Sadat regime.[61] In return the regime used the Islamists to deal with those it regarded, at the time, as its main enemies—the left: 'The regime treated the reformist wing of the Islamist movements— grouped around the monthly magazine *al-Dawa* and on the university campuses by the Islamic Associations—with benevolence, as the Islamicists purged the universities of anything that smelled of Nasserism or Communism'.[62]

Egypt was shaken by a wave of strikes, demonstrations and riots in all its 13 main cities in January 1977, in response to the state putting up the price of bread and other main consumption items. This was the largest uprising in the country since the 1919 nationalist revolt against the British. Both the Muslim Brotherhood and the Islamic Associations condemned the rising and sent messages of support to the state against what they called a 'Communist conspiracy'.

For such Islamist 'reformism' what matters is changing the morals of society, rather than changing society itself. The stress is not on the reconstitution of the Islamic community (*umma*) by a transformation of society, but on enforcing certain sorts of behaviour within existing society. And the enemy is not the state or the internal 'oppressors', but external forces seen as undermining religious observance—in the case of *al-Dawa* 'Jewry', 'the crusade' (meaning Christians, including the Copts), 'communism' and 'secularism'. The fight to deal with these involves a struggle to impose the *sharia* (the legal system codified by Islamic jurists from the Koran and the Islamic tradition). It is a battle to get the existing state to impose a certain sort of culture on society, rather than a battle to overthrow the state.

Such a perspective accords neatly with the desires of the traditional social groups who back a certain version of Islamism (the remnants of the old landowning class, merchants), with those who were once radical young Islamists but who have now made good (those who made money in Saudi Arabia or who have risen to comfortable positions in the middle class professions) and to those radical Islamists who have lost heart in radical *social* change when faced with state repression.

But it does not fit at all with the frustrated aspirations of the mass of the impoverished students and ex-students, or with the mass of ex-peasants who they mix with in the poorer parts of the cities. They are easily drawn to much more radical interpretations of what the 'return to the Koran' means—interpretations which attack not just extraneous influences in the existing Islamic states, but those states themselves.

Thus a basic text for the Islamists in Egypt is the book *Signposts*, written by one of the Muslim Brothers hanged by Nasser in 1966, Sayyid

Qutb. This does not merely denounce the bankruptcies of the Western and Stalinist ideologies, but also insists that a state can call itself Islamic and still be based on anti-Islamic barbarism (*jahiliyya*, the name given by Muslims to the pre-Islamic society in Arabia).[63]

Such a state of affairs can only be rectified by 'a vanguard of the *umma*' which carries through a revolution by following the example of the 'first Koranic generation'[64]—that is, which withdraws from existing society as Mohammed did when he left Mecca in order to build up a force capable of overthrowing it.

Such arguments went beyond seeing the only enemy as imperialism, and instead, for the first time, attacked the local state directly. They were very embarrassing for the moderates of the neo-Muslim Brotherhood, who are supposed to revere their author as a martyr. But they have inspired many thousands of young radicals. Thus in the mid-1970s one group, *al Taktir Wal Higra*, whose leader, Shukri Mustafa, was executed for kidnapping a high religious functionary in 1977, rejected as 'non-Islamic' existing society, the existing mosques, the existing religious leaders and even the neo-Muslim Brotherhood associated with *Dawa*.[65] Its attitude was that its members alone were genuine Muslims and that they had to break with existing society, living as communities apart and treating everyone else as infidels.

At first the Islamic Associations in the universities were very much under the influence of the moderate Muslim Brotherhood, not only condemning the uprising against the price increases but even disavowing Shukri when he was hanged later in the year. But their attitudes began to shift, particularly when Sadat began the 'peace process' with Israel late in 1977. Soon many of the university activists were embracing ideas in some ways more radical than Shukri's: not only did they turn aside from existing society, they began organising to overthrow it, as with the assassination of Sadat by Abd al-Salam Faraj's *Jihad* group in October 1981.

Faraj spelt out his harsh criticisms of the strategies of different parts of Islamic movement—those sections who restricted themselves to working for Islamic charities, those (the neo-Muslim Brotherhood) who try to create an Islamic party which can only give legitimacy to the existing state, those who base themselves on 'preaching' and so avoid *jihad*, those who advocate withdrawal from society on the lines of Shukri's group, and those who saw the priority as fighting against the external enemies of Islam (in Palestine or Afghanistan). Against all of them, he insisted immediate armed struggle, '*jihad* against the iniquitous prince', was the duty of all Muslims:

> *The fight against the enemy at home takes priority over the fight against the enemy abroad... The responsibility for the existence of colonialism or imperi-*

alism in our Muslim countries lies with these infidel governments. To launch a struggle against imperialism is therefore useless and inglorious, a waste of time.[66]

Faraj's argument led straight to a perspective of insurrection against the state. But this did not stop there being significant differences within his own group between the Cairo section, built round the prime objective of destroying the infidel state, and the other section in the middle Egyptian city of Asyut, who 'considered Christian proselytism the main obstacle to the propagation of Islam'.[67]

In practice this meant the Asyut group directed most of its fire against the Coptic minority (mostly poor peasants)—a policy which had already been followed with horrific success by the *jamaa* students earlier in the year, when it ignited murderous inter-communal fighting first in the middle Egypt town of Minya and then in the Cairo neighbourhood of Al-Zawiyya al-Hamra: 'The *jamaa* did not hesitate to fan the flames of sectarian tension in order to place the state in an awkward position and to demonstrate they were prepared to supplant the state, step by step, so to speak.'[68]

The Asyut section of *jihad* was, then, following a tried and proven method of gaining local popular support through a strategy of encouraging communal hatreds. This enabled it briefly to seize control of Asyut in the aftermath of the assassination of Sadat. By contrast, the Cairo activists, with their stress on the state as the enemy, 'enjoyed no networks of complicity or sustenance, and their isolated act—the assassination of Sadat—was not followed by the uprising of the Muslim population of Cairo so ardently sought by Faraj and his friends'.[69]

Instead of the assassination leading to the Islamists being able to seize state power, the state was able to take advantage of the confusion created by the assassination to crush the Islamists. As thousands were arrested and many leaders executed, repression significantly weakened the movement. However, the causes which had led so many young people to turn to the Islamists did not disappear. By the end of the 1980s the movement had regained confidence and was starting to grow rapidly in some quarters of Cairo and Alexandria. This was coupled with an effective terrorist campaign against the police and the security forces.

Then in December 1992 the state launched a new and unprecedented campaign of repression. Slum areas in Cairo, such as Imbaba, were occupied by 20,000 troops with tanks and armoured cars. Tens of thousands were arrested and death squads set out to kill those activists who escaped. The main mosques used by the radical Islamists were blocked with concrete. Parents, children and wives of activists were arrested and tortured.

Again as in the early 1980s the campaign of state terror was successful. The Islamist movement was not able to, and did not even try to, mobilise support in the form of demonstrations. Instead, it moved to a totally terrorist strategy which did not seriously shake the Mubarak regime, even if it did virtually destroy the tourist industry.

Meanwhile, the Muslim Brotherhood has continued to behave like a loyal opposition, negotiating with the regime over the gradual introduction of the *sharia* into the state legal code and holding back from protests at the repression.

The contradictions of Islamism: Algeria

The story of the rise and radicalisation of Islamism in Algeria is similar in many ways to that in Egypt. The Algerian dictator of the late 1960s and 1970, Boumediénne, encouraged moderate Islamism as a counterbalance to the left and to his historic opponents within the liberation movement that had ended French colonialism.

In 1970 the state initiated an Islamisation campaign under Mouloud Kassim, minister of education and religion, which denounced the 'degradation of morals' and 'Western influences' behind 'cosmopolitanism, alcoholism, the snobbism that consists in always following the West and dressing half naked'.[70] The Islamicists were able to climb on this bandwagon to increase their own influence, getting money from landowners worried about the agrarian reform to propagate a message which could appeal to the most impoverished layers in society:

> *The theme of the integrists' propaganda was that Islam was menaced by atheistic and communist intrusion of which the agrarian reform was the bearer... The integrists...spread their own ideas in the most unfavoured neighbourhoods, after building improvised mosques which were later made into solid constructions. Untouched by the agrarian revolution, workers and unemployed, discontented by their conditions, listened to the integrists.*[71]

Then in the mid-1970s they got support from sections of the regime to undermine the left in the colleges: 'Between 1976 and 1980 the integrists succeeded, with the connivance of the regime, in reducing to nothing the influence of the Marxists'.[72]

In the early 1980s a section of the regime continued to look towards the more 'moderate' versions of Islamism to bolster itself. The minister of religious affairs until 1986, Chibane, hoped to build such an Islamist tendency, and to this end helped the Islamists to get money for building mosques from industrialists and commercial interests.[73] But this could not stop the development of radical interpretations of Islam which rejected the regime. Thus in the city of Constantine, one study tells:

> *Integrism replaces among large sections of Constantine opinion the traditional conceptions by the popularity of a new Islamic vision standing for a resurgence of the Community of the Prophet. This integrism gets its strength from the social frustrations which afflict a large part of the youth, those left out of account by the social and economic system.*[74]

The strength of this interpretation of Islam was such as to be able to force the ministry of religious instruction to employ its people as *imams* (preachers) in the mosques rather than those who accepted 'moderate' views.

The regime was losing control of the very mechanism it had encouraged to deal with the left. Instead of controlling the masses for the regime, Islamism was providing a focus for all their bitterness and hatred against those leaders who harked back to the liberation struggle of the 1960s but who had grown into a comfortable ruling class. The economic crisis which hit Algerian society in the mid-1980s deepened the bitterness—just as the ruling class turned back to the Western capitalists it had once denounced in an effort to come to terms with the crisis. And the Islamist agitation against those who spoke French and were 'corrupted by Western morals' could easily become an attack on the interests of 'the small but influential stratum of highly educated technocrats who constitute the core of a new salaried and bureaucratised class'.[75]

The regime began to turn against the Islamists imprisoning certain of their leaders in the mid-1980s, with the regime's head, Chadli, accusing the *imams* of 'political demagogy'.[76] The effect, however, was not to destroy the Islamists, but to increase their standing as *the* opposition to the regime.

This became clear in October 1988. All the bitterness against the ruling class and the regime exploded in upheaval very similar to that which was to take place in Eastern Europe a year later. The movement, beginning as a series of spontaneous strikes in the Algiers area, soon turned into massive street clashes between young people and the police: 'The people, like a freed prisoner, rediscovered their own voices and their sense of liberty. Even the power of the police no longer frightened them'.[77] 'The insurrection of October 1988 was above all a revolt of young people against their conditions of life after a quarter of a century of military dictatorship.'[78]

The revolt shook the regime to its core. As in Eastern Europe all sorts of political forces that had been repressed now came out into the open. Journalists wrote freely for the first time, intellectuals began to speak openly about the real condition of Algerian society, exiled politicians of both left and right returned from abroad, a women's movement emerged to challenge the regime's Islamic family law, which gave women fewer rights than men. But it soon became clear that outside the Berber speaking areas the Islamists were the hegemonic force among the opposition. Their influence was in many ways like that of the 'democrats' in Eastern Europe and the USSR in the following year. The tolerance shown to them by sections of the regime in the past, and the support they continued to get from some powerful foreign states (for instance, finance from Saudi Arabia) combined with their ability to articulate a message that focused the bitterness of the mass of the population:

> *By their number, their network of mosques, and their tendency to act spontaneously as a single man, as if obeying the orders of a secret central committee, the Islamists appeared as the only movement capable of mobilising the masses and influencing the course of events. It was they who would come forward as the spokesmen of the insurgents, able to impose themselves as future leaders of the movement... Not knowing who to talk to, after quietening its machine guns, the regime was looking for 'leaders', representatives capable of formulating demands and controlling a crowd as violent as they were uncontrollable. So Chadli received Madani, Belhadj, and Nahnah* [the best known Islamist figures].[79]

So influential did the Islamist movement, now organised as the FIS, become in the months that followed that it was able to win control of the most important municipalities in the June 1990 local elections and then the biggest share of the votes in the general elections of December 1991, despite being subject to severe repression. The Algerian military annulled the elections in order to stop the Islamists forming a government. But this did not stop the massive support for the Islamists creating near civil war conditions in the country, with whole areas falling under effective control of Islamist armed groups.

Yet the rise of Islamist influence was accompanied by growing confusion as to what the FIS stood for. While it was in control of the country's major municipalities between June 1990 and May 1991,

> *The changes it brought about were modest: the closing of bars, the cancellation of musical spectacles, campaigns, at times violent, for 'feminine decency' and against the ubiquitous satellite dishes that 'permitted reception of Western pornography'... Neither Madani* [the FIS's best known leader] *nor its consultative assembly drew up a true politico-social programme or convened a congress to discuss it. Madani limited himself to saying that this would meet after they had formed a government.*[80]

What the FIS did do was show opposition to the demands of workers for improved wages. In these months it opposed a dust workers' strike in Algiers, a civil servants strike and a one day general strike called by the former 'official' union federation. Madani justified breaking the dust workers' strike in a newspaper interview, complaining that it was forcing respectable people like doctors and professional engineers to sweep up:

The dustmen have the right to strike, but not the right to invade our capital and turn our country into a dustbin. There are strikes of trade unions that have become terrains for action by the corrupters, the enemies of Allah and the fatherland, communists and others, who are spreading everywhere because the cadre of the FLN have retreated... We are reliving the days of the OAS.[81]

Such a respectable stance fitted neatly with the interests of the classes who had financed the Islamists from the time of the land reform onwards. It also suited those successful members of the petty bourgeoisie who were part of the FIS—the professors, the established *imams* and the grammar school teachers. And it appealed to those in the countryside whose adhesion to the former ruling party, the FLN, had enabled them to prosper, becoming successful capitalist farmers or small businessmen. But it was not enough either to satisfy the impoverished urban masses who looked to the FIS for their salvation or to force the ruling class and the military to sit back and accept an FIS government.

At the end of May 1991, faced with threats by the military to sabotage the electoral process rather than risk a FIS victory, the FIS leaders turned round and 'launched an authentic insurrection which recalled October 1988: molotov cocktails, tear gas, barricades. Ali Belhadj, the charismatic *Imam*, launched tens of thousands of demonstrators on to the streets.'[82] For a time the FIS took control of the centre of Algiers, supported by vast numbers of young people to whom Islam and the *jihad* seemed the only alternative to the misery of the society the military were defending.

In reality, the more powerful the FIS became, the more it was caught between respectability and insurrectionism, telling the masses they could not strike in March 1991 and then calling on them to overthrow the state two months later in May.

The same contradictions have emerged within the Islamist movement in the three years since, as guerrilla warfare has grown in intensity in both the cities and the countryside. 'The condemnation of Abasi Madani and Ali Belhadj to 12 years in prison...provoked a major radicalisation of the FIS and a fragmentation of its rank and file. The detention of thousands of members and sympathisers in camps in the Sahara spread urban terrorism and rural guerrilla warfare'.[83] Two armed organisations emerged, the Armed Islamic Movement (MIA, recently renamed AIS) and the Armed Islamic Groups (GIA), which were soon getting the support of armed bands right across the country. But the underground movements were characterised by 'internal dissension':[84]

> As against the presumed 'moderation' of the MIA, which 'only' executes the representatives of the 'impious regime', the GIA opposes an extreme **jihad**, whose chosen victims are journalists, writers, poets, feminists and intellectuals...since November 1993 killing 32 moderate Islamic **imams** and unveiled women...
>
> Fratricidal fights between the MIA and the GIA have led to dozens of casualties...the deaths of seven terrorists are imputed to these quarrels by some people, but to the death squads of the police by others...[85] The GIA accuses the historical leaders of the FIS of opportunism, treachery and abandoning their programme of the complete application of the **Sharia**.[86]

Splitting two ways

The experience of Islamism in Egypt and Algeria shows how it can split over two different questions: first over whether to follow the course of more or less peaceful reform of the existing society or to take up arms; second over whether to fight to change the state or to purge society of 'impiety'.

In Egypt the present day Muslim Brotherhood is based on a policy of reform directed at the state. It attempts to work within existing society building up its strength so as to become a legal opposition, with MPs, a press of its own, control over various middle class professional organisations and influence over wider sections of the population through the mosques and the Islamic charities. It also tends to stress the fight to impose Islamic piety through campaigning for the existing regime to incorporate the *sharia* into the legal code.

This is a strategy which also seems to appeal to a section of the imprisoned or exiled leadership of the FIS in Algeria. In the first few months of 1994 there were reports of negotiations between them and a section of the regime, with a perspective of sharing power and implementing part of the *sharia*. Thus the *Guardian* could report in April 1994 that Rabah Kebir, an exiled leader of FIS, welcomed the appointment of a new prime minster for Algeria, the 'technocrat', Redha Malek, as 'a positive act'[87]—only two days after the FIS had denounced the latest package agreed between that government and the IMF.[88]

Some perceptive commentators see such a deal as providing the best way for the Algerian bourgeoisie to end the instability and preserve its position. Thus Juan Goytisolo argues that the military could have saved itself a lot of trouble by allowing the FIS to form a government after the 1991 elections:

> The conditions in which it acceded to power would have limited in a very effective way the application of its programme. The indebtedness of Algeria, its financial dependence on its European and Japanese creditor, the economic chaos and the hostile reservations of the Armed Forces would have constituted a difficult obstacle for a FIS government to overcome... Its inability to fulfil its electoral promises were fully predictable. With a year of a government so tightly constrained by its enemies, the FIS would have lost a good part of its credibility.[89]

'Islamist reformism' fits the needs of certain major social groups—the traditional landowners and merchants, the new Islamic bourgeoisie (like those of the Muslim Brotherhood who made millions in Saudi Arabia) and that section of the Islamic new middle class who have enjoyed upward mobility. But it does not satisfy the other layers who have looked to Islamism—the students and impoverished ex-students, or the urban poor. The more the Muslim Brotherhood or the FIS look to compromise, the more these layers look elsewhere, seeing any watering down of the demand for the installation of Islam of the Koranic years as betrayal.

But their reaction to this can be in different directions. It can remain passive in the face of the state, urging a strategy of withdrawal from society, in which the stress is on preaching and purifying the Islamic minority, rather than on confrontation. This was the original strategy of the Shukri group in Egypt in the mid-1970s, and it is the approach of some of the radical preachers who are aware of the power of the state today.

Or it can turn to armed struggle. But just as peaceful struggle can be directed against the state or against impiety alone, so armed struggle can be armed struggle to overthrow the state, or armed actions against 'the enemies of Islam' among the population at large—the ethnic and religious minorities, unveiled women, foreign films, the influence of 'cultural imperialism' and so on. The logic of the situation might seem to push people towards the option of armed struggle *against the state*. But there is a powerful counter-logic at work, which is rooted in the class composition of the Islamist following.

As we have seen, the sections of the exploiting classes which back Islamism are naturally drawn to its more reformist versions. Even where they find little choice but to take up arms, they want to do so in ways which minimise wider social unrest. They look to coups d'etat rather than mass action. And if this erupts despite them, they seek to bring it to an end as quickly as possible.

The impoverished new petty bourgeoisie can move much further towards a perspective of armed action. But its own marginal social position cuts it off from seeing this as developing out of mass struggles like strikes. Instead it looks to conspiracies based on small armed groups—conspiracies that do not lead to the revolutionary change their instigators want, even when, as with the assassination of Sadat, they achieve their immediate goals. It can cause enormous disruption to existing society but it cannot revolutionise it.

This was the experience of the populists in Russia before 1917. It was the experience of a generation of students and ex-students right across the Third World who turned to Guevarism or Maoism in the late 1960s (and whose successors still fight on in the Philippines and Peru). It is the experience of armed anti-state Islamists in Egypt and Algeria today.

The only way out of this impasse would be for the Islamists to base themselves on the non-marginal groups among the urban poor today—among the workers in medium and large scale industry. But the basic notions of Islamism make this all but impossible since Islam, in even its most radical form, preaches the return to a community (*umma*) which reconciles the rich and the poor, not an overthrow of the rich. Thus the economic programme of the FIS puts forward as an alleged alternative to 'Western capitalism' a blueprint for 'small business' producing for 'local needs' which is virtually indistinguishable from the electoral propaganda of innumerable conservative and liberal parties right across the world.[90] And its attempt to create 'Islamic unions' in the summer of 1990 laid stress on the 'duties of workers', because, it was claimed, the old regime gave them too many rights and 'accustomed the workers to not working'. The class struggle, it insisted. 'does not exist in Islam', for the sacred texts do not speak of it. What is needed is for the employer to treat his workers in the same way the Koran tells the faithful to treat their domestic slaves—as 'brothers'.[91]

It is not surprising that nowhere have any of the Islamist groups ever succeeded in building a base in the factories even one tenth as strong as they built up in the neighbourhoods. But without such a base they cannot on their own accord determine the direction of social change, even if they do succeed in bringing about the collapse of an existing regime. Those on the margins of society can occasionally provoke a great crisis within an already unstable regime. They cannot determine how the crisis is resolved.

The Islamist groups may be able to provoke such a crisis in one of the existing regimes and so force out its existing leaders. But that will not prevent an outcome in which the ruling class, which has prospered beneath these leaders, does a deal with the less militant Islamists to hold on to power. And short of such a crisis the militant Islamists themselves face an enormous toll of deaths at the hands of the state.

It is this pressure from the state which encourages some of them to turn away from direct assault on the regime to the easier task of assaulting the 'impious' and the minorities—an approach which in turn can bring them back closer to the mainstream 'moderate' reformist Islamists.

There is, in fact, a certain dialectic at work within Islamism. Militant anti-state Islamists, after bearing the brunt of unsuccessful armed struggle, learn the hard way to keep their heads down and instead turn to fighting to impose Islamic behaviour either directly or through Islamic reformism. But neither imposing the Islamic behaviour nor reforms can deal with the immense dissatisfaction of the social layers that look to Islamism. And so new militants are continually arising who split off to return to the path of armed action, until these too learn the hard way the limitations of armed actions which are cut off from an active social base.

There is no automatic progression from seeing the limitations of Islamic reformism to moving to revolutionary politics. Rather the limitations of reformism lead either to the terrorism and guerrillaism of groups that try to act without a mass base, or in the direction of a reactionary attack on scapegoats for the problems of the system. And because each of the approaches expresses itself in the same religious language, there is often an overlap between one and the other. People who do want to attack the regime and imperialism do attack the Copts, the Berbers and unveiled women. People who have an instinctive hatred of the whole system do fall into the trap of wanting to negotiate over the imposition of the *sharia* by the state. And where there are divisions between rival groups—sometimes so bitter that they start killing each other as 'apostates' (renegades from true Islam)—the divisions are expressed in ways which obscure the real social causes behind them. If one upwardly mobile Islamist abandons the struggle, that only proves that he personally is a 'bad Muslim' (or even an apostate); it does not in itself prevent another upwardly mobile Islamist from being a 'good Muslim'.

The Iranian experience

The Islamic regime in Iran dominates discussions on Islamic revivalism, much as the record of Stalinism dominates discussions on socialism. And often, even on the left, very similar conclusions are drawn. The Islamists are seen, much as the Stalinists were once seen, as the most dangerous of all political forces, able to impose a totalitarianism that will prevent any further progressive development. In order to stop them it is necessary for the left to unite with the liberal section of the bourgeoisie,[92] or even to support non-democratic states in their repression of the Islamist groups.[93] It is a view that overrates the cohesion of Islamism and ascribes to it an ability to dictate historical events which in reality it does not have. And it rests on an erroneous understanding of the role of Islam during and after the Iranian Revolution of 1979.

That revolution was not a product of Islamism, but of the enormous contradictions that arose in the Shah's regime in the mid to late 1970s. Economic crisis had heightened the deep divisions which existed between sections of modern capital associated with the state and other, more 'traditional', sections centred around the bazaar (which was responsible for two thirds of wholesale trade and three quarters of retail trade) at the same time as deepening the discontent of the mass of the workers and the vast numbers of recent ex-peasants who had flooded into the cities. Protests of intellectuals and students were joined by the disaffected clergy and spread to involve the urban poor in a series of great clashes with the police and army. A wave of strikes paralysed industry and brought the all important oil fields to a standstill. And then early in February 1979 the left wing guerrillas of the Fedayeen and the left-Islamist guerrillas of the People's Mojahedin succeeded in fomenting large scale mutinies in the armed forces, so bringing about a revolutionary collapse of the old regime.

Much of the rising movement had identified with the exiled Islamist Ayatollah Khomeini. His name had come to symbolise opposition to the monarchy, and his residence outside Paris had been the point of contact between representatives of the different forces involved—the *bazaaris* and the clergy who were close to them, the liberal bourgeois opposition, the professional associations, the students and even the left guerrillas. On his return to Tehran in January 1979 he became the symbolic leader of the revolution.

Yet at this stage he was far from controlling events, even though he had an acute sense of political tactics. The key events that brought the Shah down—the spread of the strikes, the mutiny inside the armed forces—occurred completely independently of him. And in the months after the revolution Khomeini was no more able to impose a single authority over the revolutionary upheaval than anyone else. In the cities various local committees (*Komitehs*) exercised de facto power. The universities were in the hands of the left and the Mojahedin. In the factories *shoras* (factory councils) fought for control with management, often forcing out those associated with the Shah's regime and taking over the organisation of production themselves. In the regions inhabited by ethnic minorities—Kurdistan in the north west and Khuzistan in the Arab speaking south west—movements began to fight for self determination. And at the top, overseeing this process, was not one body but two. The provisional government was run by Bazargan, a 'moderate' Islamist linked to modern sections of the bourgeoisie (he had founded the Islamic students' associations in the 1950s and then the Islamic Engineers Association). But next to it, acting as an alternative centre of authority, was a revolutionary council nominated by Khomeini, around which coalesced a group of clerics and Islamist intellectuals with links with the bazaars.

The group around Khomeini were eventually able to establish near total power for themselves and their Islamic Republican Party (IRP). But it took them two and a half years of manoeuvring between different social forces which could easily have overwhelmed them. For most of 1979 they collaborated with Bazargan in an effort to clamp down on the *shoras* within the factories and the separatist nationalist movements. They used Islamic language to mobilise behind them sections of the lumpen proletariat into gangs, the Hizbollah, which would attack the left, enforce Islamic 'morality' (for instance, against women who refused to wear the veil) and join the army in putting down the separatist revolts. There were instances of brutal repression (the execution of about a hundred people for 'sexual crimes', homosexuality and adultery, the killing of some left wing activists, the shooting down of protesters belonging to the national minorities), as in any attempt to restore bourgeois 'normality' after a great revolutionary upheaval. But the overall balance sheet for the IRP was not very positive in the early autumn of 1979. On the one hand, those successes they had enjoyed in checking the revolution had strengthened the position of the grouping around Bazargan with whom they were increasingly at odds. As a study of Bazargan's movement has put it:

> *One year after the fall of the Shah it was becoming clear that the better educated middle classes and the political forces they were supporting* [ie Bazargan] *were rapidly expanding their influence, being dominant in sensitive positions in the mass media, state organisations and especially educational institutions... With the disintegration of the unity of the Islamic forces, the Islamic committees were not capable of having a large majority of the employees of the organisations behind them.*[94]

On the other, there was a growing ferment that threatened to escape from the Khomeiniites' control, leading to a massive growth of both the secular left and the Islamic left. The left was dominant among the students, despite the first wave of repression against it in August 1979. The *shoras* in the factories had been weakened by this same repression, but many remained intact for another year,[95] and the workers' willingness to struggle was certainly not destroyed—there were 360 'forms of strikes, sit-ins and occupations' in 1979-80, 180 in 1980-1 and 82 in 1981-2.[96]

The IRP could only regain control itself by making a radical shift in November 1979—organising the minority of students who followed its banner rather than that of the Fedayeen or People's Mojahedin to seize the US embassy and hold its staff hostage, provoking a major confrontation with the world's most important imperialist power. Another study of this period says: 'The fundamentalist student of the "Islamic Associations" who a few weeks earlier had been looked on by their rivals as reactionaries and fanatics, were now posing as super-revolutionaries and were cheered by masses of people whenever they appeared at the gate of the Embassy to be interviewed by reporters'.[97]

The shift to an apparently radical anti-imperialist stance was accompanied by radicalisation of the IRP's policies in the workplaces. From defending many of the old managers it moved to agitating for their removal—although not for their power to be taken over by the factory councils, but by 'Islamic managers' who would collaborate with Islamic councils from which the left and the Mojahedin were automatically excluded as 'infidels'.

This radical turn gave new popularity to the IRP. It seemed to be putting into effect the anti-imperialism which the group around Bazargan had propagated during their long years of opposition to the Shah but which they were now abandoning as they sought to cement a new relationship between Iran and the US. It was also acting in accord with some of the main and most popular slogans raised in the months since the revolution by the growing forces of both the secular and the Islamic left:

> *The taking over of the American Embassy helped the fundamentalists to overcome some of their difficulties... The outcome helped those groups that advocated the sovereignty of the clergymen to implement their polices and take over the sensitive organisations that were manned and controlled by the better educated middle class. When the students who were loyal to the clergymen invaded the gates of the US embassy, those who had been identified as 'reactionaries' re-emerged as the leading revolutionaries, capable of dumping the modernist and secularist forces altogether... It was the beginning of a new coalition in which certain clergy and their **bazaari** associates were the leaders and large groups from the lower middle class and the urban lower class were the functionaries.*[98]

The group around Khomeini was not just gaining in popularity, it was also creating a much wider base for itself as it displaced, or at least threatened to displace, the old 'non-Islamic' managers and functionaries.

In industry, the media, the armed forces, the police, a new layer of people began to exercise control whose careers depended on their ability to agitate for Khomeini's version of Islamism. And those who remained from the old hierarchies of power rushed to prove their own Islamic credentials by implementing the IRP line.

What the group around Khomeini succeeded in doing was to unite behind it a wide section of the middle class—both the traditional petty bourgeoisie based in the bazaar and many of the first generation of the new middle class—in a struggle to control the hierarchies of power. The secret of its success was its ability to enable those who followed it at every level of society to combine religious enthusiasm with personal advance. Someone who had been an assistant manager in a foreign owned company could now run it under state control and feel he was fulfilling his religious duty to serve the community (*umma*); someone who had lived in deep poverty among the lumpen proletariat could now achieve both material security and a sense of self achievement by leading a hizbollah gang in its attempts to purify society of 'indecency' and the 'infidel Communists'.

The opportunities open to those who opted for the Khomeini line were enormous. The flight from the country of local and foreign managers and technicians during the early months of revolutionary upheaval had created 130,000 positions to be filled.[99] The purging of 'non-Islamic' managers, functionaries and army officers added enormously to the total.

The interesting thing about the method by which the group around Khomeini ousted their opponents and established a one party regime was that there was nothing specifically Islamist about it. It was not, as many people horrified by the religious intolerance of the regime contend, a result of some 'irrational' or 'medieval' characteristic of 'Islamic fundamentalism'. In fact, it was very similar to that carried through in different parts of the world by parties based on sections of the petty bourgeoisie. It was the method used, for instance, by the weak Communist Parties of much of Eastern Europe to establish their control after 1945.[100] And a prototype for the petty bourgeois who combines ideological fervour and personal advance is to be found in Balzac's Pére Goriot—the austere Jacobin who makes his fortune out of exploiting the shortages created by the revolutionary upheaval.

A political party based on organising a section of the petty bourgeoisie around the struggle for positions cannot take power in just any circumstances. Most such attempts come to nothing, because the petty bourgeois formations are too weak to challenge the power of the old ruling class without a mobilisation of the mass of society which they then cannot control. Thus in the Portuguese Revolution of 1974-5 the Communist Party's attempts to infiltrate the hierarchies of power fell apart in the face of a resistance co-ordinated by the major Western capitalist powers on the one hand and of an upsurge of workers' militancy from below on the other. Such attempts can only work if, for specific historical reasons, the major social classes are paralysed.

As Tony Cliff put it in a major piece of Marxist analysis, if the old ruling class is too weak to hang on to power in the face of economic crisis and insurgency from below, while the working class does not have the independent organisation to allow it to become the head of the movement, then sections of the intelligentsia are able to make a bid for power, feeling that they have a mission to solve the problems of society as a whole:

> *The intelligentsia is sensitive to their countries' technical lag. Participating as it does in the scientific and technical world of the 20th century, it is stifled by the backwardness of its own nation. This feeling is accentuated by the 'intellectual unemployment' endemic in these countries. Given the general economic backwardness, the only hope for most students is a government job, but there are not nearly enough of these to go round.*
>
> *The spiritual life of the intellectuals is also in a crisis. In a crumbling order where the traditional pattern is disintegrating, they feel insecure, rootless, lacking in firm values.*
>
> *Dissolving cultures give rise to a powerful urge for a new integration that must be total and dynamic if it is to fill the social and spiritual vacuum, that must combine religious fervour with militant nationalism. They are in search for a dynamic movement which will unify the nation and open up broad vistas for it, but at the same time will give themselves power...*
>
> *They hope for reform from above and would dearly love to hand the new world over to a grateful people, rather than see the liberating struggle of a self conscious and freely associated people result in a new world for themselves. They care a lot for measures to drag their nation out of stagnation, but very little for democracy... All this makes totalitarian state capitalism a very attractive goal for intellectuals.*[101]

Although these words were written about the attraction of Stalinism, Maoism and Castroism in Third World countries, they fit absolutely the Islamist intelligentsia around Khomeini in Iran. They were not, as many left wing commentators have mistakenly believed, merely an expression of 'backward', bazaar-based traditional, 'parasitic', 'merchant capital'.[102] Nor were they simply an expression of classic bourgeois counter-revolution.[103] They undertook a revolutionary reorganisation of ownership and control of capital within Iran even while leaving capitalist relations of production intact, putting large scale capital that had been owned by the group around the Shah into the hands of state and parastate bodies controlled by themselves—in the interests of the 'oppressed', of course, with the corporation that took over the Shah's own economic empire being named the Mustafazin ('Oppressed') Foundation. As Bayat tells:

> The seizure of power by the clergy was a reflection of a power vacuum in the post-revolutionary state. Neither the proletariat nor the bourgeoisie was able to exert their political hegemony. The reason for their inability must be sought in their historical development which is a testimony to the weakness of both.[104]

Or, as Cliff put it of the intelligentsia in Third World countries: 'Their power is in direct relation to the feebleness of other classes and their political nullity'.[105]

It was because they depended on balancing between the major social classes to advance their own control over the state and a section of capital that the Khomeini group had to hit first at the left organisation and then at the established bourgeois organisations (Bazargan etc) before being able to consolidate their own power. In 1979 this meant working with Bazargan against the left to subdue the revolutionary wave, and then making certain gestures to the left at the time of the seizure of the US Embassy to isolate the established bourgeoisie. During the 1980s it meant another zigzag, allowing another Islamic figure linked to the established bourgeoisie, Bani Sadr, to take the presidency and then working with him to smash the bastion of the left, the universities. When the IRP suggested sending the Islamic gangs, the Hizbollah, into the universities to purge them of 'anti-Islamic elements', Bani Sadr was happy to comply:

> Both the IRP leaders and the liberals agreed to the idea of cultural revolution through direct action by the people who were mobilised to march on university campuses... For the liberals it was a means to get rid of the leftist agitators in the public institutions, the factories and the rural areas, so that economic and political stability could be restored to the country...
> The gangs of the Hizbollah invaded the universities, injured and killed members of the political groups who were resisting the cultural revolution, and burned books and papers thought to be 'un-Islamic'. The government closed all universities and colleges for three years, during which university curricula were rewritten.[106]

Yet even at this time the Khomeiniites continued to preserve part of their own 'left' image, using anti-imperialist language to justify what they were doing. They insisted the fight to impose 'Islamic values' was essential in the struggle against 'cultural imperialism', and that, because the left resisted this, it was in reality working for imperialism.

External events helped them to get away with these arguments. These were the months of the abortive US attempt to recapture the embassy by sending in armed helicopters (which crashed into each other in the desert), of Shiite demonstrations against the government of Bahrin, of pro-Khomeini riots in the oil rich Saudi province of Hasa, of the seizure of the Grand Mosque in Mecca by armed Sunni Islamists, and of the attempt by Saddam Hussein of Iraq to ingratiate himself with the US and the Arab Gulf sheikdoms by launching an invasion of Iran. The Khomeiniites could proclaim, rightly, that the revolution was under attack from forces allied to imperialism, and, wrongly, that they alone could defend it. No wonder Khomeini himself referred to the attack as a 'godsend'. The need for all out mobilisation against the invading forces in the winter of 1980-1 allowed his supporters to justify increasing their control, at the expense of both the left and the Bani Sadr group, until in June-July 1981 they were able to crush both, establishing a near totalitarian structure.

But why were the left not able to deal with the advance of the IRP? In retrospect, it is often argued that the fault lies with the failure of the left to understand in time the need for an alliance with the 'progressive', 'liberal', bourgeoisie. This is Halliday's argument.[107] But, as we have seen, the liberal bourgeoisie under Bazargan and then Bani Sadr were united with Khomeini in the campaign against the *shoras* in the factories and the campaign to purge the universities. What divided them was who was going to get the fruits of their successes against the left. It was only when he finally found that he had lost out that Bani Sadr (but not, interestingly, Bazargan, whose party continued to operate legally but ineffectively) joined with the left Islamists of the People's Mojahedin in an abortive attempt to overthrow the regime.

The Khomeiniites were able to out manoeuvre the allegedly 'liberal' section of the bourgeoisie because, after beating the left, they were then able to use anti-imperialist rhetoric to mobilise sections of the urban poor against the established bourgeoisie. They could play on the obvious gap between the miserable lives of the masses and the 'un-Islamic' lifestyles of the well to do. The left could not resist this manoeuvre by lining up with the well to do Westernised section of the bourgeoisie.

The key to genuinely undercutting the Khomeiniites lay in mobilising workers to fight on their own behalf. This would have thrown both the allegedly 'liberal' section of the bourgeoisie and the IRP on to the defensive.

The workers' struggles played a central role in the overthrow of the Shah, and in the aftermath there were major struggles in the large factories between the factory councils and the management. But once the Shah was removed, the workers' struggles rarely went beyond the confines of individual factories to contest the leadership of all the oppressed and exploited. The factory councils never became *workers'* councils on the pattern of the soviets of Russia in 1905 and 1917.[108] And because of that failing they did not succeed in attracting behind them the mass of casual labourers, self employed, artisans and impoverished tradesmen— the 'lumpen proletariat'—who the Khomeiniites mobilised against the left under religious slogans.

This weakness of the workers' movement was partly a result of objective factors. There was a division within the working class between those in the modern sector of large factories and those in the traditional sector of small workshops (many operated by family members or their owners). The areas that workers lived in were often numerically dominated by the impoverished sectors of the petty bourgeoisie: there were 750,000 'merchants, middlemen and small traders' in Tehran in 1980, as against about 400,000 workers in large industrial enterprises.[109] Very large numbers of workers were new to industry and had few traditions of industrial struggle—80 percent came from a rural origin and every year 330,000 more ex-peasants flooded into the towns.[110] Only a third were fully literate and so able to read the left's press, although 80 percent had televisions. Finally, the scale of repression under the Shah meant that the number of established militants in the workplaces was very small.

But the inability of the workers' movement to take the leadership of the wider mass movement was not just a result of objective factors. It was also a result of the political failings of the considerable left wing forces that existed in the post-revolutionary months. The Fedayeen and People's Mojahedin boasted of meetings many thousands strong, and the Mojahedin picked up a quarter of the votes in Tehran in the elections of the spring of 1980. But the traditions of the Fedayeen and the Mojahedin were guerrillaist, and they paid little attention to activity round the factories. Their bastions of support were the universities, not the factory areas. Thus the People's Mojahedin had five 'fronts' of activity: an underground organisation for preparing 'armed struggle', a youth front, a women's front, a *bazaari* front and, clearly not the top priority, a workers' front.

What is more, the large left organisations had little to say, even when worker activists did join them. In the vital first eight months of the revolution they made only limited criticisms of the new regime and these consisted mainly of its failure to challenge imperialism. The People's Mojahedin, for instance:

Scrupulously adhered to a policy of avoiding confrontations with the clerical shadow government. In late February when the Fedayeen organised a demonstration of over 80,000 at Tehran university demanding land reform, the end of press censorship and the dissolution of the armed forces, the Mojahedin stayed away. And early in March, when Western educated women celebrated international women's day by demonstrating against Khomeini's decrees abrogating the Family Protection Law, enforcing the use of the veil in government offices, and pushing the 'less impartial gender' from the judiciary, the Mojahedin warned that 'imperialism was exploiting such divisive issues'. In late March when zealous club wielders attacked the offices of the anti-clerical paper **Ayandegan**, *the Mojahedin said nothing. They opposed a boycott of the referendum over the Islamic republic and Kurdish struggle for autonomy. If the nation did not remain united behind Imam Khomeini, the Mojahedin emphasised, the imperialists would be tempted to repeat their 1953 performance.*[111]

In August the Mojahedin kept silent when armed gangs attacked the Fedayeen headquarters, and they avoided challenging IRP candidates in the 1979 elections for the Assembly of Experts.

After the occupation of the American embassy, the left became even less critical of Khomeini than before. Khomeini,

Was able to split the left opposition completely. Khomeini now declared that all problems arising in the factories, among women and among national minorities were due to US imperialism. It was US imperialism that was fighting the government in Kurdistan, in Tabriz, in Torkamansahra and in Khuzistan. Women opposing Islamic laws were US and Zionist agents. Workers resisting **shoras** *were imperialist agents.*

The Tudeh party fell in behind Khomeini's argument and backed his line. The biggest left organisations—the Fedayeen, the Mojahedin and the Paykar—also broke away from the struggle, abandoning the militant workers, the women and the national minorities, among whom they had some significant presence.[112]

The Tudeh (pro-Russian Communist) Party and the majority of the Fedayeen continued to support Khomeini until he had fully consolidated his power in 1982, whereupon he turned on them.

As time went on, the left compounded one mistake with another. While the majority of the Fedayeen dropped all criticism of the regime after the takeover of the US embassy, the People's Mojahedin eventually moved in the opposite direction, coming out in open opposition to the regime by the end of 1980 (after the regime's attack on its supporters in the universities). But its guerrilla strategy then led it to play straight into the regime's hands by joining with Bani Sadr to launch a direct struggle for power which was not rooted at all in the day to day struggles of the mass of people. When mass demonstrations failed to bring the regime down, its leaders fled into exile, while its underground activists launched armed attacks on key figures in the regime: 'The bombing of the IRP's headquarters in June 1981, which resulted in the death of Ayatollah Beheshti [IRP chairman] and many other leaders and cadres of the IRP, provided the *ulama* [ie clergy] with the excuse to unleash a reign of terror against the opposition unheard of in contemporary Iranian history'.[113]

The left was uniting with a representative of the established bourgeoisie in a campaign of assassinations directed against figures who the mass of people saw as playing an anti-imperialist role. It was hardly surprising that the impoverished petty bourgeois and lumpen supporters of the IRP identified with its leaders in the onslaught against the left. These leaders found it easy to portray the left as working hand in hand with imperialist opponents of the revolution—an argument which gained even greater credibility a couple of years later when the People's Mojahedin joined in the onslaught against Iran waged by the Iraqi army.

In fact, the Mojahedin was displaying all the faults which characterise the radical new petty bourgeoisie in many Third World countries, whether it is organised in Islamist, Maoist or nationalist parties. It sees the political struggle as dependent upon a minority acting as a 'vanguard' in isolation from the struggle of the masses. The battle for power is reduced to the armed coup on the one hand and the alliance with existing bourgeois forces on the other. With 'leadership' such as this, it is not surprising that the most radical workers were not able to build the militant struggles in individual factories into a movement capable of uniting behind it the mass of urban poor and peasants, and so left a vacuum which the IRP was able to fill.

Not all the left were as bad as the Mojahedin, the Fedayeen majority or the Tudeh Party. But these constituted the major forces to which those radicalised by the revolutionary experience looked. Their failings were a very important factor in allowing the Khomeini group to retain the initiative and to rebuild a weakened state into a powerful instrument capable of the most bloody repression.

Finally, even those on the left who did not make mistakes on the scale of the Mojahedin, Fedayeen and Tudeh Party made mistakes of their own. They had all been brought up on Stalinist or Maoist traditions which made them search for a 'progressive' section of the bourgeoisie or petty bourgeoisie to lead the struggle. If they decided a certain movement was of the 'progressive' or 'anti-imperialist' petty bourgeoisie, then they would dampen down any criticism. If, on the other hand, they decided a certain movement was not of the 'progressive petty bourgeoisie', then they concluded it could never, ever, engage in any conflict with imperialism. They had no understanding that again and again in Third World countries bourgeois and petty bourgeois leaders who are pro-capitalist and extremely reactionary in their social attitudes have, despite themselves, been drawn into conflicts with imperialism. This was, for instance, true of Kemal Ataturk in Turkey, of Grivas and Makarios in Cyprus, of Kenyatta in Kenya, of Nehru and Gandhi in India, and most recently of Saddam Hussein in Iraq. This has often given them a popularity with those they are intent on exploiting and oppressing.

The left cannot undercut that either by extolling them as 'progressive, anti-imperialist' heroes, or by pretending that the confrontation with imperialism does not matter. Instead the left has at all costs to preserve its own political independence, insisting on public criticism of such figures both for their domestic policies and for their inevitable failings in the struggle with imperialism, while making it clear that we want imperialism to be defeated much more than they do.

Unfortunately, virtually the whole of the Iranian left flip flopped from one mistaken position to another, so that they ended up taking a neutral stand in the final months of the first Gulf War when the US fleet intervened directly to tilt the balance against Iran. They did not understand that there were ways of taking an anti-imperialist stance that would have strengthened the fight against the Iranian regime at home (denouncing the refusal of the regime to make the rich pay for the war, criticising the barbaric and futile 'human wave' tactics of sending lightly armed infantry into frontal attacks on heavily defended Iraqi positions, condemning the failure to put forward a programme that would arouse the Iraqi workers and minorities to rise against Saddam Hussein, denouncing the call for war reparations as making the Iraqi people pay for their rulers crimes, and so on). Instead, they adopted a position which cut them off from anyone in Iran who remembered what imperialism had done to the country in the past and who could see that it would do so again if it got the chance.

The victory of Khomeini's forces in Iran was not, then, inevitable, and neither does it prove that Islamism is a uniquely reactionary force against which the left must be prepared to unite with the devil (or rather, the Great Satan) of imperialism and its local allies. It merely confirms that, in the absence of independent working class leadership, revolutionary upheaval can give way to more than one form of the restabilisation of bourgeois rule under a repressive, authoritarian, one party state. The secret ingredient in this process was not the allegedly 'medieval' character of Islam, but the vacuum created by the failure of the socialist organisations to give leadership to an inexperienced but very combative working class.

The contradictions of Islamism: Sudan

Iran is not the only country in which Islamists have exercised power. In the last few years the Sudanese Islamic Brotherhood, the *Ikhwan al Muslimin*, has become the decisive influence in a military government through the National Islamic Front (NIF).

The Sudanese Brotherhood began in the 1940s as an offshoot of Banna's Muslim Brotherhood in Egypt, but took on a life of its own with its own doctrines, after the crushing of the parent organisation by Nasser in the 1950s. The organisation originated in Khartoum University, where it battled with the Communists for influence over the students. This led to its first leadership emphasising the radical elements in Islamism. But in the 1960s a new leadership, under Hassan al-Turabi, succeeded in widening the base of the organisation, adding thousands of newcomers to its 2,000 hardcore members. 'The membership also witnessed a significant diversification by the involvement of *ulama*, mosque *imams*, merchants, sufi leaders and others, although the proportion of non-modern educated elements remained small in the active membership'.[114] In the 1980s it grew further, aided by the emergence (under state encouragement) of an 'Islamic' financial sector: 'The employment policy of the Islamic Bank, which favoured religious people, was helpful to *Ikhwan*'. The Islamic institutions led to 'the evolution of a totally new class of businessmen who became rich overnight' and 'opened up avenues of economic mobility for many who would otherwise have been, at most, higher civil servants'. The Brotherhood did not own the Islamic banks—they were financed by a combination of Saudi money and local capital. But it exerted enormous power by its ability 'to influence loans and other advances to customers'.[115] This translated itself into support for the Brotherhood among some of the new rich and within the state machine itself: 'The movement continued to be based on a hard core of activists, mostly modern educated professionals, but a significant contingent of businessmen (or professionals turned executives) started to acquire prominence'.[116]

In the 1986 elections after the overthrow of the Nimeiry dictatorship the Brotherhood's front, the NIF, won only 18.5 percent of the total vote, most votes going to the traditional parties. But it picked up no fewer than 23 out of 28 of the seats elected by university graduates only, and it soon became clear it had enough support among a section of the urban middle classes and businessmen to be the natural ally of key figures in the armed forces. A coup in 1989 gave power to General Bashir, but effective power seemed to be in the hands of the NIF. And since then Khartoum has become one of the centres of the international Islamist movement, a pole of attraction to rival Tehran and Riyadh for the activists.

Yet the Sudanese Brotherhood's rise to power has not been an easy one. It has repeatedly come close to losing many members and much of its support. And its tenure in power is not likely to be secure.

Turabi has sought to build the Brotherhood's influence when his rivals have been in government by agitating among the students, the middle class and, to some extent, the workers—but he has then seized every chance of participating in government himself so as to increase the Brotherhood's influence within the hierarchies of the state. This he first did in the early 1960s. The Brotherhood's agitation among students helped precipitate the October 1964 revolution of students, middle class professionals and workers. It then used its position in the new government to dampen down the wave of radicalisation and to push for the banning of the Communists—so winning to it some of the conservative privileged groups.

It followed the same manoeuvre again after a military coup put General Gaafar al-Nimeiry in power in May 1969. He repressed the Brotherhood along with the traditional parties for a period. But its spell in opposition allowed it to rebuild some of the popular support it had lost while in government, taking the lead in agitation over student conditions and leading an unsuccessful student rising against the regime in 1973. Then in the late 1970s it seized on an offer from Nimeiry of 'National Reconciliation' to join his regime, with Turabi becoming attorney general 'in charge of the review of laws to make them conform to the *sharia*'.[117] It was during this time that it used the development of the Islamic financial sector to get roots among the owners of capital. It was also during this period that it began to win over certain army officers.

Yet these manoeuvres created continual tensions within the Brotherhood and repeatedly threatened its wider base of support. The original cadres of the Brotherhood from the early 1950s were not at all happy with its leader's cultivation of sections of the traditional elite and of the new rich. Turabi's methods did not seem at all to fit the original notion of an Islamic vanguard which they had held as radical students in the 1940s. He seemed, to them, to be watering down Islamic ideas in order to gain respectability—especially when he set out to recruit women, supported them having the vote and produced a pamphlet asserting that 'genuine' Islam should give them the same rights as men.[118] To the dissidents it seemed that he was simply out to pander to the secular middle classes. On top of this Nimeiry was someone who was notorious for his non-Islamic behaviour—particularly his drinking. A group of older members preferred the radicalism of someone like Qutb, and finally split away to form an organisation of their own linked to the Egyptian Muslim Brotherhood.[119]

Collaboration with an increasingly unpopular regime began to undercut the Brotherhood's wider support. The early 1980s saw a growing wave of popular agitation against Nimeiry, with student demonstrations in 1981-2, a strike by rail workers in 1982, mutinies by southern troops in 1983 followed by strikes of judges and doctors. Through this period the Brotherhood became the only force outside the regime itself supporting Nimeiry, and began to fear being destroyed alongside the dictator when he eventually fell.

Then Nimeiry took a last gamble. He announced the immediate introduction of the *sharia* into law. The Brotherhood had no choice but to throw their weight behind him. For more than 30 years the 'return to the *sharia*' had been their answer to all of Sudan's problems. It was the single, simple slogan which connected their brand of reform with the Islamic traditions of the mass of people outside the urban middle class. And so they began agitation to support implementation of the *sharia*, in the face of resistance from the judges and much of the legal system. A million people joined a Brotherhood demonstration for an international conference on the implementation of the *sharia*, and Brotherhood members helped man the special *sharia* courts set up by Nimeiry.

This increased the Brotherhood's pull among certain traditionalist circles, especially when the courts began to pick upon certain prominent people and expose their corruption. And the new power it exercised increased its attraction to those in the state machine looking for promotion. But while making the Brotherhood popular among some traditionalist sections of the population and more influential among those who ran the state, the measures also massively increased resentment against them elsewhere. It upset those who were seculist or supporters of non-Islamic religions (the majority of the population in the south of the country) without being, in reality, able to improve the conditions of the Islamic masses. The myth of the *sharia* was that of a new legal system which would end all injustices. But this could not be brought about by any reform that was merely a legal reform, and least of all one introduced by a corrupt and unpopular regime. So all the new law really meant was a resort to *sharia* punishments, the *hudud*—amputation for theft, stoning for adultery, and so on.

In the 1960s the Brotherhood had been able to build itself among the urban intelligentsia in part because it down played this aspect of the *sharia*. The Islamic orthodoxy accepted by Turabi was to 'skirt the issue by insisting the *hudud* was only applicable in an ideal Islamic society from which want had been completely banished'.[120] Now, however, the most tangible evidence that the *sharia* was changing the legal system became the use of such punishments, and Turabi did a 180 degree turn, attacking those who claimed you could not impose morality on people by legislation'.[121]

Associated with resentment against the *sharia* courts was resentment against the Islamic financial sector. This had enabled some members of the middle class to move upwards into important business sectors. But it necessarily left many, many more disappointed:

> *Resentment was created in the business community and among thousands of aspirants who believed the main reason they were deprived of the benefits of the new system was **Ikhwan** favouritism... In the end, allegations about **Ikhwan**'s abuse of the Islamic banking system were the single most damaging liability that emerged from the Nimeiry era and discredited them in the eyes of large sections of the population.*[122]

Finally, the Brotherhood's alliance with Nimeiry over the *sharia* forced it to excuse everything else he did, at a time when there was a growing agitation against him. Even though Nimeiry, under US pressure, finally moved against the Brotherhood just before a popular rising overthrew him, it was too late for the Brotherhood to be identified in any sense with the revolution.

It survived, to take greater power than ever into its hands within four years, because it offered to those army officers who had finally turned against Nimeiry something no one else had—thousands of active members prepared to back them in their bitter civil war against non-Muslim rebels in the south of the country and in their repression of discontent in the towns of the north. The coalition of secular forces that had led the uprising against Nimeiry were paralysed by their opposed class interests, unable either to focus the discontent into a movement for a complete transformation of society, including massive redistribution of wealth and the granting of self determination to the south, or to crush it. This allowed the Brotherhood increasingly to offer itself to the army officers as the only force capable of imposing stability, showing its strength visibly by organising a large demonstration against any concessions to the the southern rebels. So it was that in 1989 when the military seized power once more, in order to pre-empt a proposed peace agreement between the government and the rebels, it connived with the Brotherhood.

In power, however, the Brotherhood has known only one answer to the problems that face the regime—increasingly severe repression wrapped in religious terminology. In March 1991 the *sharia* was reintroduced together with the *hudud* punishments. The war in the south has now been matched by repression against other non-Arab communities, including the Fur and the Nuba, despite Turabi's claims, when in opposition, to oppose any form of Islam based on Arab chauvinism. Typical of the repression against those who oppose the war in the south were the death sentences handed out two years ago to a group of people in Dafur for 'inciting war against the state and possessing weapons'. One man was sentenced to be hanged and then his body to be publicly crucified.[123] In the run up to elections in trade union and professional bodies there were reports of intimidation, arrests and torture.[124] Even some of the traditionalists who supported the campaign of Islamisation are now on the receiving end of repression. The regime has been tightening its grip on Sufi sects 'whose sermons are believed to be nurturing popular discontent',[125] and most people blame the regime and the Brotherhood for a bomb attack on a Sufi mosque earlier this year which killed 16 people.

Repression has not, however, provided more than temporary stability to the regime. There were a series of riots in the towns two years ago as a result of shortages and price increases. Initial gestures of defiance to the IMF have been followed by an Economic Salvation Programme based upon 'economic liberation' which 'involves many policies previously advocated by the fund',[126] leading to new negotiations with the IMF. This has led to a sharp decline in living standards, further discontent and further riots.

Meanwhile, the regime is isolated internationally from the other major Islamic regimes: the Brotherhood fell out with Iran by lining up against it in the first Gulf War, and with Saudi Arabia by supporting Iraq in the second Gulf War. Presumably because of this it has tried to present itself as a pole of attraction to Islamists elsewhere who are disaffected with these two countries and with the Egyptian Muslim Brotherhood—even though Turabi's own policies have been, for 30 years, a long way from the radicalism these Islamist groups espouse.

Yet the Sudanese Brotherhood itself is under enormous pressure. 'There are rumours that the NIF might split in two, with the zealots being sidelined and the relatively more moderate faction joining the conservative wings of the Umma Party and the DUP [the two main traditional parties]. There are divisions between the NIF's older generation who are prepared to accommodate with the secular parties and the younger and uncompromising zealots'.[127]

One final point is worth making about Sudan. The rise of the Brotherhood to power there has not been because of any magic powers on its own part. Rather the cause lies in the failure of other political forces to provide the way out of the progressively deeper impasse in the country. In the 1950s and the 1960s the Communist Party was a stronger force than the Brotherhood. It had competed with the Brotherhood for influence among the students and built up a following among urban trade unionists. But in 1964 and 1969 it chose to use this influence, not to present a revolutionary programme for change, but to enter nonrevolutionary governments, which then turned on it once it had calmed down the wave of popular agitation. It was, in particular, its support for Nimeiry in his first years that gave the Brotherhood the chance to take the lead in university agitation and undercut the Communists' base.

Conclusions

It has been a mistake on the part of socialists to see Islamist movements either as automatically reactionary and 'fascist' or as automatically 'anti-imperialist' and 'progressive'. Radical Islamism, with its project of reconstituting society on the model established by Mohammed in 7th century Arabia, is, in fact, a 'utopia' emanating from an impoverished section of the new middle class. As with any 'petty bourgeois utopia',[128] its supporters are, in practice, faced with a choice between heroic but futile attempts to impose it in opposition to those who run existing society, or compromising with them, providing an ideological veneer to continuing oppression and exploitation. It is this which leads inevitably to splits between a radical, terrorist wing of Islamism on the one hand, and a reformist wing on the others. It is also this which leads some of the radicals to switch from using arms to try to bring about a society without 'oppressors' to using them to impose 'Islamic' forms of behaviour on individuals.

Socialists cannot regard petty bourgeois utopians as our prime enemies. They are not responsible for the system of international capitalism, the subjection of thousands of millions of people to the blind drive to accumulate, the pillaging of whole continents by the banks, or the machinations that have produced a succession of horrific wars since the proclamation of the 'new world order'. They were not responsible for the horrors of the first Gulf War, which began with an attempt by Saddam Hussein to do a favour for the US and the Gulf sheikdoms, and ended with direct US intervention on Iraq's side. They were not to blame for the carnage in Lebanon, where the Falangist onslaught, the Syrian intervention against the left and the Israeli invasion created the conditions which bred militant Shiism. They were not to blame for the second Gulf War, with the 'precision bombing' of Baghdad hospitals and the slaughter of 80,000 people as they fled from Kuwait to Basra. Poverty, misery, persecution, suppression of human rights, would exist in countries like Egypt and Algeria even if the Islamists disappeared tomorrow.

For these reasons socialists cannot support the state against the Islamists. Those who do so, on the grounds that the Islamists threaten secular values, merely make it easier for the Islamists to portray the left as part of an 'infidel', 'secularist' conspiracy of the 'oppressors' against the most impoverished sections of society. They repeat the mistakes made by the left in Algeria and Egypt when they praised regimes that were doing nothing for the mass of people as 'progressive'—mistakes that enabled the Islamists to grow. And they forget that any support the state gives to secularist values is only contingent: when it suits it, it will do a deal with the more conservative of the Islamists to impose bits of the *shariah*—especially the bits which inflict harsh punishment on people—in return for ditching the radicals with their belief in challenging oppression. This is what happened in Pakistan under Zia and the Sudan under Nimeiry, and it is apparently what the Clinton adminstration has been advising the Algerian generals to do.

But socialists cannot give support to the Islamists either. That would be to call for the swapping of one form of oppression for another, to react to the violence of the state by abandoning the defence of ethnic and religious minorities, women and gays, to collude in scapegoating that makes it possible for capitalist exploitation to continue unchecked providing it takes 'Islamic' forms. It would be to abandon the goal of independent socialist politics, based on workers in struggle organising all the oppressed and exploited behind them, for a tail-ending of a petty bourgeois utopianism which cannot even succeed in its own terms.

The Islamists are not our allies. They are representatives of a class which seeks to influence the working class, and which, in so far as it succeeds, pulls workers either in the direction of futile and disastrous adventurism or in the direction of a reactionary capitulation to the existing system—or often to the first followed by the second.

But this does not mean we can simply take an abstentionist, dismissive attitude to the Islamists. They grow on the soil of very large social groups that suffer under existing society, and whose feeling of revolt could be tapped for progressive purposes, providing a lead came from a rising level of workers' struggle. And even short of such a rise in the struggle, many of the individuals attracted to radical versions of Islamism can be influenced by socialists—provided socialists combine complete political independence from all forms of Islamism with a willingness to seize opportunities to draw individual Islamists into genuinely radical forms of struggle alongside them.

Radical Islamism *is* full of contradictions. The petty bourgeoisie is always pulled in two directions—towards radical rebellion against existing society and towards compromise with it. And so Islamism is always caught between rebelling in order to bring about a complete resurrection of the Islamic community, and compromising in order to impose Islamic 'reforms'. These contradictions inevitably express themselves in the most bitter, often violent, conflicts within and between Islamist groups.

Those who treat Islamism as a uniquely reactionary monolith forget that there were conflicts between the different Islamists over the attitude they should take when Saudi Arabia and Iran were on opposite sides during the first Gulf War. There were the arguments that led the FIS in Algeria to break with its Saudi backers, or Islamists in Turkey to organise pro-Iraqi demonstrations from Saudi financed mosques during the second Gulf War. There are the bitter armed battles which wage between the rival Islamist armies in Afghanistan. Today there are arguments within the Hamas organisation among Palestinians about whether or not they should compromise with Arafat's rump Palestinian administration—and therefore indirectly with Israel—in return for its implementing Islamic laws. Such differences in the attitude necessarily arise once 'reformist' Islam does deals with existing states that are integrated into the world system. For each of these states is in rivalry with the others, and each of them strikes its own deals with the dominant imperialisms.

Similar differences are bound to arise every time there is a rise in the level of workers' struggle. Those who finance the Islamist organisations will want to end such struggle, if not break it. Some of the radical young Islamists will instinctively support the struggle. The leaders of the organisations will be stuck in the middle, muttering about the need of the employers to show charity and the workers forbearance.

Finally, the very development of capitalism itself forces the Islamist leaders to do ideological somersaults whenever they get close to power. They counterpose 'Islamic' to 'Western values'. But most so called Western values are not rooted in some mythical European culture, but arise out of the development of capitalism over the last two centuries. Thus a century and a half ago the dominant attitude among the English middle class to sexuality was remarkably similar to that preached by the Islamic revivalists today (sex outside of marriage was forbidden, women were not supposed to bare even their ankles, illegitimacy was a taint people could not live down), and women had fewer rights in some respects than most versions of Islam grant them today (inheritance was to the eldest son only, while Islam gives the daughter half the son's portion; there was no right at all to divorce, while Islam grants women that right in very restricted circumstances). What changed English attitudes was not something inbuilt into the Western psyche or any alleged 'Judeo-Christian values', but the impact of developing capitalism—the way in which its need for women's labour power forced it to change certain attitudes and, more importantly, put women in a situation where they could demand even greater changes.

That is why even in countries where the Catholic church used to be immensely strong, like Ireland, Italy, Poland and Spain, it has had to accept, reluctantly, a diminution in its influence. The countries where

Islam is the state religion cannot immunise themselves from the pressure for similar changes, however hard they try.

This is shown by the experience of Iranian Islamic Republic. Despite all the propaganda about women's main role being as mothers and wives and all the pressure to drive them out of certain professions like the law, the proportion of women in the workforce has grown slightly and they continue to make up 28 percent of government employees, the same as at the time of the revolution.[129] Against this background, the regime has had to shift its stance on birth control, with 23 percent of women using contraceptives,[130] and on occasions to relax the strict enforcement of the veil. Although women are denied equal rights with men when it comes to divorce and family law, they retain the vote (there are two women MPs), attend school, get a quota of places in university in all disciplines and are encouraged to study medicine and to receive military training.[131] As Abrahamian notes of Khomeini:

> *His closest disciples often mocked the 'traditionalists' for being 'old fashioned'. They accused them of obsessing over ritual purity; preventing their daughters from going to school; insisting that young girls should be veiled even when no men were present; denouncing such intellectual pursuits as art, music and chess playing; and, worst of all, refusing to take advantage of newspapers, radios and televisions.*[132]

None of this should really be surprising. Those who run Iranian capitalism and the Iranian state cannot dispense with female labour power in key sections of the economy. And those sections of the petty bourgeoisie who have formed the backbone of the IRP started sending their daughters to university and to seek employment in the 1970s precisely because they wanted the extra salaries—to enlarge the family income and to make their daughters more marriageable. They have not been willing in the 1980s to write these off in the interests of religious piety.

Islamism cannot freeze economic and therefore social development any more than any other ideology can. And therefore again and again tensions will arise within it and find expression in bitter ideological disputes between its proponents.

The Islamist youth are usually intelligent and articulate products of modern society. They read books and newspapers and watch televisions, and so know all the divisions and clashes within their own movements. However much they may close ranks when faced with 'secularists', whether from the left or from the bourgeoisie, they will argue furiously with each other—just as the pro-Russian and pro-Chinese wings of the apparently monolithic world Stalinist movement did 30 years ago. And these arguments will begin to create secret doubts in the minds of at least some of them.

Socialists can take advantage of these contradictions to begin to make some of the more radical Islamists question their allegiance to its ideas and organisations—but only if we can establish independent organisations of our own, which are not identified with either the Islamists or the state.

On some issues we will find ourselves on the same side as the Islamists against imperialism and the state. This was true, for instance, in many countries during the second Gulf War. It should be true in countries like France or Britain when it comes to combatting racism. Where the Islamists are in opposition, our rule should be, 'with the Islamists sometimes, with the state never.'

But even then we continue to disagree with the Islamists on basic issues. We are for the right to criticise religion as well as the right to practise it. We are for the right not to wear the veil as well as the right of young women in racist countries like France to wear it if they so wish. We are against discrimination against Arab speakers by big business in countries like Algeria—but we are also against discrimination against the Berber speakers and those sections of workers and the lower middle class who have grown up speaking French. Above all, we are against any action which sets one section of the exploited and oppressed against another section on the grounds of religion or ethnic origin. And that means that as well as defending Islamists against the state we will also be involved in defending women, gays, Berbers or Copts against some Islamists.

When we do find ourselves on the same side as the Islamists, part of our job is to argue strongly with them, to challenge them—and not just on their organisations' attitude to women and minorities, but also on the fundamental question of whether what is needed is charity from the rich or an overthrow of existing class relations.

The left has made two mistakes in relation to the Islamists in the past. The first has been to write them off as fascists, with whom we have nothing in common. The second has been to see them as 'progressives' who must not be criticised. These mistakes have jointly played a part in helping the Islamists to grow at the expense of the left in much of the Middle East. The need is for a different approach that sees Islamism as the product of a deep social crisis which it can do nothing to resolve, and which fights to win some of the young people who support it to a very different, independent, revolutionary socialist perspective.

Notes

1   Thus a perceptive study of the Egyptian Muslim Brotherhood could conclude in 1969 that the attempt at the revival of the movement in the mid-1960s 'was the

predictable eruption of the continuing tensions caused by an ever dwindling activist fringe of individuals dedicated to an increasingly less relevant Muslim "position" about society.' R P Mitchell, *The Society of the Muslim Brothers* (London, 1969), pvii.
2   Article in the *New Statesman* in 1979, quoted by Fred Halliday himself in 'The Iranian Revolution and its Implications', *New Left Review*, 166 (November-December 1987), p36.
3   Interview with the Communist Movement of Algeria (MCA) in *Socialisme Internationale* (Paris, June 1990). The MCA itself no longer exists.
4   F Halliday, op cit, p57.
5   For an account of the support given by different left organisations to the Islamists see P Marshall, *Revolution and Counter Revolution in Iran* (London, 1988), pp60-68 and pp89-92; M Moaddel, *Class, Politics and Ideology in the Iranian Revolution* (New York, 1993), pp215-218; V Moghadan, 'False Roads in Iran', *New Left Review*, p166.
6   Pamphlet quoted in R P Mitchell, op cit, p127.
7   A S Ahmed, *Discovering Islam* (New Delhi, 1990), pp61-64.
8   For an account of Afghan sufism, see O Roy, *Islam and Resistance in Afghanistan* (Cambridge, 1990), pp38-44. For sufism in India and Pakistan, see A S Ahmed, op cit, pp90-98.
9   I Khomeini, *Islam and Revolution* (Berkeley, 1981), quoted in A S Ahmed, op cit p31.
10 O Roy, op cit, p5. A leading Islamist, Hassan al-Turabi, leader of the Sudanese Islamic Brotherhood, argues exactly the same, calling for an Islamicisation of society because 'religion can become the most powerful motor of development', in '*Le nouveau reveil de l'Islam*', *Liberation* (Paris), 5 August, 1994.
11 E Abrahamian, *Khomeinism* (London, 1993), p2.
12 Ibid.
13 'Who is responsible for violence?' in *l'Algerie par les Islamistes*, edited by M Al-Ahnaf, B Botivewau and F Fregosi (Paris, 1990), pp132 and following.
14 Ibid, p31.
15 G Kepel, *The Prophet and the Pharoah, Muslim Extremism in Egypt* (London, 1985), p109.
16 See, for example, K Pfeifer, *Agrarian Reform Under State Capitalism in Algeria* (Boulder, 1985), p59; C Andersson, *Peasant or Proletarian?* (Stockholm, 1986), p67; M Raffinot and P Jacquemot, *Le Capitalisme d'état Algerien* (Paris, 1977).
17 J P Entelis, *Algeria, the Institutionalised Revolution* (Boulder, 1986), p76.
18 Ibid.
19 A Rouadia, *Les Frères et la Mosque* (Paris, 1990), p33.
20 O Roy, op cit, pp88-90.
21 A Rouadia, op cit, p82.
22 Ibid, p78.
23 Ibid.
24 For an account of these events, see D Hiro, *Islamic Fundamentalism* (London, 1989), p97.
25 H E Chehabi, *Iranian Politics and Religious Modernism* (London, 1990), p89.
26 E Abrahamian, *The Iranian Mojahedin* (London, 1989), pp107, 201, 214, 225-226.
27 M Moaddel, op cit, pp224-238.
28 A Bayat, *Workers and Revolution in Iran* (London, 1987), p57.
29 A Tabari, 'Islam and the Struggle for Emancipation of Iranian Women', in A Tabari and N Yeganeh, *In the Shadow of Islam: the Women's Movement in Iran*.
30 O Roy, op cit, pp68-69.
31 M Al-Ahnaf, B Botivewau and F Fregosi, op cit.
32 A Rouadia, op cit.

33 Ibid.
34 Ibid.
35 In 1989, of 250,000 who took exams, only 54,000 obtained the bac, ibid, p137.
36 Ibid, p146.
37 Ibid, p147.
38 See R P Mitchell, op cit, p13.
39 See ibid, p27.
40 Ibid, p38.
41 M Hussein, 'Islamic Radicalism as a Political Protest Movement', in N Sa'dawi, S Hitata, M Hussein and S Safwat, *Islamic Fundamentalism* (London, 1989).
42 Ibid.
43 S Hitata, 'East West Relations', in N Sa'dawi, S Hitata, M Hussein and S Safwat, op cit, p26.
44 G Kepel, op cit, p129.
45 Ibid, p137.
46 Ibid, pp143-44.
47 Ibid, p85.
48 Ibid, p95-96.
49 Ibid, p149.
50 For an account of this period see, for example, A Dabat and L Lorenzano, *Conflicto Malvinense y Crisis Nacional* (Mexico, 1982), pp46-8.
51 M Al-Ahnaf, B Botivewau and F Fregosi, op cit, p34.
52 Phil Marshall's otherwise useful article, 'Islamic Fundamentalism—Oppression and Revolution', in *International Socialism* 40, falls down precisely because it fails to distinguish between the anti-imperialism of bourgeois movements faced with colonialism and that of petty bourgeois movements facing independent capitalist states integrated into the world system. All his stress is on the role these movements can play as they 'express the struggle against imperialism'. This is to forget that the local state and the local bourgeoisie are usually the immediate agent of exploitation and oppression in the Third World today—something which some strands of radical Islamism do at least half recognise (as when Qutb describes states like Egypt as 'non-Islamic').

It also fails to see that the petty bourgeoisie limitations of Islamist movements mean that their leaders, like those of movements like Peronism before them, often use rhetoric about 'imperialism' to justify an eventual deal with the local state and ruling class while deflecting bitterness into attacks on those minorities they identify as local agents of 'cultural imperialism'. Marshall is therefore mistaken to argue that revolutionary Marxists can follow the same approach to Islamism as that developed by the early, pre-Stalinist Comintern in relation to the rising anti-colonial movements of the early 1920s. We must certainly learn from the early Comintern that you can be on the same side as a certain movement (or even state) in so far as it fights imperialism, while at the same time you strive to overthrow its leadership and disagree with its politics, its strategy and its tactics. But that is not at all the same as saying that the bourgeois and petty bourgeois Islamism of the 1990s is the same as the bourgeois and petty bourgeois anti-colonialism of the 1920s.

Otherwise we can fall into the same mistake the left in countries like Argentina did during the late 1960s and early 1970s, when they supported the nationalism of their own bourgeoisie on the grounds that they lived in 'semi-colonial states'.

As A Dabat and L Lorenzano have quite rightly noted, 'The Argentine nationalist and Marxist left confused...the association (of their own rulers) with the interests of the imperialist bourgeoisie and their diplomatic servility in the face of the US army and state with political dependency ("semi-colonialism", "colonialism"), which led to its most radical and determined forces to decide to call for an armed struggle for "the second independence". In reality, they were faced with something quite different. The behaviour of any government of a relatively weak capitalist country (however independent its state structure is) is necessary "conciliatory", "capitulationist" when it comes to meeting its own interests...in getting concessions from imperialist governments or firms...or consolidating alliances...with these states. These types of action are in essence the same for all bourgeois governments, however nationalist they consider themselves. This does not affect the structure of the state and its relationship with the process of self-expansion and reproduction of capital on the national scale (the character of the state as a direct expression of the national dominant classes and not as an expression of the imperialist states and bourgeoisies of other countries). *Conflicto Malvinense y Crisis Nacional*, op cit, p70.

53 E Abrahamian, *Khomeinism*, op cit, p3.
54 Ibid, p17.
55 O Roy, op cit, p71.
56 M Al-Ahnaf, B Botivewau and F Fregosi, op cit, pp26-27.
57 R P Mitchell, op cit, p145.
58 Ibid, p116.
59 Ibid, p40.
60 Book by Hudaybi, quoted in G Kepel, op cit, p61.
61 Ibid, p71.
62 Ibid.
63 See quote in ibid, p44.
64 Ibid, p53.
65 For details, see ibid, p78.
66 For a long account of Faraj's views in his book, *The Hidden Imperative*, see ibid, pp193-202.
67 Ibid, p208.
68 Ibid, p164.
69 Ibid, p210.
70 A Rouadia, op cit, p20.
71 Ibid, pp33-4.
72 Ibid, p36.
73 Ibid, p144.
74 Ibid, p145-146.
75 J P Entelis, op cit, p74.
76 A Rouadia, op cit, p191.
77 Ibid, p209.
78 M Al-Ahnaf, B Botivewau and F Fregosi, op cit, p30.
79 Ibid.
80 J Goytisolo, 'Argelia en el Vendava', in *El Pais*, 30 March, 1994.
81 *El Salaam*, 21 June 1990, translated in M Al-Ahnaf, B Botivewau and F Fregosi, op cit, pp200-202.
82 See the account of these events in J Goytisolo, op cit, 29 March 1994. This is now the course recommended by the British big business daily, the *Financial Times* (see the issue of 19 July 1994) and apparently by the US government.
83 J Goytisolo, op cit, 30 March 1994.
84 Ibid.
85 Ibid.
86 Ibid, 3 April 1994.
87 *Guardian*, 15 April 1994.
88 *Guardian*, 13 April 1994.
89 J Goytisolo, op cit, 29 March 1994.

90 See the translation on economic policy in M Al-Ahnaf, B Botivewau and F Fregosi, op cit.
91 Ibid, p109.
92 This is the view put forward by F Halliday, op cit. It was the view put forward in relation to Stalinism by Max Schactman and others. See M Schactman, *The Bureaucratic Revolution* (New York, 1962), and, for a critique, T Cliff, 'Appendix 2: The theory of Bureaucratic Collectivism', in *State Capitalism in Russia* (London, 1988).
93 The position of much of the left today in both Algeria and Egypt.
94 H E Chehabi, op cit, p169.
95 For details, see A Bayat, op cit, pp101-102, 128-129.
96 Figures given in ibid, p108.
97 M M Salehi, *Insurgency through Culture and Religion* (New York, 1988), p171.
98 H E Chehabi, op cit, p169.
99 The figure is given in D Hiro, op cit, p187.
100 See ch 3 of my *Class Struggles in Eastern Europe, 1945-83* (London, 1983).
101 T Cliff, 'Deflected Permanent Revolution', *International Socialism*, first series, no 12 (Spring, 1963), reprinted in *International Socialism*, first series, no 61. Unfortunately, this very important article is not reprinted in the selection of Cliff's writings, *Neither Washington nor Moscow*, but it is available as a pamphlet from Bookmarks.
102 Still less did they represent, as Halliday seems to contend, 'the strength of pre-capitalist social forces', op cit, p35. By making such an assertion Halliday is only showing how much his own Maoist-Stalinist origins have prevented him understanding the character of capitalism in the present century.
103 As P Marshall seems to imply in an otherwise excellent book *Revolution and Counter Revolution in Iran*, op cit.
104 A Bayat, op cit, p134.
105 T Cliff, op cit.
106 M Moaddel, op cit, p212.
107 F Halliday, op cit, p57.
108 Maryam Poya is mistaken to use the term 'workers' councils' to translate 'shoras' in her article, 'Iran 1979: Long Live the Revolution...Long Live Islam?' in *Revolutionary Rehearsals* (Bookmarks, London, 1987).
109 According to M Moaddel, op cit, p238.
110 A Bayat, op cit, p42.
111 E Abrahamian, *The Iranian Mojahedin*, op cit, p189.
112 M Poya, op cit.
113 M Moaddel, op cit, p216.
114 Abdelwahab el-Affendi, *Turabi's revolution, Islam and power in Sudan* (London, 1991), p89.
115 Ibid, pp116-117.
116 Ibid, pp117.
117 Ibid, pp115.
118 For his position on women, see summary of his pamphlet in ibid, p174. See also his article, '*Le Nouveau Reveil de l'Islam*', op cit.
119 Affendi, op cit, pp118.
120 Ibid, pp163.
121 Ibid, pp163-164.
122 Ibid, pp116.
123 Amnesty International report, quoted in *Economist Intelligence Unit Report, Sudan*, 1992:4.
124 Ibid.
125 *Economist Intelligence Unit Report, Sudan*, 1993:3.

126 *Economist Intelligence Unit, Country Profile, Sudan,* 1993-4. Turabi himself has been keen to insist that 'the Islamic awakening is no longer interested in fighting the West... The West is not an enemy for us'. 'Le nouveau Reveil de l'Islam', op cit.
127 *Economist Intelligence Unit Report, Sudan,* 1993:1.
128 This was the quite correct description of the ideas of the People's Mojahedin provided by the section of the leadership and membership who split away in the mid-1970s to form the organisation that later took the name Paykar. Unfortunately, this organisation continued to base itself on guerrillaism and Maoism rather than genuine revolutionary Marxism.
129 V Moghadam, 'Women, Work and Ideology in the Islamic Republic' *International Journal of Middle East Studies,* 1988, p230.
130 Ibid, p227.
131 Ibid.
132 E Abrahamian, *Khomeinism,* op cit, p16.

In the heat of the struggle
25 years of *Socialist Worker*

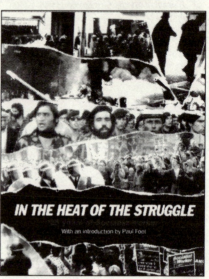

Large format, over 250 illustrations. With an introduction by Paul Foot.

In 1968 the world was rocked by student struggles, disaster for America in Vietnam, the biggest strike in history in France, ghetto risings across the US.
The weekly *Socialist Worker* was born out of those battles with a commitment: to report, analyse and organise every such struggle. 25 years on, *Socialist Worker* sticks by that pledge. This collection brings together the best articles, pictures and cartoons from those years—our history, as it was made.
£12.50 / $19.50

BOOKMARKS

Available from all good bookshops and Bookmarks, 265 Seven Sisters Road, London N4 2DE
081-802 6145
Add 15% for postage

What is changing in Ireland?

KIERAN ALLEN

James Connolly, Ireland's leading Marxist of the early 20th century, bequeathed an ominous prediction to his followers: a partitioned Ireland would lead to a 'carnival of reaction'. The division of Ireland between a Protestant dominated North and a Catholic dominated South would 'help the Home Rule and Orange capitalists to keep their rallying cries before the public as the political watchwords of the day' and so drown out any form of class politics.[1]

Connolly's prediction has been more than confirmed for most of this century. In Northern Ireland the state was built around the exclusion of Catholics. Local authorities and Orange employers discriminated against Catholics. Basil Brooke, a future prime minister, set the tone when he told fellow landowners that:

> he had not a Roman Catholic about his own place...[they] *were endeavouring to get in everywhere and were out in force and might to destroy Ulster...he appealed to Unionists everywhere to employ good Protestant lads and lassies*.[2]

In order to deal with the disgruntled minority of Catholics internment was introduced regularly. An auxiliary police force of B Specials was recruited from local Orange halls.[3] Catholics were forbidden to hold any sort of march or protest through the centres of the major towns of Derry and Belfast.

By and large, the Protestant working class supported this regime. The votes of Protestant workers ensured that a one party Unionist regime was established. In the 50 years that Unionist rule lasted, only one opposition bill was ever passed—the Wild Bird Conservation Act. In the early part of the century 60 percent of Protestant men were members of the Orange

Order and while there was a slow decline, the Order still held the allegiance of many Protestant workers.[4] The main challenger to Unionism inside the Protestant working class, the Northern Ireland Labour Party, pandered to sectarianism and bigotry. Speeches in favour of the Orange Order were regularly made from its platforms and leading members displayed their orange sash.[5] The NILP failed to condemn the use of internment or massacres such as Bloody Sunday when 13 people were shot dead in Derry by the parachute regiment. It even refused to back measures which called for 'one man, one vote' when thousands of both Catholics and Protestants were marching for this demand in 1968.[6] The unions were also contaminated by this atmosphere of sectarianism. One union, the Boilermakers Union, which organised skilled Protestant workers was actually found guilty of practising discrimination itself in membership applications.[7] Protestant workers accepted the argument that the slightest fissure in the Unionist community would open the way to the Southern government to impose a united Ireland and Rome Rule on loyal Ulster.

The South, of course, was a mirror image of the Northern regime. Fianna Fail and the Unionist party fed off and reinforced each other. Fianna Fail claimed to pursue two goals—the reunification of Ireland and the restoration of the Gaelic language. Neither was taken particularly seriously but both provided arguments around which to construct a 'national movement'.[8] From 1932 to 1973 Fianna Fail was only out of office for eight years. It presided over one of the most repressive Catholic regimes in the world. Divorce and even information on contraception were banned. Control of the hospitals and schools was vested in the hands of the church. Many of the writings of the leading Irish writers from Joyce to O'Casey were banned. Laws were passed giving the state the right to exclude married women from the workforce. And again Southern workers, by and large, supported this setup.

Fianna Fail prided itself on being the party of 'workers and small farmers'. The close links between Fianna Fail and some of the union leaders was symbolised when Charles J Haughey became prime minister in 1981. He was heralded into the Fianna Fail conference by the Irish Transport and General Workers Union band playing 'A Nation Once Again'! Just as in the North, the Labour Party was marginalised and forced to conform to the ethos set by Fianna Fail. The Labour Party leader in the 1960s, when the *left* rhetoric was at its height, was Brendan Corish who proclaimed that 'he was a Catholic first and a socialist afterwards'.[9] The Irish Labour Party has traditionally received one of the lowest votes of any Labour Party in Europe. Throughout the 1980s, for example, the average left vote in the Republic of Ireland stood at 12.8 percent compared to a Western European average of 37 percent.[10]

These conditions provided the stoniest grounds for building any serious left wing party. Yet the history of the Irish left is punctuated by flashes of real hope, times when a large audience seemed to emerge— only to be followed by periods of deep despair and demoralisation. Some of the wounds were self inflicted. Republicanism exercised an almost magnetic pull on the left. Some sections of the left saw it as the natural vehicle for advance in Irish conditions. Others recoiled in horror from any involvement with 'Catholic nationalism'.

Amongst the older generation of Irish left wingers the failures of the past linger like nightmares. But the Irish left also had a ready made alibi for those failures. Ireland, it was claimed, was a backward country. There was only a tiny working class, hopelessly divided by its communal identities. The 'objective conditions' made the prospect for constructing a serious socialist presence difficult, if not impossible, in Ireland. This article will argue that the alibis have now been proved false. The socialist movement in Ireland is at a watershed. Developments in both the North and South of the country open up new opportunities—and dangers. Whether or not there are major advances made in Ireland now depends on whether revolutionaries in Ireland can actually make the step to transform themselves into a small but significant revolutionary party that becomes a factor in the shaping of Irish history. That means breaking with the idea that socialists are bound to play a marginal role in Irish society. We shall start by looking at how the two bastions of conservatism in the South, Fianna Fail and the Catholic church, won their base—and at the serious challenges they are now facing.

Fianna Fail

The Fianna Fail party used to be an awesome phenomenon. Not only did it dominate the government of the Republic of Ireland for decades, almost as a one party state, its tentacles were everywhere. It had a relatively large and active membership for a bourgeois party. Until the 1980s the party's membership was numbered between 70,000 and 80,000 in a country whose total population was less than 3.5 million adults and children. Everywhere one looked the influence of the party was present. The Gaelic Athletic Organisation (the major sports organisation) was often organised at local level by Fianna Fail activists. The political nominees of the primary teachers' union were Fianna Fail members. If you wanted a job or a local authority house, you often had to approach the local Fianna Fail councillor. It drew its votes from right across the class spectrum. It never got less than 40 percent of the votes of the skilled and unskilled manual working class. Whilst its local leadership has traditionally been drawn from the petty bourgeoisie, there have also been a fair proportion of workers who were members. As late as 1986 it could organise a major conference for its trade union members and supporters.

Irish bourgeois commentators have been mystified by how the party won this base. The only book which has appeared on Fianna Fail was written by an *Irish Times* journalist, Dick Walsh. He claimed that at the heart of the party was 'a blazing mystique [which had] no social content'.[11] Academic writers have fared no better in their explanation. J P O'Carroll, who has written extensively on the party's founder, de Valera, has argued that the strength of his politics 'lay in the fact that it drew on much that was beyond the rational'.[12] Another has analysed Fianna Fail's base in terms of it being the political expression of 'Gaelic Romanticism'.[13]

Fianna Fail has in fact been a product of the underdevelopment and backwardness of Irish society. When he formed the party in the 1920s, de Valera described the Irish economy, accurately it has to be said, as an 'outgarden for the British'.[14] Some 97 percent of its exports went to Britain and these were overwhelmingly agricultural. A full 18 percent of the value of these exports was derived from live animals and another 40 percent was composed of food and drink. The proportion of the labour force employed in manufacturing was tiny. The party grew out of that section of the IRA which had been defeated in the civil war in 1922-3. It came to represent sections of the intelligentsia employed as teachers and civil servants in the urban areas as well as the smaller capitalists who sought to remove the shackles of economic domination.

Officially, the party decried partition and demanded the unification of Ireland. But the opposition remained entirely at a rhetorical level. Those who were later to take the rhetoric of the Southern establishment seriously and join the IRA would find themselves interned, tortured and even hanged by Fianna Fail.

For Fianna Fail, partition represented a collective symbol of a national wrong that was to be used to smother class divisions and impose a uniformity on Southern society. The real focus of Fianna Fail politics was the establishment of full national sovereignty and economic development for the South. Its principal target in its early days was the agro-export model which benefitted the larger farmers and the commercial capital. These groupings opposed any form of protectionism and state intervention.

In order to achieve their goals, Fianna Fail set out to win a base among workers. In a letter smuggled out of prison at the end of the civil war, de Valera pointed to the possibility of class politics emerging and advised his followers to 'lean more on the economic side' and insist on raising a 'national programme for the common good not a class programme'.[15] Within these strictures Fianna Fail engaged in a quite radical rhetoric. Its paper, *The Nation,* and later, the *Irish Press* denounced the 'pro-British financiers who control our economic system and visit us with all our sorrows wanton and without cause'.[16] They attacked the Free State police and demanded the aboilition of the standing army.[17] Some of their MPs expressed admiration for Stalin's Five Year Plan in Russia. One prominent deputy, Gerry Boland, claimed that 'in Russia, they treat labour on a human basis not as a commodity to be bartered with'.[18] In its attacks on imperialism and profession of sympathy with workers, Fianna Fail more than matched the left rhetoric that Sinn Fein used in the 1980s.

The nearest parallel to Fianna Fail in the 1920s and 1930s was in the populist movements in Latin America. Like Varga in Brazil, Cardenas in Mexico and Peron in Argentina, de Valera sought to create an 'industrial bloc' which united workers and small capital in a fight against the agro-export model which held their countries in a state of backwardness. In Ireland, however, there were no latifundia (large estates). Prior to their departure from the South, the British ruling class had encouraged a series of measures which enabled the old landlord class to hand over their land in return for generous compensation. The conflicts between the large farmers who relied on open access to the British market and Fianna Fail's aspirations were important, but not as intense as similar conflicts in Latin America. Fianna Fail therefore did not need the same degree of mobilisation of workers which Peron needed to achieve power in Argentina. Nevertheless de Valera sought to build a major voting base among workers and a tight network of supporters.

Irish workers responded to Fianna Fail's populism for a variety of reasons. As Trotsky pointed out, the Irish working class was 'formed in an atmosphere saturated with heroic memories of national rebellion and coming into conflict with the egotistically narrow and imperially arrogant trade unionism in Britain, has wavered between nationalism and syndicalism'.[19] The high points of workers' struggle had often coincided with upsurges of struggle against the British Empire. Indeed, the greatest expansion of the Irish trade unions occurred during the War of Independence when workers went on several local general strikes and formed soviets both to help drive out the British army and improve their own conditions. Not surprisingly then, a party which argued for continuing opposition to British colonialism was bound to get support among Irish workers.

Moreover, at the time of Fianna Fail's formation the syndicalist instinct of Irish workers was in decline. After 1923 the Irish trade union movement suffered tremendous defeats. Trade union membership fell from 126,522 in 1923 to 70,573 in 1930.[20] The best militants who supported the syndicalist traditions of Jim Larkin found themselves in disarray. The defeats coincided with a recomposition of Irish labour. The traditionally militant groupings in the transport and docks declined and the labour movement came to be dominated by sections of workers who had no previous tradition of militant struggle. By the time of the Wall Street Crash, the agro-export model was discredited. The weakness of the workers' movement meant that Fianna Fail's message that there had to be national development before there could be any social advance took serious roots.

From 1932, when they first took power, up to recent times Fianna Fail won and held a mass base among Irish workers through its nationalist message. It refused to pay land annuities—repayment on loans to buy land from the former landlord class—to Britain even though the Irish Labour Party had previously recommended that they be paid as a legal debt.[21] It faced down the fascist Blueshirts who had the backing of the big farmers in the 1930s. It refused to enter the Second World War on the side of Britain despite the virulent opposition of Churchill. Moreover, for a period, its strategy of protectionism seemed to work. Thousands of new jobs were created and an extensive house building programme was established.

Fianna Fail was able to win a base more easily among workers because of the activities of the trade union leaders and, to a lesser extent, the left. The leaders of the ITGWU forged a close alliance with Fianna Fail after the 1930s. They supported its efforts to drive women out of the workforce. They ran an hysterical campaign against 'British based' unions with the open support of Fianna Fail. In 1943 they split the Labour Party and later the Trade Union Congress for ten years on the basis of establishing a more open alliance with Fianna Fail.[22] The tiny left was also hopelessly confused by Fianna Fail's nationalism. Jim Larkin, for example, supported de Valera in the early 1930s and the Communist Party regularly called for second preference votes for Fianna Fail as a 'progressive' bourgeois party.

In the 1950s Fianna Fail began to run into considerable difficulties. Its strategy of protectionism ran up against the limitations of the small Irish domestic market. Unemployment and poverty grew while the rest of Europe was experiencing the post-war boom. Emigration became a mass phenomenon. Such was the scale of the exodus that in 1955 a book appeared called *The Vanishing Irish*, which debated the possibility of the death of the Irish 'race'. Fianna Fail and Irish capitalism saved themselves by a complete about turn in strategy after 1958. They dropped the protectionist barriers, abandoned the stipulation that Irish capital had to have 51 percent control in all companies and invited in mobile multinational investment. As these firms did not compete with Irish capital for the domestic market but rather used Ireland as a 'platform economy' for exporting to Europe, native Irish capital was given new opportunities for expansion.

The small Irish left denounced the turn as a betrayal of 'national independence'. One Labour Party TD [ie a member of the Irish parliament], for example, claimed that, 'The Soldiers of Destiny [the literal translation of Fianna Fail] had become the Queen's men.'[23] In reality Fianna Fail had not abandoned its enthusiasm for building up Irish national capital—it simply found a more realistic strategy to pursue the same goals. Irish capital began to expand dramatically after 1958, producing a few multinational firms and a huge growth of local small capital. And in conditions of an expanding world economy they were able to pull themselves away from the economic domination by Britain. After 1958 Irish trade diversified away from Britain. Its composition changed from agricultural exports to items such as electronics and chemicals. US, Japanese and German firms came to employ more workers than British firms. The Irish Central Bank eventually broke its link with sterling. After the 1958 turn it became absurd to describe the Republic of Ireland as a neo-colony of Britain.

The turn also enabled Fianna Fail to maintain its working class base. The high growth rates that the Southern economy experienced right up to the 1970s allowed the party to establish a rudimentary welfare state. Free second level education was introduced. The public health system was expanded. The tax burden of this welfare state fell, of course, on workers rather than on capital. Taxes on income grew from 18 percent of central government receipts in 1958 to 21 percent in 1973 while tax on capital actually fell from 2 percent to 1 percent in the same period.[24] Nevertheless in conditions of rising living standards—an increase estimated at 50 percent in the 1960s—the tax burden was a minor irritant. Growing conflicts emerged between Fianna Fail and an expanding working class but these were never focused by a political leadership that would have allowed full scale hostility to Fianna Fail to develop.

There was therefore nothing mystical or irrational about the way in which Fianna Fail won its base. At the core of Fianna Fail's relationship with the working class has been its promise that national development could bring gains for workers. At periodic intervals the party has indulged in a militant nationalist line on the North. But given Fianna Fail's record, anti-partitionism was never sufficient to consolidate its support. Rather its political support rested on displaying a link between periodic improvements in working class living standards and its championship of Irish capital and Irish economic development. In the 1930s and 1940s protectionism and the revival of Irish capital coincided with small and very modest improvements for an impoverished Irish working class. In the 1960s and 1970s the alliance between Irish capital and the multinationals seemed to bring even more dramatic gains. It was under these conditions that Fianna Fail could develop its ideology of 'social partnership' where union and employers worked together for the good of the country. Now, however, this period is over.

The Catholic church

Catholicism has provided the second major pillar of the conservatism of the South. Over 90 percent of the population claimed to be Catholic up to the late 1970s.[25] At its high point in the 1940s and 1950s there were over 20,000 members of religious orders.[26] Few aspects of Irish life have not been touched by the power of the Catholic church. One writer in the magazine *The Bell* summarised the atmosphere in Ireland that survived right up to the 1960s as follows:

> *In 1931 we got a new Parish Priest. He condemned dancing in every form, even the kitchen dances were sinful and against the wishes of our church. Boys and girls should not be on the roads after dark. The Curate was sent out to patrol the roads and anybody found or seen on the roads had to give their names. The people who allowed boys and girls into their homes to dance were committing a grave mortal sin... Dancing was the devil's work. So was company keeping.*[27]

The labour movement was by no means immune to the influence of the Catholic church. In 1951 one of the two Irish trade union congresses sent a telegram to the Pope claiming that their affiliated unions were 'humbly prostrate at the feet of his Holiness'.[28] Trade union officials often received their first training in Catholic adult education centres which preached the virtues of anti-communism. Conferences of the Irish Transport and General Workers Union were regularly addressed by the right wing Bishop of Galway who denounced moves to any form of a welfare state as bringing about a 'slave plantation mentality'.[29] The other guest at these congresses was often the CIA attache at the US embassy.

The Catholic church in Ireland owed its tremendous power to a combination of factors. It was seen by many as a badge of identification that was opposed to colonial rule in Ireland. A number of legal measures in the distant past which discriminated against Catholicism, such as the penal laws, gave it the image of an oppressed church. The image was, of course, not entirely consistent with the truth. Every revolutionary movement that opposed British colonialism had to face the wrath of the church. The Bishop of Kerry, for example, said of the Fenians (the nationalist movement in the 19th century) that 'hell was not hot enough nor eternity long enough to punish such miscreants'.[30] Nevertheless it was not the church of the colonial oppressor and this was later to convey certain unforseen advantages. The Catholic church in Ireland, for example, never became a powerful landowner to the extent that it did in Spain and thus avoided conflict with the peasantry. While condemning the militants among the anti-colonial fighters, it was able to maintain links with the moderate forces in the nationalist movement. Thus, one of the early leaders of Sinn Fein was a priest and when Terence McSweeny, the Lord Mayor of Cork, died on a hunger strike in protest at British rule, his funeral mass was celebrated by a number of bishops and priests.

The other factor was the rural roots of the church. Prior to the great famine of 1847, the Catholic church in Ireland had a relatively loose institutional structure. In 1840 the ratio of priests to people was only one to 3,023 and there were few public places of worship.[31] It is estimated that in 1842 only 40 percent of the population could have attended mass on any given Sunday.[32] But the transformation of the Irish land structure after the great famine changed all that. A form of mini-clearances occurred in Irish agriculture. Tens of thousands of agricultural labourers were driven off the land. So too were 'cottiers' who owned between five and ten acres. In their place emerged a class of more secure farm owners.

The clergy were drawn from the wealthier section of this new property owning peasantry. The slow accumulation of wealth on the land coincided with the huge growth of the Catholic middle class in the cities from the end of the 19th century onwards. The new wealthier farming class sent their sons to the cities as lawyers, publicans, doctors—and priests. The number of priests rose by 150 percent between 1861 and 1911 despite an overall decline of the population.[33] By 1911 there was one priest for every 210 Catholics.[34]

The particularly repressive sexual morality that is so distinctive of Irish Catholicism fitted in well with the needs of the new farm owning class. For them marriage and sexuality were intimately connected with the ownership of land. The farming class dreaded anything that might lead to the breakup of their moderately sized farms. 'Illegitimate' births were regarded as a direct threat to the consolidation of land holdings. Marriage was postponed until land became available to the eldest sons. Other sons and daughters were condemned to a life of celibacy or emigration. In the 1920s, for example, over 60 percent of what the Irish Central Statistic Office classified as 'relatives assisting' never got married.[35] To encourage this sexual repression, the Virgin Mary was set up as the role model for Irish women. This morality may have been propagated by priests who came from the 'better farming stock', but it got a hearing from the majority of the population who lived in small tightly knit rural communities where life was miserable and barren.

The Catholic church was also rewarded for playing the role of the ideological policeman in Irish society by a successive accumulation of institutional power. The process had begun in the dying day of the British Empire in Ireland when the ruling class increased their support for the Catholic bishops in the hope that this might ward off the threat of revolutionary nationalism. The main training grounds for priests in Maynooth and the system of denominational education were both established under British rule. The practice was soon taken up by the first Free State government. In return for getting the church's backing in the civil war, they gave the church control over the censorship board. But ironically it was under Fianna Fail that the trade off between more power for a church that opposed any dissent reached a new height. According to de Valera's constitution of 1937 the state recognised the 'special position of the Catholic church' and dedicated its own constitution to the 'Holy Trinity'. Nor was this a matter of mere symbols. The Catholic church took full control of the schools and the humanity faculties of most of the universities. Hospitals were also controlled by the church and an 'Ethics Committee' imposed Catholic morality on medical matters. Abortion, divorce, homosexuality, were banned and contraception was restricted—that is until the 1990s.

The winds of change

The basis for the stability of these two great pillars of Irish conservatism is now under threat in a way that it has never been in the past. The key to understanding why this is the case lies in the nature of the changes that have occurred in Ireland since industrialisation began in earnest. The changes that have happened have simply confounded many sections of the left.

The republican left argued that the changes that had occurred were, in some measure, a fake. Ireland remained a neo-colony of Britain. There was no significant indigenous capitalist class in Ireland but rather a parasitic layer that served as puppets for Britain. The efforts of workers and all oppressed groupings had therefore to be directed to ending colonialism. Until partition was removed there could be no real gains in Irish society. This perspective often led to fairly obscure arguments. The women's movement in Ireland, for example, had to align itself firmly with republicanism if it was to achieve anything—despite the fact that the same organisation opposed abortion and, in the 1980s, abstained on the question of rights to divorce.

These views were given some credibility by sections of the academic left which had a small following in Irish universities. Basing themselves on a number of Latin American writers such as Carduso and Furtado, the academic left argued that the industrialisation of Ireland was of a fundamentally different character to that experienced in metropolitan countries. It did not have a 'balanced' and integrated character where the different sectors of industry articulated with each other within the framework of a national economy. This had consequences in terms of political developments in Ireland. One writer, Ellen Hazelhorn, argued that dependent development and the practice of political clientelism were linked. With the weak and dependent form of industrialisation traditional politicians got control of the state apparatus and had even more patronage to dispense. Classical Marxism had ignored the manner in which 'clientelism is a mechanism for manipulating political disorganisation among the dominated classes in society'.[36] The prediction seemed to be that Fianna Fail might actually grow stronger because of the changes underway in Irish society.

Others argued that dependent industrialisation was associated with a weak working class. Concerned to attack the supposed 'economism' in classical Marxism they argued that 'the current form of industrialisation has involved new forms of domination of the working class'.[37] Industry was deliberately located in areas where trade union traditions were weak. The multinationals were totally hostile to any shop floor organisation. Reformism in Ireland had no locus as the national state was in no position to control the activities of these firms. The result was that 'the form of industrial work in the foreign sector militated against effective class organisation'.[38]

The overall conclusion of these writers was one of overwhelming pessimism. Irish workers were seen simply as victims of the new foreign capital, condemned to wait either for the ending of partition or help from the enlightened European Union. The reality has been far different and far more contradictory.

One effect of industrialisation has been that the working class has expanded massively over the last few decades. In 1951, 38 percent of the Irish labour force worked on farms. Today the figure has declined to 15 percent. There are more unemployed people in Ireland today than there are farmers. Moreover, a very high proportion of the population *identify* themselves as workers. Some 42 percent of the Irish population regard themselves as working class—a figure that is just below the British figure.[39] The growth of the working class has been accompanied by a major increase in trade union density. Between 1945 and 1984 the number of trade unionists in Ireland more than trebled, giving Southern Ireland one of the highest trade union densities in Western Europe.[40] Worker militancy has also risen. Between 1979 and 1981, for example, there was an explosion of class consciousness as Ireland experienced its first general strike since the war of independence over the tax burden carried by workers. As in other countries, the tempo of workers' struggle has never simply been an onwards and upwards mobilisation. The 1980s brought defeats and a downturn. But industrialisation laid the basis for class conflict on an increased scale between a larger working class and a stronger local bourgeoisie.

Industrialisation has also brought changes in the lives of working women. These changes run directly counter to the ethos of the Catholic church. Despite early attempts to exclude women from the workforce, women are joining the labour force in greater numbers. Between 1971 and 1991 the number of economically active women increased by 50 percent while the number of men increased by 10 percent.[41] Today a third of the Irish labour force are women, whereas in 1961 only 5 percent of married women were in paid employment.

All of this has brought massive changes in the way in which Irish men and women are living their lives. Until the 1950s Irish family life was often characterised by late marriages and then a very high birth rate. Today all of this has changed. Irish couples are using contraception and planning the number and spacing of children. The average family size has fallen to two compared to four 20 years ago. More and more women are discarding marriage and having children outside of marriage. Some 18 percent of births are outside wedlock. Despite the bans on abortion, Irish women in the age group 18 to 23 are having the same number of abortions as women in other countries. The difference is that they have to travel to Britain.

If the republican left and the dependency theorists ignored the scale and potential of the changes that were occurring in Irish society, others drew the equally wrong conclusion that industrialisation would lead automatically to the liberalisation of Irish society. Here it was assumed that the shift away from an agricultural to a urban society would lead to a gradual whittling away of church influence. With the help of European Union (EU) social legislation it was assumed that Irish society would gradually move to resemble the other European countries.

In fact the shifts have been far more contradictory and explosive. For most of the 1980s the church and Fianna Fail were able to mount a successful rearguard action against the new pressures that were building up in Irish society. Faced with a rising working class militancy Fianna Fail attempted to use a more nationalist rhetoric to restore its base in the working class. But the 1980-81 H Block struggle and growth of republican ideas in the South for a brief period made this a dangerous strategy. Instead Fianna Fail switched to an open alliance with the SPUC (Society for the Protection of the Unborn Child) bigots and the bishops. SPUC was given a free rein to push through a referendum in Ireland which it hoped might provide an example for 'pro-life' forces in other parts of the world. In 1983 it inserted a clause in the Irish constitution which established that a foetus of a few days old had the equivalent right to life as a pregnant woman. In 1987, after Fianna Fail were thrown out of power, it worked again with the bigots to overthrow a proposal that divorce be permitted in Ireland. The participation of Labour in government at the time created ample scope for right wing populism. The bigots raised slogans such as 'jobs, not divorce' to tap into working class bitterness.

The success of the backlash of the 1980s arose from the fact that the development that occurred in Ireland was uneven and contradictory. Huge numbers left the land in the 1960s and 1970s as staunch Catholics only to find themselves in sprawling corporation housing estates where there were large pools of unemployment. Their children went to schools that were run by the church. When they went to hospital they continued to find the nuns and priests in charge. If they didn't like the situation they often got out. In the 1980s a quarter of a million people took the emigrant ship from Ireland. Emigration provided the safety valve to rid Irish society of the discontented and angry.

As a result the first signs of liberalism in Irish society often seemed to be confined to a 'Dublin 4' liberal set. When these same liberals could not fulfil their promises to end poverty and unemployment they provided a ready made target for the bigots.

Yet despite their victories in the 1980s, neither Fianna Fail nor the church could turn the clock back. There was no return to a society built around the 'comely maidens' and the 'rural homesteads.' The slow, accumulating changes that accompanied industrialisation continued to progress despite their political victories. Marxists have argued that small quantitative changes can eventually add up to a major qualitative leap forward. History does not progress through the growth of moderation and tolerance, but to huge social explosions.

This is precisely what has happened in Ireland over the last two years. The explosions have emerged in the most surprising ways. In February 1992 the new leader of Fianna Fail, Albert Reynolds, appointed one Harry Whelehan to the office of attorney general. Whelehan had been a member of the Catholic Marriage Advisory Bureau and was known to be strongly opposed to abortion. A few days after he took up office a report arrived on his desk from the police stating that they had been approached by the parents of a 14 year old girl who had been raped. They were about to accompany their daughter on a trip to Britain to have an abortion and were enquiring if a DNA test on the aborted foetus might provide useful evidence to convict the rapist. Whelehan's response was to impose an injunction to stop the 14 year old girl travelling from Ireland. In a piece of medieval barbarism known as the X case the child was to be confined to Ireland until she delivered her baby. Whelehan's decision was upheld by the High Court which had been staffed with political hacks.

The new generation which had emerged since the country voted on abortion in 1983 were outraged. They were not demoralised by the defeats of the 1980s. They took to the streets in huge numbers in demonstrations that had been organised by the tiny forces of the revolutionary left and feminist groups. In the week after the High Court decision there were pickets and demonstrations on a daily basis. In one school in Dublin 200 schoolgirls defied the nuns and walked out with a banner which said, 'Let us decide'. At the weekend demonstration 14,000 people took to the streets of Dublin. Many of those who joined the demonstration had previously voted with SPUC. But it was one thing to oppose abortion in the abstract because of Catholic principles. It was quite another to impose barbarism on a real human being. The militancy of the demonstration indicated that there would have been riots on the streets of Dublin if the 14 year old in the X case had not been freed. The Supreme Court reversed the High Court's decision and twisted the meaning of the SPUC amendment to the Irish constitution to create more openings for abortion. The bigots had been forced to eat their words.

The effects of this defeat on the Catholic church have astounded those familiar with Irish history. The X case brought about everything the bigots feared—it opened the 'floodgates'. Four months after the X case, Dublin saw its first Gay Pride march in seven years. A year afterwards homosexuality was decriminalised and the legal age of consent was set at 17, compared to the British age of 18. Later when a government minister from the Labour Party was found cruising in a gay area of Phoenix Park, the police leaked the story to the media in the hope of provoking a backlash. The atmosphere was such that he held his seat amidst statements that it was a 'personal matter'. Condoms were also made fully legal and vending machines started appearing in Irish pubs. Information on abortion was made fully legal and in the referendum in 1992 abortion was accepted under limited and restricted circumstances. In all these instances the bishops have been forced to retreat.

If the Catholic church has taken a hammering, so too has Fianna Fail. The upsurge of anger over abortion coincided with a series of scandals that started to unravel the close connections between Fianna Fail and sections of the business class. Fianna Fail has traditionally projected itself as part of the 'plain people' of Ireland. But a scandal in the beef industry showed that the leading company, Goodman International, was paying more into Fianna Fail funds than it had paid in taxes to the Irish state. Throughout the 1980s the company had only paid 1 percent of its tax bill while Irish workers were shouldering the tax burden. Other scandals soon followed as the captains of Irish industry fell out under pressure of the recession.

At the end of 1992, when a general election was called, the scale of opposition was revealed. Fianna Fail got its lowest vote since 1927. In urban areas it faced a huge decline in working class votes. In 1994 Fianna Fail got a repeat of this experience in Dublin. Its vote sunk to below 20 percent—just above that of the Green Party! A party that once had cumman (branches) in every ward and parish is seeing its membership melt away. The Fianna Fail leader recently revealed that Fianna Fail now has less than 2,000 members in Dublin where it previously had 12,000. In the rural areas the party is still holding its base—but in the cities it is treated with contempt by huge sections of workers whose fathers and mothers looked on past Fianna Fail politicians with respect.

The initial beneficiary of the move away from Fianna Fail was the weak Irish Labour Party. It became the focus of a huge desire for change. It seemed to represent the new Ireland. It had a modern image. It seemed to want to face up to the church. And it stood for some recognition of the realities of class conflict in Irish society. One of its main election themes was the need to break the 'golden circle' where Fianna Fail dispensed patronage and favours to its financial backers.

In 1992 it got its highest vote ever and trebled its vote compared to the election of 1987. The Labour Party put up only 45 candidates and most of them topped the poll under Ireland's proportional representation system. Although the vote still remained modest by the terms of European social democracy it seemed that class politics had finally arrived in the South.

However, no sooner were the elections over than Labour began to betray its supporters. Instead of calling on the two right parties, Fianna Fail and Fine Gael, to form a government, they entered into talks with Fianna Fail and formed a coalition. For the Labour leaders it was simply a decision about how best to get access to the privileges and pomp of office. But the left wing of the party also embraced the decision enthusiastically. The Labour left came from an older generation who had been influenced by milder forms of Stalinism. After the collapse of the USSR their politics shifted to 'realism' and an accommodation with the market. From outside the party, Sinn Fein offered the advice that coalition was the only realistic road. If Irish society was showing signs of entering a new period of struggle, the traditional elements of the left were still caught in their past. All the accumulated illusions about Fianna Fail being 'more progressive' than the more pro-British Fine Gael, about the need to mix the red of social democracy with the green of Irish nationalism, came to the surface.

The participation of Labour in government has been a disaster and has led to widespread disillusionment. Labour ministers have pressed the management of state companies to impose wage cuts on their workers. They have stood by the Fianna Fail leader, Reynolds, when he was found to be selling off Irish passports to a millionaire who invested in his pet food company. They have delayed introducing a referendum on divorce and backed down in a confrontation with the church over the management of schools. They have supported a vicious Public Order Bill which allows for six months imprisonment for 'abusive words' on leaflets and placards. Fianna Fail has used Labour's presence in government to present itself as more of a 'left of centre party' in the hope of relating to changes that are happening in Irish society. Meanwhile opinion polls show that support for Labour is tumbling as anger mixes with disillusionment.

While the South has been subject to major political shifts, new developments also indicate that there are also real possibilities—and dangers—in the North.

The North: Britain's declining interest

The Downing Street Declaration was issued in December 1993. It was hailed by John Major and Albert Reynolds as the document that would bring peace to Northern Ireland within weeks. In reality it was a vague, vacuous document which had been carefully scripted to allow for different meanings and interpretations. However it did contain one significant claim—namely that Britain has no 'selfish, strategic or economic interest in Northern Ireland'. It presented the British role in Northern Ireland as that of a neutral caring neighbour trying to reconcile those involved in a domestic brawl.

The reality is very different. The activities of the British army have been almost exclusively directed against the nationalist population. The case of Brian Nelson, for example, revealed clearly that the British intelligence services worked closely with the UDA to set up leading nationalist lawyers such as Pat Finucane for assassination. Nelson worked as an agent for MI5 within the ranks of the UDA and helped to organise the importation of weaponry from South Africa. These weapons later played a major role in a random loyalist murder campaign against Catholics. No wonder Amnesty International noted that it:

> Has not been convinced that the government has taken adequate steps to halt collusion, to investigate thoroughly and make known the full truth about political killings of suspected government opponents, to bring to justice the perpetrators and dismantle 'pro-state' organisations dedicated to political violence or otherwise deter such killings.[42]

Nevertheless, despite the stupendous hypocrisy involved, there is an important truth involved in the statement about Britain's lack of a strategic or economic interest in Northern Ireland today. This represents a major change from the situation in the early 20th century when Britain's rulers had a vested interest in the partition of Ireland. The 'revisionist school' of Irish history, which has sometimes adopted a pseudo-Marxist analysis, is wrong when it claims that 'British capitalism had no need to partition Ireland to protect its interests, for it was not an essential source of raw materials nor a vital market for British goods'.[43] Britain's rulers had three main areas of interest in partitioning Ireland.

Firstly, Britain had key economic and military interests in Northern Ireland. Between 1870 and 1910 the labour force in shipbuilding grew five times and Belfast became a key provider of ships for the British Empire. Around the shipbuilding industry there grew a major engineering industry that formed part of an industrial triangle linking Belfast to Manchester and Glasgow. According to one historian:

> *Linen and shipbuilding were the dominant industries in the north east* [of Ireland]... *But Belfast had many other industries as well, most of them springing up to meet the needs of these two giants. Spinning machines, scutching and hacking equipment were made in the city. So were steam engines, foundry products, ropes and heating and ventilating equipment. Manufacturers diversified and produced tea-drying equipment, stable fittings, agricultural machinery, motor cars, mineral waters and cigarettes.*[44]

Most of this industry was owned by British firms or by sections of Ulster's ruling class that looked to Britain. Northern Ireland also provided key military bases for the British army which played an important role in the Second World War.

Secondly, the Irish War of Independence represented a major political threat to the empire itself. The First World War had accelerated the development of national movements in other parts of the empire. A full scale victory of Irish republicanism would have had major repercussions beyond Ireland. The war of independence in Ireland was accompanied by a tremendous wave of workers' militancy. Towns like Limerick were taken over by trade unionists and a 'soviet' was proclaimed.[45] A general strike forced Britain to grant political status to republican prisoners. Railway workers refused to transport British munitions.[46] There was huge sympathy for the Bolshevik revolution. One commentator noted that Catholic communities are:

> *Generally hostile to socialism and so the socialistic enthusiasm which swept over Ireland during 1919 puzzled many. But there the fact was. Never was*

Ireland more devoutly Catholic than today...yet nowhere was the Bolshevik revolution more sympathetically saluted.[47]

The British ruling class feared that the victory of a increasingly radical national movement would set new examples for countries such as Egypt and India. Its own weakness forced it to retreat—but by imposing partition it split the national movement and salvaged some of its status.

Thirdly, partition helped to lock the South of Ireland into a neo-colonial relationship with Britain for nearly four decades after formal political independence. The eventual financial settlement which was imposed on the Irish Free State subjected it to a large annual levy for the British exchequer. Cut off from the industrialised North, the South became an economy that was built around the supply of raw materials to Britain. In reality Britain lost little from the independence of the South. Lionel Curtis, an advisor to Winston Churchill, put it a little strongly when he claimed that 'the making of the Irish Treaty was one of the greatest achievements of the Empire',[48] but he did indicate the sense of relief in British ruling class circles.

These direct interests of Britain ensured a close and friendly relationship with the Unionist party. The Tory party was known as the Conservative and Unionist Party. Both the Conservative and Labour governments turned a blind eye to the bigotry and discrimination which the Unionists imposed on Northern Ireland. A convention developed in the British House of Commons whereby the 'internal affairs' of Northern Ireland were never discussed. Every spurious piece of rhetoric from Southern politicians led to new assurances from Britain that the link with Northern Ireland would never be broken.

However, soon after the Northern state was established, difficulties began to emerge. Initially the Northern state was expected to generate a financial surplus and make a contribution to the empire. But the depression of the 1930s weakened Northern industry and by 1938 the British government officially recognised that it would have to subsidise Northern Ireland.[49] By the end of the 1950s the landscape had changed even more dramatically. Northern Ireland's main industries were in decline and the state had to turn to multinational capital to help start industries such as artificial fibres. The South too had started to make a shift from a closed protectionist economy that restricted access from British capital to one that was also open to multinational capital. These changes were recognised by Eamonn McCann in his major Marxist account of modern Ireland written in 1974:

> *By the end of the fifties the economic basis of partition was being eroded. The interests of the dominant classes, North and South, converged. And by the same token, the British interest in Ireland changed... The British interest now*

lay not in giving uncritical support to the Orange government in the North, but in balancing between the Orange and the Green, between North and South, between Protestant and Catholic capitalism in Ireland.[50]

Since this was written the changes have accelerated and deepened. Northern Ireland's manufacturing industry has been rocked to its very foundations. Table 1 illustrates the scale of the decline in employment in some of the key traditional industries.

TABLE 1: EMPLOYMENT IN MANUFACTURING IN NORTHERN IRELAND (IN THOUSANDS)

	1950	1990	percent change
SHIPBUILDING	24.2	2.5	-89.7
TEXTILES	72.8	17.3	-87.0
CLOTHING	32.5	17.3	-46.8
TOTAL (Manufacturing)	195.5	104.0	-46.8

[*Source: Northern Ireland Economic Council, Economic Strategy in Northern Ireland 1991, p11*]

In the case of shipbuilding, for example, losses have risen dramatically. In 1977, for example, Harland and Wolff lost £11.9 million. By 1987 the figure rose to £57.8 million.[51]

However, it is not simply that older manufacturing industries are in decline. There has also been a flight of foreign capital and, in particular, British capital. Employment in externally owned plants has fallen by 53 percent between 1973 and 1990.[52] The largest decline has been in British owned plants which dominated the textile and artifical fibre industries. US companies are now one of the main sources of foreign capital. Ironically, the only other group of foreign capitalists to step up their investments in the North are those from Southern Ireland.

The result has been a sharp decline in the activities of private capital and a greater reliance on the state. Total private sector employment in the North has fallen from 352,200 in 1960 to 288,200 in 1988.[53] By contrast employment in the public sector—including the security sector—has escalated. In 1960, 97,100 were employed in the public sector. By 1988 it had risen to 223,900.[54] No wonder the *Economist* screamed in horror:

Northern Ireland's economy resembles more closely that of an Eastern European country than Margaret Thatcher privatising Britain. The ratio of public spending to GDP has been rising inexorably to 78 percent while it has been falling for Britain as a whole.[55]

The result has been a huge rise in British subvention for the North. In 1972 at the beginning of direct rule the British subsidy to Northern Ireland was £100 million. By 1988-9 it has increased to £1.9 billion.[56]

The policy and strategy of the British ruling class has never been shaped by a crude reading of their profit and loss account. They have been willing to lay out considerable sums in the past in military spending that did not seem to have immediate economic benefits. But in the case of Northern Ireland it is no longer a case of short term losses. There has been a withdrawal of key sections of British capital. There has been an effective liquidation of much of Orange capital into the stock exchange and property markets of London. The British army has probably learnt as much as it needs to know about dealing with 'civil disorders' by their involvement in the North and now find their overall priorities distorted by this seemingly endless conflict. On top of all this is an awareness in ruling class circles that Britain itself is a shrinking political power in a more dangerous and less stable world. These have all raised major questions about Britain's continuing interest in the province. Moreover, while Britain has essentially pursued an ad hoc policy over the last 20 years that rested on establishing 'an acceptable level of violence', the decline of Britain itself and its growing public sector deficit has added a new urgency to the questioning that is going on in ruling class circles.

This does not mean that Britain is pulling out immediately. The ideal solution that British and Irish rulers favour is the establishment of joint sovereignty under which they both undertake the running of Northern Ireland. The central thrust of the Downing Street Declaration is therefore to *institutionalise* the sectarian identities of the North by presenting Britain's rulers as the guardians of Protestant interest and the Southern rulers as guardians of Catholic interests. After a longer period they hope that this might lay the basis for some form of united Ireland.

This shift of Britain's rulers' has already meant a further distancing from the Unionist establishment. Unionist politicians, and the Paisleyite Democratic Unionist Party in particular, are regarded as political dinosaurs who may still have to be tolerated for a brief period. Britain's rulers have not dismantled the sectarian state—but they have sought to create the space for a more vibrant Catholic middle class to emerge. They increasingly talk about the need to recognise 'both identities'. This in turn has raised major question marks over the relationship of the Unionist party to the Protestant working class.

The Protestant working class

At the start of 'the troubles' the dominant view on the British and Irish left was that the Protestant working class formed a 'labour aristocracy'.

They were supposed to live a privileged existence that arose from the bribes that imperialism could bestow on them. Michael Farrell used the term 'labour aristocracy' to describe Protestant workers explicitly in his important book, *Northern Ireland: The Orange State*.[57] Geoff Bell was even more direct about the issue:

> *What privileges there were in Ireland were enjoyed by the Protestant community. The main area of Protestant concentration in Ireland, in the North East, has a higher standard of living, comparable at some levels to that in Britain.*[58]

This characterisation of Protestant workers was always wrong and led to disastrous conclusions. It implied that a socialist movement could only be built inside the Catholic working class and even that a civil war might be necessary to bring about a 'progressive' solution to the national question.

The notion of Protestant workers being any sort of privileged caste ignored the elementary truth that in a divided working class every worker lost out. Racism and sectarianism are not in the interest of any section of the working class.[59] By dividing workers, by encouraging some to believe that a boss is part of their 'community', racist ideas leave workers more open to increased exploitation. If the 'labour aristocracy' theory was always wrong, the changes over the last two decades make it even more absurd.

Today Northern Ireland is experiencing a period of mass unemployment which makes it the main jobless blackspot of the UK. By the end of the 1980s unemployment in Northern Ireland was 50 percent worse than Wales or the North of England and three times higher than the rate in the South East of England.[60] Almost 50 percent of the unemployed are long term unemployed compared to a UK average of 27 percent.[61] Huge numbers have found themselves in dead end 'training schemes'. These levels of unemployment bring all the familiar evils with them. Infant mortality in Northern Ireland, for example, is 120 percent of the level for the UK.[62]

For those at work the situation is also worse for both Catholic and Protestants. Average weekly earnings in Northern Ireland are only 85 percent of the British average even though prices in the region are higher.[63] One quarter of the workers are on part time contracts.[64] The level of desperation that part time workers experience is reflected in the polite language of the Northern Ireland Economic Council:

> *Part time work tends to be low paid. However, Northern Ireland's workers exhibit substantial attachment to their jobs suggesting that this employment is not as temporary as has been suggested.*[65]

Despite improvement in the notorious housing conditions of the North, a recent Northern Ireland housing survey showed that 8.4 percent of all housing stock is unfit to live in.[66] That is almost twice the British figure. Undoubtedly this is also linked to the high death rate from pneumonia which Northern Ireland experiences. In 1990 the rate of death from pneumonia was four times the UK average.[67]

It may be argued that these average figures hide the divisions between workers. It is certainly that case the Catholic workers experience hardship disproportionately. But Protestant workers are increasingly experiencing low wages, unemployment and poor housing. A report from the Community Development in Protestant Areas group looked at two Protestant working class housing estates in Belfast—Taughmonagh and Clarawood. In Taughmonagh, less than half the workforce was in full time employment. Over two thirds of households had an income of less than £110 a week. Three quarters over 16 year olds had no formal qualifications. In Clarawood over half the households had an income of less than £90 a week.[68] This poverty shows up in terrible educational deprivation. Northern Ireland still implements the vicious 11-plus system which discriminates against all working class pupils. But in the heartland of the Protestant working class, the Shankill Road, only 4 percent of eligible pupils passed the 11-plus in 1988.[69]

In the 1960s the dominant image of the Protestant worker was of the skilled craftsman who worked in shipbuilding or engineering on high wages. Today the typical Protestant worker is likely to experience spells of unemployment, to be working for the public sector, to be earning low wages and to be working alongside Catholics.

These worsening material conditions have coincided with a growing awareness among Protestants of Britain's changing interest. The result has been high levels of disillusionment as many see that their 'loyalty to Queen and Country' is thrown back in their faces. Traditional institutions are now more likely to be treated with contempt by many Protestants. Tens of thousands of Protestant workers, like many others throughout the rest of Britain, now see the monarchy as parasites. The close relationship with the RUC has broken down in many areas. The Unionist parties may still get the vote—but there is a scepticism and a contempt about their inability to bring any improvement. After the Anglo-Irish agreement, which gave Dublin a voice in the running of Northern Ireland, the Unionist vote fell from 43.9 percent of the electorate in 1986 to 36.7 percent in 1987.[70] While this reflected a temporary fluctuation, Unionist politicians have been unable to mobilise many Protestant workers into active opposition to the Anglo-Irish agreement. Paisley's attempt to form a quasi-military Ulster resistance movement was a fiasco. Even when he denounced the 1993 ICTU led peace marches tens of thousands of

Protestant workers turned a deaf ear to him. One survey in a Protestant housing estate in Derry summed up the mood when it argued that the residents felt that 'the old Unionist Corporation had done nothing to improve their poor social conditions'.[71]

The rise of the Catholic middle class

If the Protestant working class have experienced major changes there have also been important developments within the Catholic population. Throughout the 25 years of the Northern conflict there has been an assumption that all Catholics formed a 'community'. Politicians from John Hume to Bernadette McAliskey have spoken eloquently about the wrongs suffered by this 'community'. Few mentioned the *class* divisions among Catholics. The newspaper of Sinn Fein, *Republican News*, for example, regularly reports on strikes in the South but ignores them in the North. Just as Fianna Fail in the South presented itself as the party of the 'plain people', so too have Northern nationalist politicians pretended that to be Catholic in Northern Ireland was to be oppressed *and* to be poor.

The reality is different. A recent book by Fionnula O'Connor on Northern Catholics has revealed the scale of the class divisions. It shows how a confident Catholic middle class has emerged over the last two decades.[72] Before the troubles the Catholic middle class consisted mainly of the publicans, builders, head teachers and auctioneers who served their own community. One woman interviewed by O'Connor described them as follows:

> *I associated them with the **Gaeilgeori** [Irish language users] and clean faces...small shopkeepers, say on the Falls Road, whose kids went to the same school as me, the respectable people.*[73]

The removal of the old Stormont regime and the imposition of direct rule from Britain changed this. What has emerged is a situation which has close parallels with the US.

Thirty years after Martin Luther King started the civil rights movement, the situation for the mass of black people is worse now than it ever was. The median income of black families fell during the 1980s and death from diseases such as asthma rose by 50 percent.[74] A black newborn infant is now twice as likely to die before the age of one than a white baby. But for the black middle class it has been a different story. Despite the fact that they continue to suffer racial prejudice, they have seen their situation improve dramatically. They are the real victors of the civil rights struggle. According to Marable:

In the quarter of a century after the passage of the Civil Rights Act, the number of African American elected officials increased from barely one hundred to nearly 7,000. The number of African Americans enrolled in colleges and universities quadrupled; the gross receipts of black owned businesses and financial institiutions increased more than eightfold; the size of the African American middle class and number of professionals significantly expanded.[75]

The US government responded to the black civil rights movement by a programme of 'affirmative action' which was partially a concession to the movement and partially a deliberate strategy to create a substantial middle class that could give it a lever inside the civil rights movement.

The British government has reacted in a similar fashion. It has imposed a fairly strong 'fair opportunities' code—but the main beneficary has not been the Catholic working class who continue to live in ghettoes of high unemployment, but rather a new middle class. The civil service, which is the North's biggest employer and was once a bastion of discrimination, is now 35 percent Catholic at management level.[76] Catholics, it has to be remembered, now make up 40 percent of the population of the North. In December 1992 the Northern Ireland Office announced that it set as its goal a 25 percent representation of Catholics in the top policy related posts.[77] Outside the civil service there have also been gains for the Catholic middle class. Fully 60 percent of the annual intake of trainee barristers are now Catholic[78] and 30 percent of managers in the private sector are Catholic.[79]

The change is best symbolised in the Malone Road which was once the symbol of Protestant privilege. In the past there was a tiny Catholic chapel on the Malone Road which was mainly used by Catholic domestic servants of the Unionist rich. Today the same Catholic church has been greatly expanded and 'twinned' with the poor parish of Twinbrook in West Belfast. The leafy Malone Road is now mainly Catholic.

Similar developments in Derry are noted by Eamonn McCann in the most recent edition of *War and an Irish Town*:

In the courthouse in Bishop St it is now usually a Catholic lawyer who'll represent the Crown—unheard of a generation ago. Just along the street, Derry's only gentleman's club, the Northern Counties, which did not admit Catholics in the 1960s, now has a majority of Catholic members. Down in the Diamond, the city's biggest department store, owned until the early 1970s by the ascendancy Austin family, is now in the hands of the Catholic Hassons.[80]

With the growth of this class there has also been a change in their political orientation. In the past the Catholic middle class who operated outside their ghettoes attempted to ingratiate themselves with the Unionist establishment. Right up to the 1980s they mainly voted for the softer Unionist party, the Alliance party, and presented themselves as loyal citizens of the UK. But today the Catholic middle class are brimming with a new confidence. They want to assert their Irishness and see no reason to bow the knee to Orangeism. They support Gaelic games and are openly proud of it. They don't see why they cannot sing the Irish national anthem or commemorate 1916. One Catholic businessman interviewed by O'Connor expressed their sentiments:

> *I remember being in the Balmoral Golf Club on Saturday night when there was a dance and then they played 'God save the Queen'. Looking around, I realised, God, 60 percent of the people here are Catholic: who's insisting on this?...*
>
> *What I see is, among people of my children's age and people like me who've got this far in their lives, we do want to be part of Ireland, to say we're Irish—but we're not going to let anything go on up here that we are not part of. This is our place too, and it's taken us long enough to get this far.*[81]

For this class of Catholic the goal of a united Ireland is a dream that they identify with—but they can wait. In the meantime they want to be able to assert their 'cultural identity' and to have a real recognition of 'the two traditions'. Yuppie nationalism finds its symbol in John Hume but it increasingly reaches beyond him. The new confidence of the Catholic middle class means that they also want to assume their 'rightful place' as leaders of their own communities. As Marable has pointed out with regards to the black middle class in the US, the very precariousness of their position means that the middle class that has emerged from a civil rights movement want some degree of mobilisation to assert their goals.[82] In the case of the black middle class this takes the form of voter registration drives to build up their power block in the Democratic Party.

In Northern Ireland the Catholic middle class also need to call on extra political reserves to safeguard and expand their new positions. This can mean calling on Dublin for additional support. The Anglo-Irish agreement created a space for the Dublin government to be consulted on the running of the North. But the Catholic middle class would like to see the process go further and have clear recognition given to the fact that Dublin can function as their protector.

But this can only happen if some settlement is at hand. This is not unlikely. Developments inside Sinn Fein and the IRA indicate that they are looking for a way out of the conflict.

The republicans: coming in from the cold?

The left in Ireland has traditionally adopted one of two attitudes to Irish republicans. Organisations such as the Democratic Left—which grew out of the Workers Party—continue to regard them as 'quasi-fascists' who are engaged in mindless violence. Others take a similiar, though not as extreme, view. The *Militant* organisation regularly equates the IRA with the UDA/UVF and effectively brands it as the cause of violence in the North by refusing to call for a withdrawal by the British army. On the opposing side are remnants of groups like Peoples Democracy which have had some impact in the past. These believed that the IRA and Sinn Fein contained the vanguard of the Irish revolution. The role of the left was to act as their advisors.

Neither approach is correct. The IRA was born out of a movement that fought oppression. In 1968, when tens of thousands started marching for civil rights, the IRA was a tiny, disorganised and demoralised grouping.[83] But when the civil rights movement was met by the violence of the Northern state, thousands started to look for a political response. They soon found themselves in confrontation with the British army which wanted to shore up and protect the Northern state before gradually weaning the Unionist politicians towards reform. A series of events between 1968 and 1972 laid the basis for the building of a mass base for republicanism—August 1969 saw attacks on Catholic areas from the RUC and B specials; in 1970 the Falls Road was placed under curfew by the British army and five civilians were murdered; in August 1971 hundreds of Catholics were interned and tortured; in January 1972 14 civilians were murdered by the British army in Derry. Each event added to the scale and tempo of recruitment to the IRA. By 1971, for example, the previously demoralised IRA had recruited 1,000 members to its Belfast brigade alone.[84] It is precisely because the IRA emerged out of the fight against oppression that revolutionaries can find themselves on the same side against the British state.

But it is necessary for socialists to go much further. Struggles against oppression, particularly when they are not going forward, are often surrounded by moralism. The hardship and sufferings that are experienced by the oppressed, combined with the relative weakness of those involved, leads to demands for 'loyalty' and no criticism. This has to be resisted. The experience of history has always been that nationalist movements eventually seek to make their peace with the system—their fight is not against capitalism itself. As a result, whatever gains that are made invariably accrue to the middle class or the upper class. It is not simply a matter of the final outcome of nationalist movements. In the case of Ireland the nationalist politics of the IRA has led to a complete underestimation of the strength of organised labour. The focus of all struggle becomes an armed campaign.[85]

In reality this tactic has become more and more counterproductive. The bombing of mainly Protestant towns has helped drive hundreds into the ranks of the UDA. It has alienated the thousands of workers throughout the South who despise the British army but today cut themselves off from any involvement in what is happening in Northern Ireland. It has helped to bring about a situation where mass protests in Catholic working class areas today increasingly have a ritualistic character about them. Most of the big marches are for anniversaries of events which happened over 20 years ago. It has tragically confirmed Trotsky's prediction about any guerrilla campaign which seeks to substitute its own energy for the organisation of the masses:

It belittles the role of the masses in their own consciousness, reconciles them to their powerlessness and turns their eyes and hopes towards a great avenger and liberator who some day will come and accomplish his mission.[86]

The approach of revolutionaries in Ireland has therefore been clear. They have neither seen the IRA as a 'sectarian' force nor as potential agents for the liberation of Catholic workers, still less the wider working class. Instead revolutionaries have pointed to the British army and the Northern state as the principal causes of violence in Ireland. The objection to republicanism has been that its politics and tactics could not offer a way of defeating these forces and removing sectarianism.

This standpoint is more relevant now than ever before. The strategy which dominated republicanism in the 1980s has run out of steam. This involved a combination of the armed struggle and use of the ballot box. It also meant using a more left wing rhetoric in the hope of building a base among workers in the South. But Sinn Fein's vote in the North has now reached a plateau and it finds itself under greater military attack from loyalist forces. The attempt to expand into the Southern working class has been a dismal failure. The view that the South was a 'neo-colony' of Britain and therefore that workers could be won to a vague 'anti-imperialism' has proved a fantasy.

The collapse of this strategy has meant that Sinn Fein has lowered its sights. Gone is the talk of winning a united Ireland in the short term. Instead Sinn Fein President Gerry Adams has not ruled out 'interim measures' such as joint sovereignty. The fact that Sinn Fein is looking for compromise is what has made the Downing Street Declaration possible.

Here Sinn Fein is part of the common pattern of national liberation movements around the world. Gerry Adams has hailed the Israel-PLO deal as 'courageous first steps' and claimed that the lesson was that 'a peace process is possible in the most difficult of conflicts'.[87] In the 1980s organisations such as the African National Congress in South Africa, the Palestine Liberation Organisation, and the FMLN in El Salvador were seen as the focus of opposition to the system. Today they are increasingly becoming proponents of moderation and sacrifice before the dictates of world capital. The FMLN, for example, which was once regarded as one of the most left wing guerrilla organisations of the world, is now engaged in a peace pact with the butchers of ARENA and has argued for an amnesty of those found guilty of human rights abuses.[88] This shift has been associated with the fall of communism. In fact, its roots go far deeper.

Nationalist movements in the 20th century have often sought to win a working class base by a left wing or populist language. But the working class is invariably seen as a battering ram to open the doors for a new nationalist elite. The suffering and the heroism of the poor are celebrated by nationalist ideologues but there is a cold scepticism about the ability of that same class to liberate itself. The goal of these movements remains the development of their particular nation rather than the advance of the working class. Because they do not set out to fight the overall system, they eventually come to a compromise with it. There is no reason to believe that Irish republicans will behave any differently.

Indeed, the rhetoric of republicanism has already registered a significant shift. Their key aim now is to forge an alliance with the right wing leader of Fianna Fail, Albert Reynolds. Sinn Fein President Gerry Adams has already attacked 'the fiction that Sinn Fein is out to undermine the authority of the Southern state'.[89] At the Sinn Fein conference in 1994, not a word of criticism was to be heard of Reynolds despite the fact that Fianna Fail is increasingly loathed by many Southern workers. Instead, Adams told the delegates that their aim was 'winning the backing of the Dublin government and co-operating to obtain powerful international allies'.[90] The reference to international allies may be a little mystifying. But today Sinn Fein is tremendously impressed by the way that the Irish lobby in the US has won a hearing with Bill Clinton. It hopes that US pressure can be used to nudge Britain towards a settlement. This explains why Sinn Fein has pressed Clinton to send a 'peace envoy' to the North. All of this has political implications. When the US ambassador was visiting Derry, Sinn Fein members were told to have nothing to do with a picket that protested about the continuing sanctions directed at Iraq.

This shift in republican politics has occurred before any settlement has been reached. It merely indicates what is yet to come. There can be little doubt of the desire of the Sinn Fein leadership to make the full transition to a proper party that operates within the system. But so far it has received little by way of concrete inducements from the British government. The Downing Street Declaration made no reference to the freeing of the hundreds of republican prisoners. It gave no concrete promises that the RUC or the British army might be withdrawn from the areas where they are hated and despised. The British ruling class may have a long term desire to disengage from the North, but they are, for the moment, nervous about dealing openly with a guerrilla movement on their own doorstep. This means that the 'peace process' between Sinn Fein and the British may be more protracted than was originally thought.

Prospects

For the moment then Irish politics are dominated by two central themes—the growing social tensions in the South and the prospects of the 'peace process' in the North. This is the terrain on which the left has to start building—and building quickly. The stakes are high. A failure to build a fighting socialist force in Ireland raises new prospects of growing ethnic conflicts about 'identities' and even a regression from the social advance that has occurred in the South.

One key area for the left is the Protestant working class. The declining interest of Britain and the worsening material conditions of Protestant workers have led to a crisis of confidence in Unionism. How this is to be resolved is an open question. One real possibility is a growth of the extreme right. Recent estimates put the current strength of the UDA/UVF at 2,300.[91] The youth organisation of the UDA, Young Militant, may contain over 1,000 members on a loosely organised basis. These organisations are stronger in areas of high unemployment where fewer Protestants meet Catholics through work. However, it has also become apparent that these organisations are now receiving active support from a section of the Unionist middle class who find themselves in growing competition with their Catholic counterparts, and who fear that any constitutional adjustments will further undermine their access to privilege.

This explains why the former mayor of Belfast, Sammy Wilson, from the Paisleyite Democratic Unionist Party, has praised the UDA's plans for the ethnic cleansing of Catholics from particular areas of the North as 'realistic'. Other Unionist figures are not far behind in their attempted rapprochement with the killer squads. The 'liberal' Unionist Christopher McGimpsey has admitted having had talks with the UDA about the Downing Street Declaration. Spokespersons for the UDA have in turn pointed to their links with the respectable elements of Unionism. One of them boasted that 'they had unlimited financial assistance and the ability through business contacts on the continent to procure a steady supply of weapons and explosives'.[92] This shift by some Unionist politicians towards greater collusion with loyalist terror gangs was inadvertently alluded to by Reynolds in a remark that was simply glossed over by the media. Reynolds stated that a number of 'good, solid, Unionists' told him that they felt under siege and that 'the traditional way to break out of the siege is to go out and murder some Catholics. People have actually said those words to me'.[93]

The Unionist middle class have much to fear. While the the former captains of Orange industry have simply upped and left, the nature of their social position means that the middle classes are left behind, more dependent on state employment and more subject to increased competition. The Anglo-Irish Agreement of 1987 set up a structure whereby the Dublin government won a consultative voice in the day to day running of Northern Ireland. In practice it opened a new avenue whereby the middle class SDLP could use Dublin's civil servants who sat on the inter-governmental conference at Maryfield to channel more funds and resources to its areas. It has meant that the former bastions of middle class privilege such as Queen's University are now subject to considerable scrutiny and have been forced to accept policies designed to employ more Catholics. The fear of the Unionist middle class is that greater involvement of Dublin will further erode their position which has already been made more insecure by recession and the decline of the Northern economy.

The UDA/UVF have a long way to go before the major sections of the Unionist middle class step into an open alliance with them. The majority of the Unionist middle class look to the Unionist party and, to a lesser extent, the DUP as their main defenders. For the moment, the loyalist paramilitaries are seen by the 'good solid Unionists' as a reserve force which can be used to increase their leverage with the British and Irish governments. The Unionist politicians merely express 'understanding' of the rhetoric and activities of the UDA/UVF. All of this means, however, that they have a stake in whipping up sectarianism. When the UDA claims that Catholic community centres and youth clubs get more resources than those in Protestant areas because of the violence of the IRA, the Unionist leaders do not demur. Indeed, their whole attitude indicates sympathy with this argument.

However, a rise in sectarianism and growth in support for the UDA/UVF is only one possibility. There are also signs that sections of Protestant workers are sickened by the logic of loyalism. In the past the Unionist state sought to bar Catholics from certain jobs. Today the UDA/UVF try to achieve the same end through the use of terror tactics. Among their prime targets for assassination are Catholics who stray out of their area and seek jobs in areas traditionally held by Protestants. But attacks on fellow workers have driven a wedge between the loyalist killer squads and the Protestant workers. When a Catholic contractor was murdered in the overwhelmingly Protestant Shorts factory, 1,000 workers walked out. When Catholic workers on Belfast's buses were threatened by the UVF, Protestant and Catholic workers took strike action to demand that the threats be withdrawn. Most impressively of all, when Maurice O'Kane, a Catholic welder, was murdered by the UVF at Harland and Wolff, the shop stewards convened a meeting and walked off the site. As one of the stewards put it, 'Maurice has three sons working in the yard. We had a duty to protect them. Working class lives are hard enough without these threats of murder'.[94] It was the first time the shipyards had ever taken such action. In the past, the Harland and Wolff shipyard was notorious for launching pogroms against Catholics.

It is not just in the workplaces that there is opposition to the loyalist thugs. The UDA/UVF regularly include coded messages in their publications about individual Protestants who have been seen going out with 'Fenians and papists'. They also try to target Protestants who are involved in mixed marriages. All of these activities are held in contempt by the vast majority of Protestant workers. The most dramatic indication of this disgust came after the murder of Margaret Wright. She went to a late night drinking club run by the UVF in the Village area in Belfast. She was mistaken for a Catholic and beaten to death on the dance floor of the club. Afterwards, 600 local people gathered and demanded that the UVF club be bulldozed down.

As conditions worsen, as Protestant workers become more aware that Britain's rulers have no interest in their loyalty, they are presented with a choice: either they are pulled into the orbit of the thugs of the UDA who are achieving a greater weight within the politics of Unionism, or they begin to break from the logic of loyalism and seek to identify with those Catholic workers who are under threat.

Here is where the scale, intensity and outcome of the class struggle in Britain over the next period are so important. Notions of class and class solidarity have always featured strongly in the lives of Northern workers, co-existing in uneasy and contradictory ways with the intense sectarianism. Union membership in Northern Ireland stands at 38 percent of the workforce, similar to that in Britain itself.[95] More union members in Northern Ireland have been on strike than their counterparts in Britain.[96] Belfast on May Day is probably one of the few cities in the UK that resembles Yorkshire in its traditional observance of workers' day as 1,000 trade unionists regularly take to the streets. A rise in industrial militancy across Britain will inevitably affect the North as well. When Catholic and Protestant workers fight alongside each other, it makes the propaganda of the UDA appear even more disgusting. If some of those struggles end in victory, it can broaden the horizon of workers and help to make class appear as a more important source of identity than sectarianism.

That at least has been the experience of the past. The only time sectarianism has been overcome in the North has been in the heat of class struggle. In the near revolutionary upheavals of 1919, Catholic and Protestant workers fought together. During the unemployment crisis of the 1930s the Falls and the Shankill fought together against the RUC. Even in the midst of the Second World War, when patriotic fervour was at its height, Catholics and Protestants fought together in 1944 against the arrest of their shop stewards.[97] This history makes Northern Ireland fundamentally different to Israel and South Africa, to which it is sometimes compared.

But if the class struggle in Britain is important, so too is the struggle in Southern Ireland. At the start of the troubles in 1968, the average Protestant worker could make a relatively easy transition between 'being British' and seeing him or herself as relatively superior to workers in the impoverished Southern state. Today when 'being British' means being part of Europe's cheap labour economy that transition is not so easy. But though the old illusions are dying, there is still a big question about the nature of the South for many Protestant workers.

Here is where the current struggles in the South can make a difference. If Southern workers begin to take on their employers and also start to break from the domination of the church then this can have a tremendous influence on Protestant workers. But of course, none of this is automatic. The upturn in struggle in the South began at a political level before it touched the workplaces. There were more delegations, for example, from girls' schools on the X case march than there were from workplaces. Few trade union banners have appeared on the big demonstrations against Thorp, the nuclear reprocessing station, or the demonstrations in solidarity with the anti-fascist struggles in Europe. This represented a major weakness.

For one thing, the Catholic right are still a force waiting on the wings of Southern society. The defeats they suffered on the abortion issue were serious but not fatal. For decades the Catholic right had the ear of the Fianna Fail politicians either directly or indirectly through the bishops. They believed—with some justification—that they represented the 'real Ireland'. In the aftermath of the X case, however, they shifted from being regarded as an important pressure group to being seen as a liability. This shift in their status has forced the Catholic right to reconsider their tactics. They are now being pulled in two directions. A minority around Youth Defence are more willing to use violence against their left wing opponents and women's activists. A recent picket at the Irish parliament, for example, found itself subject to an attack by Youth Defence fanatics.

But the majority of the bigots are adopting a more political strategy. They have formed an organisation called Solidarity and have started to broaden their agenda beyond the issues of abortion and sexuality. Their propaganda focuses on the need to preserve 'family farms'. They want more indigenous Irish industry to replace the multinationals which they blame for creating unemployment. They want more support for married women to stay at home. They want a stronger reassertion of Irish culture and a more militant stance against 'the Brits'. In a more sinister development, they point to the Jewish background of the Labour minister for equality, Mervyn Taylor, who they claim is undermining 'Christian values'.[98] Their aim is the creation of an extreme right wing populist movement which can relate to the growing anger in Southern society. In the longer term, it cannot be ruled out that such a movement can shift from right wing social Catholicism to an embrace of fascist politics similar to that of Dolfuss in the 1930s in Austria.

However the Catholic right have only just started to regroup and are a long way from relating to the anger that presently exists. Southern Ireland still resembles the experience of Italy in the 1960s and 1970s.[99] In both countries, the process of modernisation did not lead to a gradual shift to a more liberal society. Instead big struggles developed as the old order was shaken. In the process significant numbers became radicalised. But, as Italy shows, radicalisation alone is not sufficient to remove the right wing who occupy positions of power. In Ireland, the bigots still have friends in high places. The Irish Medical Council, for example, has been taken over by groups of right wing doctors and now refuses to implement any form of abortion. High Court judges, such as Justice O'Hanlon, speak out openly against a government which has 'decriminalised sodomy'.[100] The right wing still have a network of schools and parish institutions at which they can rebuild their base. And most important they have a target: a government with Labour ministers who have severely disappointed their supporters. The son of the disgraced Fianna Fail leader, Haughey, gave an indication of the type of attack that the right can mount. He denounced 'the steamroller approach of the Labour party on abortion and divorce' and connected it with the party's desire for 'Mercs, perks and expensive hotels'.[101]

Whether or not the political radicalisation that has emerged in the South is sustained therefore depends on whether there is shift from an adherence of alternative lifestyles and values to a real engagement with working class struggles. Without that shift, the gains that have been made in the South can be turned aside and the right can re-emerge as a force.

Fortunately, the political radicalisation is now matched by a rise in working class militancy. Ever since Fianna Fail returned to power in

1987, it adopted a strategy of co-opting the union leaders and managing the economy through social partnership agreements where workers are tied to centrally negotiated pay norms. These agreements have included no-strike clauses which gave the employers a free hand to push through major changes at the level of the workplace which resulted in big increases in productivity. Workers are now becoming keenly aware that their sacrifices have not been matched by the employers. Unemployment still stands at 18 percent of the workforce. A full 27 percent of Southern workers are earning less than £150 a week.[102] Everywhere there are attempts to introduce 'yellow pack workers'—workers who start on lower pay rates and enjoy no holiday or sick pay benefits.

The mood among workers has therefore started to shift. In the past tens of thousands emigrated—but today they are more likely to be forced to stay in Ireland and start thinking about collective responses to their situation. The mood of anger still co-exists with the legacy of defeat in the 1980s. Workers want to fight—but they are not yet sure they can win. Beyond the top union bureaucracy there is a wide layer of shop stewards who have accepted the arguments about 'new realism' and still desire partnership with their employers. The shift in mood and the continuing problems are illustrated most clearly in a dispute at Team-Aer Lingus. The company demanded wage cuts and layoffs in the national airline. When the issue first emerged, socialists who took their banners on workers' marches were thrown off as troublemakers. But almost a year later there is a good awareness of what happened during the Air France dispute, because socialists have been leafleting the workplace. No Team march takes place now without a speaker invited from socialist organisations. Yet the mood of militancy still clashes with the pessimism of the shop steward leadership who believe that industrial action does not win.

This is where politics count. Many of the thousands who shifted to the left during the fight against the power of the church will find their way into the workplace. So too will those—often the same people—who are moved by the threat of fascism in Europe today. They know that militancy can overcome the defeats of the past. These radicalised political layers can play a major role in overcoming the inertia of some of the older working class leaderships. But they have to be convinced to argue this with their fellow workers. And the type of politics that emerge in the workplace do not just stop at how to fight redundancies or wage cuts—but can also include arguments about the position of women in Irish society or how the problem of the North is to be solved.

The emergence of a working class movement in the South which fused the anger about economic 'sacrifice' with a desire to break the grip of Fianna Fail and the church would have a major impact on Northern Protestant workers. It would help make class the touchstone of identity rather than appeals to a sectarian past. By contrast, the sectarian bigots of the North and South can also help to reinforce and strengthen each other. The re-emergence of the Catholic right in the South could become a major factor in persuading Protestant workers that there is no hope but to defend their own.

Conclusion

The key issue in Irish politics, then, is whether class or ethnic identity come to the fore in the coming years. Every political movement has to be judged in terms of that question.

For official Irish society this, of course, is barely an issue. National identity is assumed to be intrinsic and natural. The British and Irish ruling classes may believe that the constitutional settlement of 1922 has to be readjusted to allow for a new balance of power between Catholics and Protestants. But despite all the talk of 'solving the national question' any bourgeois solution in Ireland will merely institutionalise the sectarian divisions that now exist. The British and Irish rulers will seek to create structures which allow these divisions to be managed rather than removed. In the process, they hope to keep the old right wing watchwords at the heart of Irish politics. The Fianna Fail leader, Reynolds, for example, claimed that a new Ireland could see the two 'great forces' of Fianna Fail and the Unionist party coming together and promised that one third of elite positions in any new state would be reserved for Unionist supporters.

Any settlement that emerges from the British and Irish ruling classes will be inherently unstable. Not only will sectarianism remain institutionalised but it will do so in conditions of ever growing poverty for many workers. The dangers are obvious. Europe at the moment is full of political adventurers who see the crisis as a way of winning a base for their particular shade of extreme right opinion. A rearranged constitutional settlement of Ireland would provide ample material for stirring up new ethnic and sectarian hatreds. In the process those sections of the Unionist middle class who collude with the UDA can quickly recognise their mirror image opponents among the bigots of the South. A conservative settlement in Ireland in the 1990s will have far more devastating effects than that of the 1920s.

It is against these prospects that all oppositional movements have to be evaluated. For most of its history a large section of the Irish left has viewed republicanism as the vehicle for rapid social advance. The very weakness of the working class seemed to call for a substitute force that drew on the mainspring of native radicalism. In the 1890s James Connolly saw little else on the bleak landscape of Irish working class politics and named his first organisation the Irish Socialist Republican Party. The workers' army he established in 1913, the Irish Citizen Army, dissolved itself into the republican Irish Volunteers after his death. Connolly's son Roddy set up the Irish Communist Party and focused its efforts on trying to convince the republicans to shift left. As late as the 1970s, hundreds of Irish left wingers were pulled towards the Irish Republican Socialist Party which seemed to offer the final fusion of Marxism and native radicalism.[103] Historically, that section of the left which looked to republicanism was often subjectively the most revolutionary. The others who recoiled from republicanism often became ardent supporters of the status quo. The Workers Party, for example, who regarded the republicans as 'proto-fascists' became avid defenders of censorship in the South and the RUC in the North.

Today, however, republicanism is at a turning point. As the leadership seek to follow the path of Arafat and Mandela they are keenly aware of their own history of divisions. Every time the movement has tried to move decisively towards an accommodation with the system a section has split off to engage in the age old tactic of armed struggle. When the republican leadership accepted the treaty in 1922, it provoked a civil war. When de Valera tried to move those opposed to the treaty towards involvement in parliament in 1926, he had to set up Fianna Fail and see the IRA continue its involvement in armed struggle. As late as the 1980s Adams and McGuinness, the current leadership, had to witness a split in their ranks as they argued for an end to the policy of abstention from the Irish parliament. The splits have emerged because of the divided class basis of the movement. Republicanism has always included the most conventional of would be politicians alongside radicals who have seen armed struggle as the only way of expressing their anger at the system.

It is difficult to predict with any certainty what will happen to republicanism. But broadly we can say that either significant sections of the movement will be incorporated into some form of all Ireland settlement or it will become a smaller oppositional movement that relies increasingly on the counterproductive strategy of armed struggle, shorn of any strategy or hope. At the root of the weakness of modern republicanism has been its belief that it could only identify with the aspirations of the oppressed Catholic community of the North. In the 1970s, when the revolt of the Catholic working class was at its height, republicanism could mount a real challenge to the system. Despite its right wing ideas at the time, republicanism had the confidence to believe that British imperialism would be driven out of Ireland and that the Southern state would be toppled in the process and replaced by an 'Eire Nua'(new Ireland). But when that revolt did not break through, it became more ghettoised and more cynical. The very aspects of oppression that fuelled the anger against the system as a whole also contained elements within it which saw Protestant workers as near fascists and Southern workers as pampered traitors. When the struggle was going forward these latter elements were barely expressed undercurrents. As the struggle moved towards a dead end in the 1980s, the elements of separatism and contempt for Protestant workers, in particular, became more prominent. Yet in reality the stress on separatism, on not just promoting but virtually developing a distinct 'national culture' in the Catholic areas, has only benefited the Catholic middle class and done nothing for the working class adherents of republicanism.

The manner in which republicanism can cut against the grain of working class struggle has become more obvious as the possibility of workers' unity has grown. In 1993, for example, health workers in the North faced major battles against trust status. The fate of the mainly Protestant workforce in the Jubilee hospital was bound together with that of the mainly Catholic workforce of the Royal Victoria in West Belfast. And most workers understood this. Huge protests and demonstrations brought Catholic and Protestant workers onto the streets against the Tory plans. But *Republican News* could only talk about the Catholic hospital and complained that 'jobs lost in West Belfast are less politically sensitive than elsewhere'.[104] In fact, the Tories have no sensitivity about cutting any workers' jobs. By focusing on their own community the republicans only played to the Tories' divide and rule tactics. Worse, however, was to follow. When Protestant workers in the Shorts factory walked out in defence of the Catholic murdered by the UDA, republicans simply dismissed its significance. When the Harland and Wolff shipyard stopped, the action could not be ignored and *Republican News* ran the banner headline on its front page, 'Shipyard of shame'. It discussed at length the sectarian history of the yard without once supporting the walkout by the Protestant workforce. More graphically than anything else it showed that republicans regard Protestant workers as simply the objects of history rather than part of a class which has the potential to liberate itself. Not surprisingly, Gerry Adams has claimed that what Protestants need is 'a de Klerk type figure'.[105]

The separatism which pervades republicanism makes it weaker and all the more likely to adapt to the system. One journalist aptly wrote that the republicans are 'attempting to keep the Major-Reynolds bus waiting while Adams talks the drivers into going an extra bit further in his direction'.[106] The driver will, of course, also be demanding a fare for the ticket. If and when the republicans move closer to a settlement they will use all the authority that has come out the sacrifice of struggle to promote 'realism' and 'disipline' among their supporters. That in turn would only help to increase the bitterness which sees Protestants rather than bosses as their chief competitors and enemies. Republicanism today has not only not got the slightest notion of socialism, it is also incapable of meeting the vision of its founder, Wolfe Tone, in creating an Ireland which 'unites Catholic Protestant and dissenter'.

That task falls to the still small forces of the revolutionary left.

Notes

1. *Forward*, 21 March 1914.
2. G Bell, *The Protestants of Ulster* (London, 1976), p40.
3. See M Farrell, *Arming the Protestants* (London, 1983), for how the auxiliary forces were formed along sectarian lines.
4. M Goldring, *Belfast: From Loyalty to Rebellion* (London, 1991), p123.
5. P Devlin, *Straight Left: an autobiography* (Belfast, 1993).
6. Ibid, p132.
7. A Boyd, *Have the Trade Unions Failed the North?* (Cork, 1984), p72.
8. The Fianna Fail party has often claimed to be more than a mere political party and instead to be a real movement of the Irish people. See D Walsh, *The Party: Inside Fianna Fail* (Dublin, 1986).
9. See C Kostick, *Why the Irish Labour Party Fails* (Dublin, 1993).
10. P Mair, 'Explaining the Absence of Class Politics in Ireland', in J Goldthorpe and C Whelan, *The Development of Industrial Society in Ireland* (Oxford, 1992), p386.
11. D Walsh, *The Party: Inside Fianna Fail* (Dublin, 1986), p32.
12. J P O'Carroll, 'Eamon de Valera, Charisma and Political Development', in J P O'Carroll and J A Murphy (eds) *De Valera and His Times* (Cork, 1983), p33.
13. J Praeger, *Building Democracy in Ireland* (Cambridge, 1986), p208.
14. *Dail Debates*, 12 July 1928.
15. Quoted in T Ryle Dwyer, *De Valera* (Dublin, 1991), p134.
16. *The Nation*, 5 October 1929.
17. Dail Debates, 22 March 1928.
18. Dail Debates, 2 November 1927.
19. L Trotsky, 'Lesson of the Events in Dublin', in *Lenin's Struggle for a Revolutionary International 1907-1916* (New York, 1984), p373.
20. *CSO Statistical Abstracts, 1932*.
21. The Labour Party leader, Tom Johnson, claimed that 'there was no justification in law or morality' for not paying the land annuities. *The Irishman*, 25 August 1928.
22. See C McCarthy, *Trade Unions in Ireland 1894-1960* (Dublin, 1977).
23. *Labour News*, January 1966.
24. *National Income and Expenditure Reports 1958-1973*.
25. M Nic Ghiolla Phadraig, 'Religious Practice and Secularisation' in P Clancy (ed) *Ireland: a Sociological Profile* (Dublin, 1990), p94.
26. Conference of Major Religious Superiors, *Profile of Religious in Ireland*, (Dublin 1990), p94.
27. Quoted in J Whyte, *Church and State in Modern Ireland 1923-1979* (Dublin, 1980), pp29-30.
28. Minutes of the Central Council of Congress of Irish Unions, 30 March 1951.
29. Congress of Irish Unions, *Annual Report 1951*, pp37-38.
30. Quoted in J Connolly, *Labour, Nationality and Religion* (Dublin, 1972), p10.
31. M Nic Ghiolla Phadraig, 'Religious Practice and Secularisation', op cit, p147.
32. Ibid.
33. E Strauss, *Irish Nationalism and British Democracy* (London, 1951), p104.

34   Ibid.
35   R Breen, D Hannan, D Rottman, C Whelan, *Understanding Contemporary Ireland* (Dublin, 1990), p104.
36   E Hazelhorn, 'Class, Clientilism and Political Process in the Republic of Ireland', in P Clancy (ed), *Ireland: a Sociological Profile*, op cit, p339.
37   J Wickham, 'The Politics of Divided Capitalism' in A Morgan and B Purdie, *Divided Nation, Divided Class* (London, 1980), p59.
38   Ibid.
39   J Goldthorpe and C Whelan, *The Development of Industrial Society in Ireland* (Oxford, 1992), p389.
40   W Roche and J Larragy, 'The Trend of Unionisation in the Republic' in UCD (eds) *Industrial Relations in Ireland* (Dublin, 1987).
41   B Walsh, *Labour Force Participation and the Feminisation of the Labour Force* (Dublin, 1992), p1.
42   Amnesty International, *Political Killings in Northern Ireland* (London, 1994), p2.
43   B Probert, *Beyond Orange and Green* (London, 1978), p46.
44   Quoted in R Munck, *The Irish Economy: Results and Prospects* (London, 1993), p48.
45   See E O'Connor, *Syndicalism in Ireland* (Cork, 1988).
46   See A Mitchell, *Labour in Irish Politics* (Dublin, 1985).
47   A de Blacam, *What Sinn Fein Stands For* (Dublin, 1920), pp105-106.
48   K Allen, *Is Southern Ireland a Neo-colony?* (Dublin, 1990).
49   R Munck, *The Irish Economy*, op cit, p52.
50   E McCann, *War and an Irish Town* (London, 1993), pp179-180.
51   NIEC, *Annual Report 1992-1993* (Belfast, 1993), p23.
52   Ibid.
53   NIEC, *The Private Sector in the Northern Ireland Economy* (Belfast, 1990), p7.
54   Ibid.
55   Quoted in F Gaffikin and M Morrissey, *Northern Ireland: the Thatcher Years* (London, 1990), p48.
56   Ibid, p49.
57   M Farrell, *Northern Ireland: the Orange State* (London, 1976), pp16-17.
58   G Bell, *The Protestants of Ulster,* op cit.
59   In the US, for instance, the racist south has lower wages for both black and white workers than the more integrated north. Indeed white workers in the south are lower paid than *black* workers in the north. A Shawki, 'Black Liberation and Socialism in the USA' in *International Socialism* 47, p77.
60   F Gaffikin and M Morrissey, *Northern Ireland: the Thatcher Years*, p77.
61   NIEC, *Economic Assessment 1991* (Belfast, 1992), p30.
62   NIEC, *Demographic Trends in Northern Ireland* (Belfast, 1986), p66.
63   NIEC, *The Private Sector in Northern Ireland* (Belfast, 1988).
64   NIEC, *Annual Report 1992-93* (Belfast, 1993), p4.
65   Ibid.
66   M Hewitt, *Can Protestant and Catholic Workers Unite?* (Dublin, 1991), p13.
67   Ibid.
68   Community Training and Research Services, *Poverty Amongst Plenty* (Belfast, 1993), pp5-6.
69   A Pollack (ed), *A Citizen's Inquiry: the Opsahl Report* (Dublin, 1993), p43.
70   A Hamilton, C McCartney, T Anderson and A Finn, *Violence and Communities* (Coleraine, 1990), p5.
71   Ibid.
72   F O'Connor, *In Search of a State: Catholics in Northern Ireland* (Belfast, 1993).
73   Ibid, p21.

74 M Marable, *Race, Reform and Rebellion* (London, 1991), p208.
75 Ibid, p185.
76 F O'Connor, op cit, p15.
77 Ibid.
78 Ibid.
79 Ibid.
80 E McCann, *War and an Irish Town,* op cit, p52
81 F O'Connor, op cit. pp32-33.
82 M Marable, *Black American Politics* (London, 1985), p245.
83 See J Boyer Bell, *The Secret Army* (Dublin, 1979), pp336-350
84 Ibid.
85 For an extension of this argument see K Allen, *Socialism Republicanism and Armed Struggle* (Dublin, 1991).
86 L Trotsky, *Against Individual Terrorism* (New York, 1980), p7.
87 *Socialist Worker* (Ireland), February 1994.
88 CIIR, *El Salvador: Wager for Peace* (London, 1993), p21.
89 *Socialist Worker* (Ireland), February 1994.
90 Quoted from copy of G Adams's speech at Sinn Fein Ard Fheis, 1994.
91 *Fortnight,* February 1994.
92 Ibid.
93 *Irish Times,* 16 March 1994.
94 *Socialist Worker* (Ireland), July 1994.
95 P Stringer and G Robinson (eds), *Social Attitudes in Northern Ireland* (Belfast, 1993), p68.
96 Ibid, p70.
97 The story of many of the joint struggles between Catholic and Protestant workers can be found in M Hewitt, op cit.
98 *Irish Times,* 9 July 1994.
99 For a history of the struggles in Italy see P Ginsborg, *A History of Contemporary Italy: Society and Politics 1943-1988* (London, 1990).
100 *Irish Times,* 17 March 1994.
101 *Irish Times,* 16 March 1994.
102 Figures based on 1987 data from B Nolan and T Callan, *Poverty and Policy in Ireland* (Dublin, 1994), p118.
103 See J Holland and H McDonald, *INLA: Deadly Divisions* (Torc books, 1994), for a history of the Irish Republican Socialist Party and its armed wing, INLA.
104 Quoted in M Hewitt, op cit, p32.
105 Copy of speech from G Adams to Sinn Fein Ard Fheis, 1994.
106 *Fortnight,* February 1994.

The wrong road on Russia

A review of S Clarke, P Fairbrother, M Burawoy and P Krotov, **What About the Workers? Workers and the Transition to Capitalism in Russia***, (London, 1993) £12.99*

MIKE HAYNES

The working class of the former USSR has frequently been described as a 'sleeping giant'. It was this working class that was the dynamic force in 1917, but it was this working class that was also destroyed during the civil war as the Russian Revolution remained isolated. Such was the economic and social dislocation of war that in Petrograd, of the 400,000 factory workers who had made the revolution in 1917, only 50,000 to 60,000 were left in 1922—the lowest point of the period.

The subsequent years of New Economic Policy (NEP) in the 1920s saw a recovery in numbers but few of the workers who survived seem to have returned to their jobs of 1917 and perhaps not even to the same cities where they had been so militant. Although there were important protests against the growing degeneration of the revolution, the working class as a whole was unable to stop the emergence of a new ruling class which then tried to drive the Russian economy forward to industrialise in the most rapid way possible in order to compete with its Western rivals. This industrialisation drive produced enormous social dislocation and it led to the development of a huge new working class. One measure of this is the level of urbanisation which rose from approximately 18 percent in 1926 to 33 percent in 1939, 48 percent in 1959 and 66 percent in 1989. Throughout this period the rulers of Russia kept the lid very firmly on working class resistance and smashed any attempts at protest. This repression moderated after the death of Stalin but no real space was allowed for sustained working class organisation.

It was only when the contradictions of perestroika and Gorbachev's attempts at reform from above began to go wrong that the ruling class group faltered and new opportunities arose that promised to allow open class conflict to emerge on a mass scale. In the summer of 1989 this happened with huge miners' strikes that stretched across the coalfields of the

USSR from western Siberia to the Ukraine and Kazakhstan. Finally, it seemed that the contradictions of crisis and reform would allow working class militancy to grow and the possibility of an independent workers' movement that could be the basis of a genuine left wing opposition that was against both Western capitalism and the Stalinist tradition in Russia. Alas it was not to be. Although struggles continued to erupt in 1990 and 1991 the movement faltered and the USSR, after the failure of the August 1991 coup, disintegrated into a mass of mutually suspicious successor states.

As the drama of events in Russia has unfolded over the past two years little of the struggle of the working class movement has been reported in the Western press. A book, therefore, which boldly asks 'what about the workers?' and sets out to explore the role of 'workers and the transition to Capitalism in Russia' promises to demand a place on every socialist's bookshelf. Regrettably no such endorsement is possible. *What About The Workers?* is one of the most theoretically inept books to have been published on Russia by those on the left for some years. It is empirically frustrating in the extreme and its political conclusion is mind boggling.

What About the Workers? reports the investigations of Simon Clarke, Peter Fairbrother, Michael Burawoy and Pavel Krotov into working conditions in Russia and the workers' movement based on extensive first hand investigation. The bulk of the book consists of empirical and theoretical chapters by Clarke and Fairbrother although they suggest that their work has been assisted by Krotov, a Russian sociologist and Michael Burowoy, a leading American left wing sociologist. Burowoy and Krotov's contribution, however, is restricted to one reprinted chapter on the work process in the wood industry. This has one enormous merit. Burowoy managed to get a job working for two months in a factory as a machinist and much of the discussion reports his first hand experiences. Unfortunately this is insufficient to compensate for the theoretical weaknesses of the book. Clarke and Fairbrother spent 45 weeks doing field work in Moscow, St Petersburg, the Kuzbass, Komi, Ekaterinberg (Sverdlovsk), Chelyabinsk and Samara, but little of what they write is explicitly informed by their visit.

This is a book about a working class that has been made mute by the Soviet regime for nearly 60 years. After 1989 workers again began to find a voice and the authors appear to have been given an unparalleled opportunity to investigate and report this but in the book there is not one single quotation from a Russian worker. For Clarke and Fairbrother the Russian workers are as mute as the theorists of the old regime made them. What kind of investigation is it that does not allow the authentic voice of any worker through? It cannot be that they have found nothing of interest. For example, we learn that the authors managed to contact

Vladimir Klebanov, one of the leaders of the repressed free trade unions at the turn of the 1980s.[1] He apparently told them that informal organisations of workers had existed in some plants in the 1950s. But this is all we learn for we are protected by the 'tremendous condescension of the left wing sociologist'.

This is a book about the workers' movement but it provides no systematic idea of scale either in respect of protests or the organisations that are its subject. Individual statistics are quoted but there is no attempt to give us, for example, an idea of the rhythms of the strike movement. Yet some statistics have appeared and, however inadequate they are, one might have imagined that the authors would have made it a priority to get hold of them and analyse them. We might have hoped that they would have organised their material on the size and distribution of free trade unions in a more helpful way.[2]

This is also an incredibly narrow study. Its interests are essentially the work process. Now this is important but Russian workers have a life outside their workplace and that life also interacts with life inside the workplace. But there is little or nothing of this here either. Most obviously there is no explicit consideration of the issue of nationalism and how the fracturing of the USSR has affected the possibility of building an independent working class movement.

How could a book which asks 'what about the workers' have such a limited vision? The simple answer is that the theory which the authors use—that Soviet Russia was neither capitalist nor socialist but some kind of new society—is inadequate. This is not to say that the theory can explain every deficiency of this book, rather what it has done has been to reinforce the crassness and blind spots of the authors and in such a way as to make them oblivious to what they are doing.

Exceptionalism or confusionism?

There are essentially three possible approaches to analysing the former USSR. The first sees it as some kind of socialism, however degenerate. Since, however, most commentators now agree that the working class had no power in these societies, this view must implicitly define socialism against the working class. While this poses no difficulties for the enemies of socialism, it leaves socialists in a very uncomfortable position and their discomfort is increased by the transition. Since this is pictured as a shift from socialism to capitalism they must effectively defend the old order—whatever their doubts—and so line themselves up alongside those who represent its worst elements.

The second view argues that these societies were class societies based on state capitalism. The working class was exploited and oppressed for the benefit of a ruling class which used a political rhetoric of 'socialism' to try to disguise the true nature of the regime. Now that ruling class is trying to shift more of its power towards the market and private property to maintain its overall grip in a rapidly changing world. Politically this leads to the conclusion that workers in both state and private industry have a common class identity, opposed to the common class identity of their rulers and this identity needs to be articulated and fought for as the basis of a real alternative. It is this view that has long been associated with this journal.

The third view has been described as 'exceptionalism' in the sense that it sees the USSR as neither socialist nor capitalist but some new, exceptional form. This argument also has a long history but in its modern form it has become more popular in the last two decades as socialists have rejected any claims to find any kind of socialism in the USSR but have been unwilling to concede the argument that Soviet society was a form of capitalism. Unfortunately 'exceptionalism' has never had a coherent theoretical basis and its political conclusions have often been ambiguous. Yet it is to this idea that the authors of this book look and in the process their analysis descends from 'exceptionalism' to 'total confusionism'.

Unfair? Well, consider the following: 'The underlying argument of this book is that the Soviet Union was neither state capitalist nor socialist, but that it represented a *sui generis* form of class rule, whose precise nature remains to defined.'[3] Indeed so indifferent is the main author, Simon Clarke, to the central theoretical problems of his case that he declares that he intends to leave open the issue of whether this '*sui generis* form of class rule' constitutes a 'Soviet mode of production'. More bizarrely still, having defined the issue as the existence of a new form of class rule he also declares that he wishes to leave open the issue of whether there has ever been a ruling class in the Soviet Union despite the fact that 'so many heads have been broken in debate around this question' . Instead what we are offered is a description of the old USSR and the transition in which the terminology is one of class but the analysis stresses the ambiguity of the distribution of power and control. The workers are pictured as being powerless as a class but having considerable workplace power to subvert the orders of those above them.

It does not seem to occur to either Clarke or Fairbrother that these theoretical issues are not abstract ones but crucial to any explanation of the rise and fall of the USSR, and crucial to any consistent explanation of the contradictions of the workplace. This cannot be because of ignorance of the debates, though the book makes no reference to them. In earlier issues of this journal this type of argument was subject to critiques that this author still thinks remain unanswered. But if Clarke and Fairbrother were unaware of these they surely cannot plead ignorance of a devastating critique by John Molyneux of the exceptionalist argument published in the lion's den itself—the journal *Critique*—the home in the United Kingdom of such theorising.[4]

Lest they have missed these debates and have not seen the problems as they have worked through their own arguments let us briefly summarise them.

i) The theory fails to define the subject of investigation. Burowoy in his contribution to this book clearly has in mind a general analysis since he uses the term 'state socialism' but Clarke and Fairbrother implicitly echo Hillel Ticktin's focus on the former USSR without ever confronting the wider issue of whether this analysis is intended to apply beyond the bounds of a single country.

ii) The theory assumes that the analysis of the USSR can be abstracted from the location of that economy in the wider world economy. Clarke and Fairbrother bring the world economy in as an ad hoc factor when it suits them and ignore it when it does not. Indeed at one point Clarke boldly declares that the Soviet 'disaster was not the result of unfortunate and unforseeable blows from the outside, but of the crisis of the world capitalist system of which the Soviet Union had long been an integral part'.[5] But there is no analysis of what this might mean either theoretically or historically.

iii) Exceptionalism theorists confuse the issue of whether the USSR was a class society. If they take their theory seriously they must recognise that their analysis denies the existence of a ruling class and—since class is a two sided relationship—they must also deny the existence of a working class. Some do this, explicitly talking of workers rather than a working class. But Clarke et al wish to maintain an air of radicalism and constantly evade the issue of the class nature of Soviet society while using the term working class as a rhetorical category rather than a real one.

iv) The theory offers no explanation of how the degeneration of the revolution led to this new exceptionalist form. Neither does it explain how such a bastardised structure could come into existence within the overall trajectory of historical development.

v) The theory offers no explanation of the dynamic of development of this exceptionalist structure. The USSR appears as a society lacking a dynamic. This results in a lack of any real historical sense of development and any explanation of that development. Things change but they do not move unless they are pushed by an external force—something which only makes the lack of a theorised link to the world economy even more painful.

vi) In trying to argue that the production process in the old USSR was non-capitalist, the theory tries to identify problems peculiar to the USSR but effectively exaggerates the scale of these problems compared to other difficulties. It fails to see the extent to which problems of internal control of the labour process are common to all forms of capitalism and therefore distinguished in the old USSR more by degree than kind.

It would be possible to go on but enough points have been made to suggest that any serious development of the exceptionalist argument has a formidable agenda to answer. In so far as an account of the working class is concerned the most central issue is that raised by John Molyneux about the nature of class relationships. It is simply not possible to argue that a working class exists if a two sided class relationship does not also exist. You cannot have a working class in a non-class society and an attempt to maintain the contrary can only lead to a discussion that is both theoretically and empirically impoverished. We can see this if we turn to the crucial question of class consciousness and examine the way in which these authors treat the problem.

What about the workers?

The fundamental issue in Russia today is why the working class is not fighting. In the last few years living standards have been slashed on a scale almost unique in peacetime world economic history. At the same time the rulers of Russia are flaunting their wealth in a way that now allows Third World style contrasts to be the day to day experience of large cities in Russia. This would seem to provide at least part of the basis for the biggest mass revolt in history but there is no sign yet of this happening. The *Financial Times* correspondent in Russia, John Lloyd, suggested in January 1992 that the reformers were 'creating and/or have been bequeathed the classic Marxian pre-conditions for a proletarian revolution. There is a huge working class steadily becoming impoverished in order to increase the rate of profit'. He went on to suggest that it would be an incompetent and irresponsible left wing opposition which could not mobilise some support. A year later he could write that 'the striking thing is how normal everything that is happening in Russia now seems to be. The punishing drop in living standards, the drastic shrinkages in Russian power, the sudden excision from the motherland of Russians living in the former Soviet states—all this has been absorbed and contained'. And now, bereft of an explanation, he returned to the Russian soul and slave mentality: 'the famed and self-advertised virtue of the Russians—their doleful capacity to take punishment and carry on—would appear to be borne out'.[6] But this does not mean that the working class can be completely written off. Russian politicians, including Boris Yeltsin, often quote Pushkin's line: 'I fear a Russian revolt without pity or limit' and the government, in the words of Viktor Gerashchenko, the head of the Central Bank, feels itself caught between 'the Scilla of fighting inflation and the Charybdis of social conflict'.[7]

How can we explain all of this? If we leave aside speculation on the Russian soul and character, it is not difficult to list a number of factors that go some way to explaining why the working class has not resisted more. There is obviously the debilitating effect of the catastrophic fall in living standards which has to some extent sapped the confidence to fight; there is the enormous ideological confusion which has arisen from the way that the old regime captured the language of the left and totally discredited it; there is the weakness of any independent tradition of organisation; there is the way in which the government has deliberately encouraged collusion through policies of the selected appeasement of key groups of workers, a policy that has been reflected in workplaces in the way that managers have tried to incorporate dissent; there are the enormous opportunities for corruption both of mind and pocket in the existing situation and the size of the temptation to allow oneself to be sucked in—especially given the scale of the crisis. Any adequate account will share an emphasis on these and similar factors.

But to construct an analysis it is not sufficient to make a list. The relationship between the different parts and the system must be teased out. To do this we have essentially two choices. The first is to argue that Russian society is built on a fundamental class antagonism but that factors like this are preventing the development of a class conscious movement for political change from below. To this extent, although these factors arise from within the system, and powerful though they are, they are secondary to the main contradiction and in constant tension with it. Moreover because they are secondary the possibility exists that they might be overcome and ways might be found to enable workers to organise in a way which more clearly reflects their class interests.

The second choice is to argue that Russian society is not built on a fundamental class antagonism and the quiescence and confusion of the workers therefore arises directly from the specific nature of the 'mode of production/social formation' (whatever it is) which denies workers the ability to articulate a clear class interest against those above them. This must be the position of those who see the USSR as neither capitalist nor socialist and it is the implicit position of Clarke and Fairbrother although they continually fight shy of openly drawing out this logic. Typical is their argument that in the past 'there was...a high degree of collusion by the workers in their own exploitation; and class conflict was displaced and diffused into individual, and sectional conflicts within the hierarchical structure'.[8]

But this will not do. If the USSR was a class society then it is possible, as state capitalist theory would argue, to say that 'class conflict was displaced'. If it was not a class society then conflict was not displaced—its diffusion 'into individual and sectional conflicts within the hierarchical structure' is an entirely natural consequence of the fact that class conflict is not the central divide of that society. This then affects the analysis of the transition. If class relationships are unclear it is no surprise that workers have found it hard to articulate a clear class antagonism and to organise on that basis. To the extent that workers come 'to feel an identity of interests as between themselves, and as against their rulers and employers' this lacks the central material basis Marx analysed and can therefore only be a transient phenomena. Class formation—as bourgeois sociologists argue of the west—is but a fleeting moment before it is overwhelmed by other antagonisms and fractures that are at least as important and probably more so. To analyse such a situation in the language of class is therefore to profoundly misunderstand it and it is irresponsible to offer an unrealistic political agenda based on the idea of class. The result, in other words, is complete paralysis if the argument is taken seriously. The old order cannot be defended because it is correctly seen that it was not socialist. Yet the old order cannot be practically attacked—except at the level of rhetoric because there is no central antagonism around which to hang the critique and against which to direct the fire. There is no route that can link the actual struggles of workers and the objective of a genuine socialist alternative.

Yet the new order of 'capitalism' cannot also be supported either, because as socialists we are opposed to that as well. Or can it? Well in a perverse way it can be supported, for with real capitalism will come the emergence of real class antagonism and thus a clear class alternative. This is in effect the conclusion that Clarke and Fairbrother are driven to: 'Privatisation...is only the beginning of a struggle which for the first time since the 1920's can be fought out in the workers own ground, within the enterprise, the "state within the state" which is not just the place of work, but a way of life.'[9] In other words we are effectively back to an argument popular in Russia in the late 19th and early 20th centuries —socialism is all very well but first we need capitalism to build the central antagonism which will allow the workers to fight on their own ground as a class polarised against a ruling class.

This is nonsense. Russian workers in both the state and private sectors face common problems of intensified exploitation. It does not help to try to argue that somehow or other struggles in the 'private sector' are more authentic class struggles because commodity relations are clearer.

To resolve these difficulties the Russian ruling class has at some point to assert its authority in *both* the state and private sectors. But it remains unsure of what to do. Fearing revolt it makes concessions—promises such as those made to the miners, which when faced with growing chaos, it is incapable of meeting. This contradiction cannot last forever. One symptom of this is Zhirinovsky's attempt to fill the vacuum. But it remains possible that if the state pushes harder then it will provoke a resurgence of mass conflict. This can happen without organisation, but without organisation any gains for workers would only be short term and possibly short lived. Sadly, *What about the workers?* offers no way forward and if its arguments are taken seriously they can only damage the pitifully inadequate small beginnings that already exist. All this at a time when every step forward, no matter how small, is a precious one.

Notes

1 See V Haynes, *Workers Against the Gulag* (London, 1979).
2 We should also note that the bibliography not only excludes references to works the authors are criticising but also appears to have missed a number of valuable western European discussions of the recent workers' movement.
3 S Clarke et al, *What About the Workers? Workers and the Transition to Capitalism in Russia* (London, 1993), p7.
4 J Molyneux, 'The Ambiguities of Hillel Ticktin', *Critique*, no20-21, 1987.
5 S Clarke et al, op cit, p42.
6 J Lloyd, 'Year One', *London Review of Books*, 30 January 1992, p11; 'Moscow Diary', ibid, 7 January 1993.
7 Quoted in the *Guardian*, 28 February 1994.
8 S Clarke et al, op cit, p19.
9 Ibid, p241.

Marxism and the new imperialism

Alex Callinicos, John Rees, Mike Haynes, Chris Harman

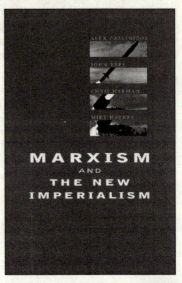

Marxism and the new imperialism provides key analysis of the shape of the modern world—in the wake of the Cold War and at the beginning of a new phase.

Marxism and the new imperialism combines the Marxist view of capitalism with masses of new and up to date detail.

The book features: **Alex Callinicos** on Marxism and imperialism today; **John Rees** on Arms and the new imperialism; **Mike Haynes** on Class and crisis—the transition in Eastern Europe; and **Chris Harman** on The return of the national question.

£6.50 / $10.00

BOOKMARKS

Available from all good bookshops and Bookmarks, 265 Seven Sisters Road, London N4 2DE
081-802 6145
Add 15% for postage

Hero and villain?

A review of D Gluckstein, **The Tragedy of Bukharin** *(Pluto, 1994) £12.95*

ROB FERGUSON

The October revolution of 1917 and Stalin's seizure of power in the late 1920s face each other across a momentous decade. Both, in different ways, were points of cleavage in the socialist movement that challenged socialists to either defend or disown the principles of working class self emancipation and internationalism. Any consideration of the historical and political importance of the October revolution and the rise of Stalinism are dominated by two closely related questions. First, what was the relationship between these two events, and second, could an alternative to Stalinism have emerged from the revolution?

For those who were dismayed by the first victorious workers' revolution, Stalinism provided 'proof' of the evils of revolution in general and Lenin and the Bolsheviks in particular. For those who wished to defend the Stalinist system the October revolution became a weapon used to legitimise every monstrous crime and betrayal perpetrated in the name of 'the workers' state'. The scale of the dilemma led many socialists to lose their grip on the principles that had once inspired them. Many slipped into a chasm believing their only choice was either to defend Stalinist Russia or to ditch socialist revolution.

In order to avoid being trapped in the jaws of this dilemma it is essential to understand how and why the revolution decayed from within. The degeneration of the Russian Revolution has been one of the most misunderstood and misrepresented periods of the 20th century. Thus *The Tragedy of Bukharin* is a refreshing breath of air. Donny Gluckstein traces in depth the political and economic questions that confronted the Bolsheviks in the decade or so following the October revolution through a study of the political thought of Nikolai Bukharin. Bukharin was a leading Bolshevik—described by Lenin as the 'favourite' of the whole party—who came to embody the degeneration of the Russian Revolution during the 1920s. Donny examines Bukharin's development as a revolutionary theorist, how he faced the enormous contradictions and pressures of his time and how, tragically, he succumbed to them. Donny seeks to demolish the claims of two groups of historians that Bukharin provided the basis for a 'humanistic', democratic and *pro-market* alternative to Stalin.[1] In doing so he also rescues Bukharin from the grasp of his latter day disciples, demonstrating that, in spite of his great faults, he remained inspired by the hope of an end to capitalism and the victory of socialism until his death.

In the interpretation and counter-interpretation of Russian history the waters have often become tremendously muddied. The Cold War warriors were happy to disregard the evidence and draw a direct line from Lenin to Stalin. Historians like E H Carr and Isaac Deutscher made important contributions to the study of the period but they saw no alternative to the rise of Stalin which they regarded as an inevitable consequence of the economic crisis at the end of the 1920s.[2] Many in the 'revisionist' school of Sovietology who focus on social history and 'history from below' have produced valuable insights but shun any examination of class relations and reach varied, contradictory and often confused conclusions.[3]

To the question, 'Was there a socialist alternative to Stalinism?' the foes of socialist revolution and the supporters of Stalin both responded with a resounding 'No!' For decades there was one discordant voice—from the Trotskyist tradition. Despite the fragmentation and tiny size of the movement which Trotsky left behind him there was no disguising the fact that the most tenacious, vehement and determined opposition to the rise of Stalin in the 1920s had come from Trotsky and the Left Opposition. For this they paid with their lives.

In the 1970s however some Western historians claimed Bukharin, rather than Trotsky, as the real alternative to Stalin. They were joined in the 1980s by a group of Soviet academics.[4] On the face of it the notion of Bukharin as an alternative to Stalin is a strange one. It is true that after 1928 he was increasingly hounded by Stalin and became a victim of the monstrous show trials, but in the crucial period of the mid to late 1920s Bukharin was Stalin's foremost ally in the politburo. He formulated the defence for the doctrine of 'socialism in one country' and presided over the Comintern (the Communist International) during a period when it imposed the most disastrous policies on the international working class movement. These policies led to working class defeat in China and Britain, reinforcing Russia's isolation and creating the conditions for the defeat of the revolution at Stalin's hands. He fought the Left Opposition who were demanding democracy within the party and the strengthening of the political weight of workers against the increasing power and influence of the bureaucracy. He provided the theoretical armoury against Stalin's opponents and was a vital component of what became known as the Stalin-Bukharin 'duumvirate' (rule by two leaders).

But Bukharin has two great attractions for his latter day adherents. His economic writings of the mid-1920s enable them, on a highly selective reading, to present him as the tribune of a market alternative to Stalin. It is a reading that has to ignore much of Bukharin's work and distort the remainder. His second attraction is that he left no revolutionary political tradition behind him. This makes it easier to remove Bukharin's life and work from the context of his times and present him as the forerunner of today's supporters of the market. In order to counter the distortion Donny traces Bukharin's political development, in all its contradictions, through some of the most momentous events in 20th century history.

One of Bukharin's most important contributions to Marxism was his analysis of imperialism.[5] Bukharin brilliantly exposed the belief of the reformists that modern capitalism could develop peacefully and that war and imperialism were an aberration. Bukharin analysed how capital increasingly merged with the state and how competition on a world scale meant war and imperialism, far from being an aberration were the natural conditions of modern capitalist development. However, from the outset Bukharin was to demonstrate a tendency for allowing his vast theoretical sweep to obliterate the complexities of social relations, particularly those posed by the class struggle itself. He opposed Lenin's demand for the right of nations to self determination, for example, on the grounds that in the age of imperialism national self determination was an illusion. His level of abstraction, while on the one hand his strength, prevented him from grasping the nature of combined and uneven development, and his argument, while correct in the abstract, simply played into the hands of national chauvinism when translated into a guide for action.

Bukharin's tendency towards what Lenin referred to as 'scholasticism' —the study of theory divorced from practice—was to become a feature of his development. In March 1918, even though the Bolsheviks had no army with which to fight, Bukharin opposed a separate peace with Germany on the grounds that to leave the field of battle was to desert the international revolution. During the civil war that lasted from summer 1918 until 1921 Bukharin wrote the *Economics of the Transition Period*. These were times of tremendous destruction. The revolution was blockaded and besieged by 14 invading armies. Industry all but collapsed, as did the soviets—the organs of workers' power. The working class itself disintegrated. Its most advanced sections joined the Red Army or took up posts in the military, state and party administration. Many workers were forced into the countryside in order to find food to survive. This was the period known as War Communism—characterised by the state takeover of industry, payment of wages in kind (if at all) and the requisition of grain from the peasantry. Bukharin described with great insight how the building of a socialist society necessarily involved destructive processes as capitalist relations were dismantled. But too often he made a virtue out of necessity. The disappearance of money for example was not, as Bukharin would have it, a consequence of the development of socialism but the result of economic collapse. Under the pressures of the time many Bolsheviks, including Lenin and Trotsky, made similar errors but a tendency that often stemmed from the need to galvanise the defence of the revolution was elevated by Bukharin to the level of theoretical principle.[6]

However, by the end of the civil war the population, and in particular the peasantry, would no longer tolerate the rigours of War Communism. With the defeat of the White army its rationale had disappeared. Peasant uprisings and strikes by workers culminated in the Kronstadt rebellion, a sailors' mutiny in what had once been a stronghold of Bolshevism and revolution. War Communism was abandoned and the era of the New Economic Policy (NEP) ushered in.

The NEP was a retreat. Given the failure of revolution in Germany and the destruction wreaked by war and blockade on what was already a backward economy, the Bolshevik government was forced to rely on the market to provide the basis for economic recuperation and restore trade between town and country. In this it was to a considerable degree successful but the price paid was heavy. Urban unemployment grew dramatically while hucksters and middlemen made small fortunes. Social inequality was displayed openly for all to see, class differentiation grew in both the towns and countryside. Most important of all the party and state bureaucracy developed into a distinct social layer, divorced from workers, with its own political outlook and interests. For as long as Bukharin had been part of a strong revolutionary party his strengths were able to flower and enrich the movement and his weaknesses were held in check. However, as the party itself began to decay, Bukharin's faults carried him into the arms of those who wished to turn their backs on the revolution.

Bukharin's theoretical approach would not allow room for an analysis of the tensions and contradictions that the retreat of the 1920s imposed. The market, whilst necessary in the circumstances, inevitably undermined the possibility for developing the productive forces on a socialist basis; the priorities of the peasant and the trader overrode the urgent need to invest in industry. Above all the NEP strengthened the conservatism of the party bureaucracy itself which adapted to the pressures of the wealthier peasant and the capitalist trader or 'nepman'.

All this imposed the need for a struggle to continually reinforce democracy within the party, to ensure that workers and poorer peasants, rather than nepmen, benefited from increased productivity, to shift resources from agriculture into industrial investment without destroying the delicate balance of a desperately backward economy. It was this struggle that Trotsky and the Left Opposition urgently tried to foster. Bukharin opposed them. Cold realities deal harshly with theoretical abstractions. Fault lines can rip apart, shattering both theory and conviction. Kronstadt had disabused Bukharin of his illusions in War Communism but now he performed a theoretical double flip. He argued that the NEP was not a retreat and that since the working class were in power the danger of capitalism from within was not a threat. He became, in effect, the tribune of the alliance between the bureaucracy and the rich peasant and nepman. His theoretical wizardry provided essential cover for Stalin and his supporters.

Despite Bukharin's faith in the NEP it could not provide for a smooth transition to socialism. Recovery reached its limits and economic crises of increasing severity forced the Soviet leadership to address their misplaced confidence in the NEP. It was at this point that Bukharin and Stalin began to diverge. Today Bukharin is praised for his belief that the manipulation of prices would lead to an increased circulation of goods in the market and that this would foster economic growth. This, his would-be disciples argue, was the alternative to Stalin's brutal collectivisation of the peasantry and forced industrialisation programme.

The problem went far deeper. The failure to resist the pressures of the peasant market in the early 1920s had deprived industry of capital investment, weakened the working class and strengthened the position of the bureaucracy. But agriculture and industry were not separate spheres. Without affordable agricultural tools and machinery, agriculture itself remained backward. With no alternative on offer the poorer peasantry were cemented politically to their richer neighbours. The hostility of both towards the towns and the state deepened. Beyond Russia's borders fascism was on the rise; in 1929 the Great Depression racked the Western economies; war scares disturbed the Soviet leaders.

The grain crisis of 1927 convinced Stalin and his supporters that they could no longer tolerate the obstacle to development posed by the peasant market. The bureaucracy had strengthened itself through the NEP but no longer wished to be shackled by it. It no longer required an alliance with the wealthy peasant and nepman. First tentatively, sometimes in panic, but then with increasing confidence, Stalin began to resort to the systematic use of force against peasant and worker in order to subjugate them to the requirements of capital accumulation. Bukharin never understood how he and his ideas had helped to cut the ground away from underneath the revolutionary tradition of which he was a part. He refused, however, to countenance Stalin's counter-revolution and became one of the most famous of its millions of victims.

Donny also compares Bukharin's development to that of Trotsky. Western supporters of Bukharin attempt to smother Trotsky in a false embrace arguing that he and Bukharin were in fact natural allies who allowed petty personal and theoretical differences to divide them. The Soviet supporters of Bukharin (and many Western historians) attempt to bury Trotsky in Stalin's grave, maintaining that in implementing forced industrialisation Stalin merely stole Trotsky's clothes. Donny elaborates the real alternative that Trotsky posed while at the same time providing an honest examination of his mistakes and weaknesses and his misestimation of the class character of Stalinism.

I have some reservations about the book, though none of them should detract from the important contribution that it is. My principal concern is that it will be largely inaccessible to the reader who does not have a thorough grounding in the history of the revolution and its defeat. Here the socialist defence of the October revolution—against the mass of misrepresentation that fills the shelves—is often taken as read. It would not have been possible to elaborate the argument at length in such a book. However, I feel Donny's argument would have been more persuasive to those not acquainted with the revolutionary tradition if some of the central myths had been debunked.[7]

The fashion for Bukharin has largely waned. The post-Soviet intelligentsia in particular no longer need the artificial theoretical bridge they required in the 1980s to span the abyss between the Russian Revolution and the market. However, this book helps fill what has been a major gap in historical and political writing. This study of the complex process of degeneration during the 1920s fulfils three essential purposes. It underlines the gulf that separates the October revolution from Stalinism. It demolishes the idea that the restoration of market relations could have provided a humane alternative to Stalinism and in doing so challenges today's orthodoxy that the market is the necessary condition for economic life. Finally *The Tragedy of Bukharin* restores Bukharin himself to his rightful place—as an often brilliant, if flawed, revolutionary theorist whose achievements and failures are so instructive to those who aspire to fight for the cause to which he dedicated his life.

Notes

1   The main Western texts are S Cohen, *Bukharin and the Bolshevik Revolution* (Oxford, 1971), and M Lewin, *Political Undercurrents in Soviet Economic Debates* (Princeton, NJ, 1974). D Gluckstein cites as Soviet examples discussions at the Thirteenth Round Table of historians, 1988, and journal articles including G A Bordyugov and V A Kozlov, 'Man in History; History in Man. Nikolai

Bukharin, Episodes of a Political Biography', in *Kommunist*, September 1988, p105.
2   See E H Carr, *The Russian Revolution from Lenin to Stalin 1917-1929* (London, 1979), and I Deutscher, *Stalin: a Political Biography* (Harmondsworth, 1974).
3   Two examples are S Fitzpatrick, *The Russian Revolution* (Oxford 1982), and J Arch Getty, *Origins of the Great Purges: The Soviet Communist Party Reconsidered 1933-38* (Cambridge, 1985).
4   See note 1.
5   N Bukharin, *Imperialism and World Economy* [1915] (London 1987).
6   N Bukharin, *The Politics and Economics of the Transition Period* [1920] (London 1979).
7   For a recent defence of the revolution see J Rees, 'In Defence of October', *International Socialism* 52, and the subsequent debate by R Service, S Farber, R Blackburn and J Rees in *International Socialism* 54. Also see D Howell, 'Bookwatch: The Russian Revolution', *International Socialism* 62.

A Nation of Change and Novelty
Christopher Hill

'Hill on top form, lambasting the "simple-minded" who want to edit out all that's radically strange.'
—*Independent on Sunday*

Christopher Hill has long been at the centre of debate about the English Revolution. This collection is grand testimony to his tradition of combining historical rigour with polemical style.
Includes chapters on literature and revolution, Gerrard Winstanley and freedom, English radicals and Ireland, plus much more.
£10.95 / $16.50

Available from all good bookshops and Bookmarks, 265 Seven Sisters Road, London N4 2DE
081-802 6145
Add 15% for postage

Suffragette style

A review of K Dodd (ed), **A Sylvia Pankhurst Reader** *(Manchester University Press, 1993) £14.95*

JANE ELDERTON

Sylvia Pankhurst is probably best known for the role she played in the fight for women's right to vote. This new collection of her writing, *A Sylvia Pankhurst Reader*, shows that in the course of her life she campaigned over many other issues. She opposed the First World War and welcomed and supported the 1917 Russian Revolution.

The articles, drawn from 1909 to 1953, reveal how her ideas developed. Unfortunately, anyone hoping the commentary provided by Kathryn Dodd, who edited and introduces this selection, will provide any guide to Sylvia Pankhurst's life will be disappointed. Dodd argues that Sylvia 'continually struggled to embrace new ideas about politics'.[1] But Dodd fails to locate Sylvia's changing ideas in the world around her. The only real explanation she offers is to look to Sylvia's style of writing.

Dodd argues that the 'available form of writing conditioned what she could express'.[2] In other words her ideas were limited by her access to different styles of writing. This is rubbish. The changes in her writing, both the content and the style, reflected Sylvia Pankhurst's changing ideas. Sylvia did not have one message which she fought to express throughout her life. Her greatest strength was the way she responded to world events, her struggle to build a mass working class base for the fight for women's right to vote and her efforts to win support in Britain for the 1917 Russian Revolution.

But she never seems to develop a theoretical understanding of either capitalism or the fight for socialism. To explain this point it is necessary to say more about Sylvia's life, and here her writings provide many useful insights.

Sylvia Pankhurst came from a comfortable, middle class, but political background. Like her mother and father she was a member of the

Independent Labour Party. She was a founder member of the Women's Social and Political Union, the organisation set up in 1903 with her mother, Emmeline, and her sister, Christabel, as a pressure group to campaign for votes for women. At that time no woman had the vote. The franchise had been further extended in 1884 but not all men had the vote.

Christabel's own description of her early efforts at militant action convey much about the nature of the suffragettes, as the press named them. She describes her efforts to get arrested to attract publicity:

> Lectures on the law flashed to my mind. I could, even with all my limbs helpless, commit a technical assault and so I found myself arrested and charged with 'spitting at a policeman'. ... It was not a real spit. But only, shall we call it, a 'pout', a perfectly dry purse of the mouth. I could not really have done it, even to get the vote, I think.[3]

Sylvia did not begin by devoting all her time to politics. She went to London as a student at the Royal College of Art. Once in London she set up a WSPU branch. By 1906 her mother and sister had both joined her, making London the centre of their organisation.

In 1907 Sylvia Pankhurst spent six months touring Northern England, painting and sketching working women. But, as Dodd points out, she gradually abandoned her art and devoted herself full time to the fight for the vote. This is the period in which she began to contribute to the WSPU journal, *Votes for Women*. She published articles on the history of women's fight for the vote and some essays on the conditions of working class women.

These descriptions of working women give you a real insight into Sylvia's background. They are written from the point of view of a middle class woman. The poverty and degradation of the working women's lives provokes pity and horror but Sylvia appeals to other middle class women to improve the workers' lot.

> Then the potato pickers rose, and straightened themselves, and came towards me where I sat watching them, and I saw them clearly for the first time. They were poor, miserable creatures, clad in vile, nameless rags, sometimes pinned, sometimes tied round them with other rags or bits of string. There were old, old women, with their skin all gnarled and wrinkled, and their purple lips all cracked. There were young women with dull white sullen faces, many with scars or black bruises round their eyes, and swollen shapeless lips. Their hair was all matted and neglected, and every woman's eyes were fiery red... I saw them standing huddled together, these poor, degraded creatures lower than the beasts of the field... Oh, can it be that we women

would have let so many things go wrong in this world, and should we have let it be so hard a place for the unfortunate, if we had had the governing power that men have had?[4]

By 1911-12 Sylvia Pankhurst was travelling all over the country speaking for the WSPU on women's fight for the vote. The WSPU had ceased to be a group exerting pressure on the ILP. In fact it had gradually moved away from connections with any political party towards militant direct action, involving increasing numbers of upper class, wealthy women. It was not just the vote that was denied women. While working class women suffered both oppression and exploitation as workers, upper class women were denied access to education and the professions simply because of their sex. Sylvia pointed out that 'opportunities for higher paid employment were severely restricted'. Christabel herself was prevented from becoming a lawyer just because she was a woman. But Sylvia Pankhurst saw the need to involve more than just these wealthy women. She wanted to build a mass movement of women. In 1913 she formed her East London Federation—creating a working class base for the WSPU in the east end of London.

The suffragettes used their militant tactics to win as much publicity as possible to pressurise government. Their campaign of direct action was often spectacular, ranging from mass window smashing to arson. But their tactics meant the women faced constant arrest and Sylvia, like many other women, was hounded by the authorities.

In 1913 the Liberal government introduced their vicious 'Cat and Mouse Act' which meant hunger striking suffragette prisoners would be let out of jail for short periods of time to allow them to recover. But they were re-arrested as soon as their strength did recover a little. As a result women's prison sentences could go on and on. Many women had their health permanently broken. These women were treated with brutality by the state despite the fact that when they were raiding parliament some of their friends and acquaintances would be sitting inside as MPs. In her book *The Suffragette Movement* Sylvia described the horrors of being force fed in prison:

Presently I heard footsteps approaching, collecting outside my cell. I was strangled with fear, cold and stunned, yet alert to every sound. The door opened—not the doctors, but a crowd of wardresses filled the doorway... I struggled, but was overcome. There were six of them, all much bigger and stronger than I. They flung me on my back on the bed, and held me down firmly by shoulders and wrists, hips, knees and ankles. Then the doctors came stealing in. Someone seized me by the head and thrust a sheet under my chin. My eyes were shut. I set my teeth and tightened my lips over them with all my strength. A man's hands were trying to force open my mouth; my breath was coming so fast that I felt as though I should suffocate. His fingers were striving to pull my lips apart—getting inside. I felt them and a steel instrument pressing round my gums, feeling for gaps in my teeth... Then something gradually forced my jaws apart as a screw was turned; the pain was like having teeth drawn. They were trying to get the tube down my throat. They got it down, I suppose, though I was unconscious of anything save a mad revolt of struggling, for they said at last: 'That's all!' and I vomited as the tube came up.[5]

In 1914 Sylvia started to publish her paper, the *Woman's Dreadnought*. She wrote in the first issue, 'The *Woman's Dreadnought* is published by the East London Federation of the Suffragettes, an organisation mainly composed of working women, and the chief duty of the *Dreadnought* will be to deal with the franchise question from the working women's point of view, and to report the activities of the votes for women movement in East London. Nevertheless, the paper will not fail to review the whole field of the women's emancipation movement.'[6]

Her paper soon addressed other issues—including support for James Connolly and the Irish struggle and the Scottish Shop Stewards Movement. But most significantly Sylvia Pankhurst used her paper to make a stand against the outbreak of the First World War.

The combination of the experience of the fight for the vote and the sharp class conflict which had engulfed Britain from 1910-14 had radicalised Sylvia's politics, in a period known as the Great Unrest. As George Dangerfield says in his account of the period, *The Strange Death of Liberal England*, parliamentary democracy was experiencing 'what looks very like nervous breakdown'.[7] A fearful Lloyd George described how 'revolt was spreading like foot and mouth disease.' However, as Sylvia's ideas developed, so Christabel Pankhurst, who was by now living in Paris, became increasingly right wing in this period. She could no longer stand Sylvia's association with left wingers and socialists. Sylvia was summoned to Paris and forced out of the WSPU.

Christabel and her mother dropped the fight for the vote to devote all their time to being avid supporters of the First World War, but Sylvia Pankhurst's paper became a major anti-war publication. In Britain such a stand took great courage. Many other socialists kept their views quiet when faced with the First World War. By 1916 Sylvia had changed the name of the East London Federation of Suffragettes to the Workers' Suffrage Federation, campaigning for 'social and economic freedom for the people'.[8] But the event which had the greatest impact on Sylvia Pankhurst's ideas was the Russian Revolution of 1917. She greeted the revolution with enthusiasm and this was reflected in her paper.

'Our eager hopes are for the speedy success of the Bolsheviks of Russia: may they open the door which leads to freedom for the people of all lands!' she wrote in 1917.[9] In 1917 she again renamed the paper. Instead of the *Woman's Dreadnought* it became the *Workers' Dreadnought*. By 1918 Sylvia was promoting the idea of workers' councils and she set up the People's Russian Information Bureau. Her efforts made available in Britain the writings of Russian revolutionaries like Lenin, Trotsky and Kollontai, as well as work by the German socialist Clara Zetkin. In 1919 Sylvia was actively working within the 'Hands Off Russia' campaign to stop the blockade of revolutionary Russia by Allied troops.

She clearly understood the impact of the revolution on politics in Britain. Here she explains how that revolutionary wave was key in women winning the vote after the First World War: 'It is interesting to observe that the legal barriers to women's participation in Parliament and its elections were not removed until the movement to abolish Parliament altogether had received the strong encouragement of witnessing the overthrow of Parliamentary Government in Russia and the setting up of Soviets.'[10] There is no doubt Sylvia was an important figure in the socialist movement in Britain. She played a part in the negotiations of 1919-20 to form a Communist Party in this country.

To explain Sylvia's ideas during this period it is necessary to say something about the nature of the left in Britain. The main socialist organisations included sections of the ILP, the British Socialist Party, the Socialist Labour Party and the Scottish Shop Stewards Movement. All the small Marxist organisations in Britain at this time, with their long history of sectarianism, spent months arguing about fusing to become a Communist Party—along the lines of the Bolshevik Party in Russia. The unity negotiations foundered. Sylvia was not alone when she refused to agree with Lenin's argument that the new Communist Party should apply for affiliation to the Labour Party. However, unlike today, the Labour Party was then made up of different affiliated groups and organisations.

Although on the surface a great gulf separated the politics and practice of the likes of Willie Gallacher of the Scottish Shop Stewards Movement and Sylvia Pankhurst, both reached the same conclusions on the question of the Labour Party.

Today her rejection of reformism can look very impressive. She argued, 'The real work for the Socialist revolution must be done outside Parliament',[11] and wrote in her paper:

> The tide of Socialism, bringing all power to the workers, is sweeping over Europe and waves of Socialist thought, of working class longing, are rising to

meet it in this country. Webb and those who are holding the reins of power in the Labour Party shrink from it, fearfully trembling. Unconscious lackeys of the capitalist system, instinctively they fear that system's fall. Is there no spirit in their souls to answer to the call of Socialist fraternity? It seems not.[12]

But her strategy risked not relating to the thousands of workers influenced by the Labour Party. Lenin wrote *Left Wing Communism—an Infantile Disorder* attacking the position of Sylvia and others in Britain. These arguments were not unique to Britain—the same debate was taking place elsewhere in Europe. In 1920 Sylvia travelled to Moscow to attend the Second Congress of the Third International and debated with Lenin.

When the Communist Party of Great Britain was formed Sylvia accepted unity but against the wishes of the leadership she insisted on keeping her own independent paper. In the early years Communist Party members faced arrest and persecution. In October 1920 Sylvia Pankhurst was arrested for publishing two articles urging the armed forces to mutiny. She was sentenced to six months imprisonment. A year later she was expelled from the Communist Party for insisting that she continue to edit her paper, the *Dreadnought*.

Kathryn Dodd's explanation for her expulsion from the Communist Party is that there was 'no place for Pankhurst's vision of an open, democratic, feminist communism in the mainstream movement'.[13] Yet the truth is Sylvia, despite her enthusiasm for the revolution, never developed any real understanding of the need to build a party of the Bolshevik type. Other than workers simply deciding to reject the bosses and their system, there is no sense in this collection of writings of how socialism could be won.

So in June 1920, a year of ruling class offensive and working class retreat in Britain, she wrote in the *Workers' Dreadnought*, 'The capitalist system must be completely overthrown and replaced by the common ownership and workers' control of the land, the industries of all kinds and all means of production and distribution.'[14] This shows how Sylvia Pankhurst understood the importance of politics but unfortunately her article does nothing to outline how this can be achieved. Instead she gives her blueprint for socialism—including soviets for households, soviets for urban areas, soviets for towns, soviets for industry, soviets for public health, soviets for education and the national council of soviets.[15] In August 1920 in her paper she even tells an imaginary tale of life under socialism.[16] Yet this was far removed from the possibilities in Britain at this time.

She also failed to understand the pressures on revolutionary Russia, which was by then under siege. The combination of attack by Allied forces and the civil war left the Russian economy in a state of collapse.

Industrial production was about a fifth of pre-war production levels. Between the end of 1918 and the end of 1920 epidemics, hunger and cold killed 9 million Russians. Sylvia Pankhurst aligned herself with Alexandra Kollontai and the Workers' Opposition in the debate on the way forward for Russia. She argued against the New Economic Policy which she saw as a 'reversion to capitalism' and questioned the democracy of revolutionary Russia.

But what Sylvia does not make clear in her writing on this period is the way the Bolsheviks encouraged debate at party meetings and in the press. In how many countries would the opposition's pamphlet outlining their point of view be circulated? This is what happened in 1921 when 250,000 copies of Kollontai's pamphlet putting the case for the Workers' Opposition were reproduced. These arguments, and ultimately the defeat of the Russian Revolution, left Sylvia Pankhurst demoralised and isolated. By 1924 she had left the east end of London and in that year the last copy of her paper was produced.

After her break with the Communist Party her political vision narrowed. She no longer writes about transforming society and this collection of her writings gives examples of Sylvia concentrating on issues that she sees as affecting women.[17]

Women over 30 years old won the vote immediately after the First World War but it was not until 1928 that both women and men won the vote from the age of 21. Sylvia Pankhurst argues that since women won the vote much has been gained. But she says, 'I for one...I want much more.'[18] However, when she writes of working class women suffering instead of working women organising themselves to fight for a better life, she returns to making pleas to the high and mighty for reform. This is clearly born of disillusionment: 'The average woman, who, by the hundred thousand, was enthused 20 years ago with the sense of a social mission, is today concerned merely with her own or her husband's financial prospects with dress and a round of visits and amusements with no great vistas.'[19]

It is in this later period that Sylvia actually wrote her own history of the suffragettes—*The Suffragette Movement*. This is a book which really inspires. It conveys the mood, the excitement and the action of the suffragettes and also shows how the movement radicalised so many women.

During the 1930s her writings are despairing as she witnesses the rise of fascism across Europe. She is sickened by the ruling class reaction to the rise of Mussolini in Italy.[20] But her writings lack any sense of what the solution could be to this horror. They convey her isolation. From the 1930s until her death in 1960 all her energy and enthusiasm went into her campaign against the Italian invasion of Ethiopia in 1935 and later the fight for Ethiopian independence. She gave her support to reactionary monarch Haile Selassie, the emperor of Ethiopia.

So how should we judge Sylvia Pankhurst? Her great strength was her ability to agitate and build roots in the working class. Her descriptions of how she built real mass support in her fight for women's right to vote, but also in other campaigns, is an inspiration. At one point it was impossible for the authorities to even arrest her because literally hundreds of workers in the east end prevented the police laying a hand on her.

There can be no doubt, Sylvia was a talented agitator. Although her actual organisation remained small, she involved many hundreds of working class women in politics. So, for example, one account of Poplarism from 1919 to 1925 makes references to working class women who worked alongside Sylvia Pankhurst in east London. Pankhurst also understood the way a socialist paper was essential to that agitation, although there is no sense of it in this collection. Writing of a meeting about striking miners in South Wales during the First World War she said:

> *The struggle of the miners was stirring the hearts of the organised workers throughout the country. The South Wales rebels were regarded as the flower of the working class, the standard bearers of the workers against compulsion and profiteering. Wherever I went to speak on these things, I found great audiences thronging the largest halls and gathering in the open air in numbers beyond the reach of a single speaker. When I had spoken, I would jump down from the platform, and thread my way amongst the audience selling our literature. Pennies were eagerly reached out to me; great piles of* **Dreadnoughts** *and pamphlets disappeared. I returned to Bow laden with heavy bags of copper.*[21]

Sylvia Pankhurst was prepared to be unpopular if that was the cost of sticking to her principles. This was evident in her opposition to the war and her support for the Russian Revolution.

Lenin recognised her importance, as can be seen in the effort he put into winning her to the revolutionary socialist movement. The tragedy is that Sylvia Pankhurst was not won to building a mass revolutionary party in Britain when that opportunity existed. But that is far more than just a personal tragedy. Had the Communist Party of Great Britain been formed in 1918 or 1919, it could have taken advantage of the rising industrial and political struggle. But in 1920-1 the working class were in retreat in the face of a ruling class offensive. The bosses won a series of victories against the engineers, the miners and the rail workers. The combination of the political situation and, importantly, the historical weakness of the left in Britain meant that opportunity was missed.

Her politics can only be understood by looking at the political tradition that existed in Britain at that time. Kathryn Dodd, the collection's editor, argues that there are parallels between the utopian socialist William Morris and Sylvia Pankhurst which Dodd says explains why Sylvia has been 'marginalised'.[22]

There is no doubt this political tradition is apparent in Pankhurst's ideas. She could not ignore the suffering and exploitation of the working class and she saw the desperate need for a very different sort of society. This led her to try and improve workers' lives both through her welfare work—her nurseries, community restaurants and factories spring to mind. But it also made her fight for a better society.

There is no doubt that after Sylvia Pankhurst's break with the Communist Party her writing and her political activity reflect the retreat in her politics. But Sylvia Pankhurst's contribution should not be underestimated. Anyone wanting to know how her ideas changed should take a look at this collection of her work. But you should do more. Her book *The Suffragette Movement* remains one of the best, if sometimes inaccurate, accounts of the suffragettes you can read.

Notes

1 K Dodd (ed), *A Sylvia Pankhurst Reader* (Manchester University Press, 1993), p8
2 Ibid, p11
3 B Castle, *Sylvia and Christabel Pankhurst* (Penguin Books, 1987), p49
4 K Dodd, op cit, p34, 35, 36
5 S Pankhurst, *The Suffragette Movement* (Virago, 1977), p443
6 K Dodd, op cit, p48
7 G Dangerfield, *The Strange Death of Liberal England* (Paladin, 1983), p75
8 K Dodd, op cit, p77
9 Ibid, p83
10 Ibid, p134
11 Ibid, p88
12 Ibid, p87
13 Ibid, p79
14 Ibid, p100
15 Ibid, p100-104
16 Ibid, p104-108
17 Ibid, p141
18 Ibid, p150
19 Ibid.
20 Ibid, p126
21 S Pankhurst, *The Home Front* (Hutchinson, 1987), p224
22 K Dodd, op cit, p4

New from Bookmarks

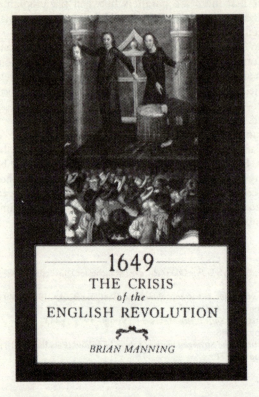

The long awaited follow up to the hugely respected *English People and the English Revolution*. This book continues Manning's unique and pathbreaking account of class struggle and the Revolution through to the execution of Charles I and beyond. With special sections on the army, youth and women.

£9.95 paperback, £19.95 hardback
Available from booksellers and Bookmarks, 265 Seven Sisters Road, London N4 2DE or PO Box 16085, Chicago, Il 60616, add 10% postage.

The two faces of modernism

CHRIS NINEHAM

Gareth Jenkins's 'Novel Questions' in *International Socialism* 62 is more than an interesting discussion of the English novel. The general points Gareth makes suggest a particular framework for a Marxist understanding of much of the culture of the last two centuries. His defence of 'strong realism' is essential reading, and his theoretical approach is crucial; we have to judge whether works of art, he says 'get to grips with the complex dynamics of social development...and not simply whether they satisfy certain formal aesthetic criteria'.[1] But Gareth applies his own criteria unevenly, and his overall account is weakened by his dismissive attitude to modernism.

Gareth is absolutely right to underline the unique qualities of the classical realist novels of the early 19th century. As the Hungarian Marxist George Lukacs first pointed out, the novels of Scott, Balzac and later Tolstoy, were written as the rising capitalist class created the conditions and the need for a fearless examination of society. The revolutionary slogan, 'Liberty, Fraternity and Equality', offered the hope of the full and free development of the individual through class struggle. In Lukacs's words capitalism had 'for the first time made history a mass experience'.[2]

The finest novels of the period captured the complex dialectic between society and the individual with a clarity unmatched before or since. Their heroes are products of social change, but they also express the need for it. 'Scott's novels marched towards the great heroes in the same way as history itself had done when it required their appearance'.[3] Some later English 19th century novels like *Middlemarch* retain an ambition to grasp society in its totality through representative characters. But Gareth Jenkins's—and Lukacs's—crucial point is that once the bourgeoisie had secured power, it rushed to bury its revolutionary origins.

By the second half of the 19th century the writer could no longer occupy an artistically privileged position at the eye of the storm. Relative social stability could sustain art that was descriptive and sometimes compassionate, but the real relations of society remain hidden beneath the calm.

The high points of 19th century culture need defending. The establishment wants to empty them of all social content and turn them into harmless heritage while sections of the left would like to junk them as 'bourgeois ideology'. Marxists understand that because capitalism excludes workers from access to so much culture we still have a great deal to learn from the culture of the past, particularly from the culture of revolutionary periods.

However, in his enthusiasm to defend 19th century realism, Gareth is too quick to write off all that has happened since. Although he accepts Brecht's point that you can't simply tell contemporary writers to 'write like Balzac', he seems basically hostile to modernism:

> *It* [modernism] *denies the potential of the human subject either by withdrawing into a private 'space' of subjectivity or by making the subject as inhuman as the forces which confront it in the public world. Either way, the condition of alienation is accepted as given, whether despaired of or rejoiced in...*
>
> *Fragmentation, plurality, the dehumanisation of the subject, the aestheticisation of experience—all of which remain key elements within the modernist movement, even at its most radical and challenging—emphasise the sphere of individual refusal as the only meaningful sphere.*[4]

The simple fact that so many modernist artists, from Picasso to Grosz and from Heartfield to Bertold Brecht were passionately interested in overcoming alienation and releasing the 'potential of the human subject', doesn't in itself prove Gareth wrong. It does suggest however that Gareth is telling only half the story of modernism. I want to take issue with three main points; that modernist art was always and only a reflection of fragmentation, that it could only be an individualistic response and therefore ignored society, and that it accepted alienation as a given.

Modernism is a term used to lump together an enormous body of artistic work in all forms—poetry, cinema, painting, architecture—that was produced roughly between the 1890s and the mid 20th century. General definitions are difficult, but modernist work tends to be formally experimental and highly self conscious—think of the Cubist paintings of Picasso or the 'flow of consciousness' of James Joyce's novels. Gareth Jenkins is right to emphasise dislocation and fragmentation as characteristics of modernism. The 'high period' of modernism from 1900-1930 was of course a time of unmatched upheaval, in which the promises of the bourgeois revolution were finally shattered by war, slump and workers' revolt. The accelerating development of technology and the penetration of mass production techniques into every sphere of life added to a deep sense of uncertainty. In Perry Anderson's words, 'European modernism in the first years of this century thus flowered in the space between a still usable classical past, a still indeterminate technical present and a still unpredictable political future'.[5]

It has been very tempting for Marxist criticism to glorify modernism given its origin in such a period of upheaval, and its—at least formal— rejection of the past. After the Russian Revolution the intellectuals of Proletkult argued for a rejection of all previous culture, claiming that modernist techniques were the basis for a brave new working class art.

Such a simple minded response misses the contradictory nature of all modernism. Gareth is right to point out that modernist work often appears as a retreat from society. Its emphasis on dislocation and alienation could open the way to a kind of rampant subjectivity. His criticism of Virginia Woolf, for example, is telling: 'one cannot escape the feeling, beneath the richness of language, of artistic impoverishment which follows from impoverished grasp of social reality'.[6] However, if the modernists often found a retreat or refuge in their art, many of them also found a form of rebellion against a society that had gone crazy, and a conventional art that was no longer adequate or honest. The Dada artist Hans Arp suggests this dual role for his art. When hiding in Switzerland from 'the slaughterhouses of war' he wrote:

We searched for an elementary that would, we thought, save mankind from the furious folly of these times. We aspired to a new order that might restore the balance between heaven and hell. This art gradually became the object of general reprobation. Is it surprising that the 'bandits' could not understand us? Their puerile mania for authoritarianism expects art itself to serve the stultification of mankind.[7]

When Marcel Duchamp chose to put a urinal on display in a gallery he may not have been exposing the dynamics of capitalism but he was rejecting complacent and cosy art that simply justified the status quo— precisely the slavish and superficial art of the 'Naturalists' that Lukacs so despised. When the Dadaists covered gallery walls with cut out images of violence and greed from magazines they may have despaired of any decent future for mankind, but this simple rebellion had its value. As Trotsky said of the modernist writer Celine, 'exposing the lie he instils the want for a more harmonious future...the very intensity of his pessimism bears with it a dose of its antidote.'[8]

Modernism, however, was more than a rebellion. While it expressed dislocation, it had to find ways to overcome it in order to survive. A famous quote from the reactionary modernist poet T S Eliot describes this process. The poet's mind, he says, is 'constantly amalgamating disparate experience; the ordinary man's experience is chaotic, irregular, fragmentary. The latter falls in love, or reads Spinoza, and these two experiences have nothing to do with each other, or with the noise of the typewriter or the smell of cooking; in the mind of the poet these experiences are always forming new wholes'.[9] Poetically, artistically, the modernists were trying to find 'new wholes' in an alarming world. This could and did lead artists in all sorts of directions. Eliot's elitism is clear from his contempt for 'the ordinary man' in the quote. The Italian Futurists found meaning in a celebration of the inhuman power of technology and the destructiveness of war.

But the search for new artistic method, and the corresponding self consciousness about the role of the artist in society, could lead to a critique of society itself. If the artist was alienated then perhaps a new art should find a new place in society. Camilla Gray describes why the prerevolutionary Russian Futurists developed a rudimentary street theatre; their 'antics and public clowning [were a] naive attempt to restore the artist's place in ordinary life, to allow him to become, as they themselves profoundly felt the need to be, an active citizen'.[10] At a time when technology was promising undreamed of transformations, when capitalism was being shaken by war and revolution, the frustrated artist could go further—perhaps a new art requires a new society. In Trotsky's words it depended 'on what angle the artist was struck by the revolution'. In Russia the Futurists went over to the side of the workers:

The workers' revolution in Russia broke loose before Futurism had time to free itself from its childish habits...before it could be officially recognised, that is, made into a politically harmless school whose style is acceptable. The seizure of power by the proletariat caught Futurism still in the stage of being a persecuted group. And this fact alone pushed Futurism towards the new masters of life, especially since the contact and rapprochement with the revolution was made easier for Futurism by its philosophy, that is by its lack of respect for old values and dynamics.[11]

For a few years before the Stalinist clampdown the Russian modernists were able to try and unite political and aesthetic revolutions. The poet Mayakovsky described the project: 'We do not need a dead mausoleum of art where dead works are worshipped, but a living factory of the human spirit—in the streets, in the tramways, in the factories, workshops and workers' homes.'[12]

The Futurists' rhetoric is sometimes childishly impatient as well as passionate. Workers cannot skip over the past and create a fully formed 'socialist' culture in a day. Time will be needed to grapple with and assimilate the achievements of past cultures. But there is no mistaking the excitement of the Russian Futurist experiment. Far from 'accepting alienation' these artists were raging against it, and searching to overcome it in practice.

Precisely because they are self conscious and self referential, the best modernist works convey the ambiguities of the artists' predicament. The Cubist paintings of Picasso or Braque are fragmented but playful at the same time. They celebrate the artists' new found freedom from perspective and an new mastery over form at the same time as threatening to dissolve into chaos. There cannot be a better insight into the age.

Moholy-Nagy, a consciously political theorist of modernism, made the link between social change and visual form explicit in his discussion of abstract art that 'projects a desirable future order'...'creates new types of spatial relationships, new inventions of forms, new visual laws—basic and simple—as the visual counterpart to a more purposeful, co-operative human society'.[13]

At its most politically conscious and sophisticated, in the work of Brecht, Eisenstein or Dos Passos amongst others, modernism could express the fragmentation of experience under capitalism *and* the potential that capitalism creates for new unity. All three of these artists consciously used montage to point out the monstrous contradictions of the system and to encourage the public to see themselves as activists who have the potential to end these contradictions.

Why does any of this matter? Modernism too is constantly attacked and trivialised. The conventional wisdom is that art and politics do not mix. To the faddish presenters of the *Late Show* the idea of a conscious social role for the artist is crude and old fashioned. That suits the establishment. We need to fight for recognition and understanding of artists who were at once angry and technically brilliant, expressive and politically committed.

The establishment itself tends to attack modernism in its most social incarnations. It condemns modernist architecture particularly. Tower blocks offend it, not because the materials used were shoddy or the lifts are not properly maintained—although these facts give its attacks a real resonance—but because they are public housing. Around them lingers the memory of an idea that cities could be planned for people, and even by people, that the architect could serve society, not just Lloyds or Natwest.

The idea of art and society coming together was most fully developed by those of the modernists who found inspiration in the revolutionary upheavals that followed 1917. In France, Le Corbusier planned utopian housing schemes for a harmonious new society. In Berlin the artists of the Bauhaus tried to develop a whole philosophy of design for a socialist order. Much of the rhetoric and some of the practice of these artistic revolutionaries seem naive and utopian to us today. There is no doubt they needed interaction with a mass movement to continue developing. But the best of them found new ways of exploring the reality of their time which could point towards ending the alienation and fragmentation of capitalism.

In his article Gareth rightly warns us against the tendency to see modernism or realism 'as a set of techniques, rather than the ability of a culture to grasp the underlying dynamics of an epoch'.[14] The techniques of modernism have indeed survived it, but they have been used in ways which can confuse the debate.

Once the revolutionary groundswell of the inter-war years had subsided, the notion of expert social planning was easily taken over by the reformists who had need of schemes to cheaply rebuild bombed out cities. The idea of an artistic 'avant garde' could also be taken up by artists who had turned their back on any social role. The revolution had been defeated, technology had been used by big business to enslave, not by workers to liberate. The post-war abstract artists may have begun in the belief that their art could be a haven from a hostile world, but some of them quickly discovered it could provide them with a passport to privilege in the post-war boom.

Earlier, modernist art had mainly outraged and offended the establishment. After the war 'avant garde' abstract painting became the officially sanctioned culture of corporate America. The paintings of Jackson Pollock and Theodore Roethke looked impressive, seemed meaningful and had absolutely no connection with any aspiration to change the world. By the 1980s no self respecting capitalist could be without a smattering of 'new art' in the office. The likes of Jeff Koons or Damien Hirst are not interested in questioning their roles as artists—they are quite happy as international celebrities, dreaming up mildly eccentric status symbols for the rich.

In the last 20 years certain 'radical' artists and critics have actually celebrated and encouraged fine art's drift into harmless obscurity. Following Althusser's disastrous claims that the realm of ideology is effectively separate from the economic base, it became fashionable to talk of a separate 'ideological struggle'. A whole generation of supposedly subversive artists became obsessed with challenging conventional 'modes of representation' and 'discourses'. The result—art that was completely self-referential and irrelevant to anyone who had not been to art school.

Just as we need to defend the great realists from their superficial imitators, so we need to disentangle the most penetrating and challenging work of the modernists from those who want to turn art into a commodity. In the next great upheavals, new artists will want to learn from their pioneering efforts to break down the barriers between art and life.

Notes

1. G Jenkins, 'Novel Questions', *International Socialism* 62, p116.
2. G Lukacs, *The Historical Novel* (Penguin, 1981), p20.
3. Balzac paraphrased by G Lukacs, ibid.
4. G Jenkins, op cit, pp114-115.
5. P Anderson, *Modernity and Revolution*, quoted in A Callinicos, *Against Postmodernism* (Polity, 1989), p40.
6. G Jenkins, op cit, p115.
7. Quoted in D Britt (ed) *Modern Art—Impressionism to Postmodernism* (London, 1989), pp210-211.
8. L Trotsky, *On Literature and Art* (Pathfinder, 1981), p202.
9. Quoted in M Bradbury and J McFarlane (eds), *Modernism* (Penguin, 1976), p83.
10. C Gray, *The Russian Experiment in Art 1863-1922*, (Revised edn London, 1986) p116.
11. L Trotsky, *Literature and Revolution* (Redwords, 1991), p160.
12. V Mayakovsky, quoted in A Callinicos, op cit, p57.
13. Quoted in D Britt (ed), op cit, p201
14. G Jenkins, op cit, p113.

New from Bookmarks

The case of Comrade Tulayev

By Victor Serge

Serge's classic novel, in print for the first time in 20 years, is set against the backdrop of Stalin's purges and the Spanish civil war. An invaluable insight into a world now collapsed, but whose legacy lives on.

£8.95

Available from Bookmarks, 265 Seven Sisters Road, London N4 2DE, or PO Box 16085, Chicago, Il 60616, US, add 10 % postage.

Three replies to 'Jazz: a people's music?'

1. MIKE HOBART

Charlie Hore writes in his article 'Jazz: a People's Music?' that jazz has been in a steady decline since the 1970s, and as a result is no longer at the cutting edge of innovation. Neither does it have a resonance with the struggle for black emancipation that it once had. He concludes that its position has been taken by other forms of black American music, or by the development of 'world music'. Charlie claims that since the 1960s there have been neither innovations of substance, nor the emergence of a figure of the stature of John Coltrane or Charlie Parker. This development, he thinks, should not be mourned, for it shows that the world proletariat has now entered the cultural stage.

The Marxist tradition has always argued that the aesthetic evaluation of art is based on objective criteria, on the grounds that it is necessary to understand the science of an art—its internal structures and forms—as well as the particular historical and political context of its creation and consumption. Charlie's assertion that there have been no fundamental innovations in jazz music since the early 1970s is simply wrong.

At every level of the music, innovation has been such that a musician armed only with the theories and techniques of the 1960s would find it nearly impossible to cope with the demands of contemporary jazz. The great diversity of approaches in contemporary jazz music has been brought about by integrating two seemingly incompatible elements, the 'commercialism' of funk/fusion and the 'academicism' which increasingly characterised free jazz. Thus musicians with such diverse backgrounds as Mike Brecker, David Murray, Wynton Marsalis, Kenny Garrett and the M Base Collective have all developed and theorised what in the 1960s was only just being discovered.[1]

Jazz music in the 1970s and 1980s combined the existing elements of jazz to create new musical relationships. These developments in jazz were in line with the overall patterns of evolution in jazz up till then. More complex musical theories allowed improvising musicians more choices of sound combinations. This has taken place across the board in rhythm, harmony, acceptable melody and in the very structures of improvising itself. It is difficult to argue that these innovations have not been fundamental, although almost certainly they have not been so rapid or intense as in other periods. It is also probably true to say that a musician of the stature of say, John Coltrane, has yet to emerge. This is certainly the opinion of Wynton Marsalis. However, to use the early 1960s as a benchmark is essentially misleading. The coincidence of a healthy jazz economy with a very high level of struggle was itself the main factor in allowing John Coltrane to fully realise his artistic potential, and for the incredibly rapid advances in jazz music. However, when the tide ebbs, it does not mean that innovation ceases. Indeed the last 20 years of jazz have not been anything like as catastrophic as the period between 1929 and 1935, which virtually eliminated existing jazz forms, or the period of 1947 to 1953, during which the jazz economy could not support a single black touring modern jazz band of stature.

Charlie goes on to argue that jazz has lost an influence which it once had. Again I find this surprising given the use of jazz on samples, the presence of jazz musicians of stature on non-jazz releases and the omnipresent figure of Quincy Jones, producer of Michael Jackson's album *Thriller*. Already the harmonic ambiguity of M Base is feeding its way into modern funk and hip hop. Perhaps Charlie feels that jazz is no longer the spokesperson for militant black America. But militant black America is still emerging from a prolonged period of depression following its defeats in the 1970s.

The emergence of successive generations of musicians such as Antonio Hart, Steve Coleman and the Marsalis brothers shows that young musicians have returned to acoustic jazz throughout the 1980s in ever increasing numbers. It is a signal for cautious optimism, since without doubt they will be unable to fully realise their music without a significant increase in the intensity of the struggle.[2]

Charlie not only gives us a wrong idea of the present, he gives a distorted and oversimplified view of the past. I will look briefly at three issues, the question of jazz influence on militant black America, the development of a world proletariat and the influence of classical music.

At the height of the ghetto uprisings the emotional power of free jazz seemed its most potent musical expression. However, it is precisely at this time that the jazz clubs which supported the music went into chronic decline. In fact many commentators blame the declining popularity of jazz in general on free jazz in particular. Looking back at the specialist jazz magazines of the time, a rather different picture emerges, which has little to do with changes of taste in the black ghettos.

The big record companies bought up the independent record companies which recorded jazz music. This was not because of jazz's popularity, but because the same labels tended to record rhythm and blues and the increasingly popular 'rock' acts. Led Zeppelin, for example, were signed by Atlantic. Basically, the record majors had no interest in jazz, with its tiny sales which just reached break even point, and wound down the jazz catalogue. This is clear from Blue Note, which was bought by Liberty, who then rushed out albums of lesser worth to fulfil contractual obligations with their artists. The other pillar of the jazz economy at the time was the jazz clubs. Musicians point out that many were closed by the police at the height of the uprisings. In addition many white patrons stayed away from the majority of jazz clubs which were located in the black areas.

As Charlie rightly pointed out, jazz funk has been almost completely dismissed as an innovative music. This needs to be emphasised since this development of jazz has been of crucial importance in the formation of new ideas in jazz during the last decade. As soul music grew in popularity, so too did albums playing jazz versions of soul hits. It is this strand, that of tenor organ groups and funky jazz, which remained economically healthy and, as Charlie says, is inseparable from the developments in black pop music and art music. Young black musicians never stopped playing jazz, they just played a jazz which jazz critics did not like. Jazz has always used the pop music of the time. When it was based on show tunes, standards, it was art. When it was based on songs written by Marvin Gaye and Curtis Mayfield it was debased commercialism. Thus, when jazz was supposed to be dying on its feet, jazz singles began entering the *Billboard* Rhythm and Blues charts in some numbers.

Another problem with Charlie's analysis is his overestimation of jazz's popularity in earlier periods. David Rosenthal analysed certified sales of jazz albums on record labels associated with hard bop and early crossover musicians like the organist Jimmy Smith. The average sales worldwide of a single issue on Blue Note records, the most influential of the specialist jazz labels, before deletion, were a mere 5,000. It took ten years for Miles Davis's album *Kind of Blue* to sell 100,000 copies. Bear in mind that by 1921 Bessie Smith saved CBS from bankruptcy with a million selling 78. However, Rosenthal goes on to point out that at least half the record sales were in shops in the black ghettos.[3] Even in London, Blue Note records were sold in the shops which imported blue beat from Jamaica.

Jazz influence has always been indirect, far greater than record sales would suggest. But at no stage has innovative jazz been anything remotely close to a mass music, even in the ghettos which are its spiritual wellspring. The musicians, however, articulate in both their music and their sentiments the spectrum of nationalist and socialist politics. Politically conscious blacks therefore often form a deep love of the music and form close relationships with individual musicians.

Charlie ends his article on a triumphant upbeat. Jazz is dying, long live the music of the world proletariat. The development of the world market and its effect on the world proletariat have been a constant element in our political analysis. However, it is not a new phenomenon. Indeed, the internationalisation of the proletariat and the internationalisation of working class culture begin at the very beginnings of world capitalism. Peter Linebaugh's excellent *The London Hanged* gives tantalising glimpses of this process in 18th century London.

Jazz itself has played a central role in the development of an international music culture. It both absorbs influences from musical cultures it comes into contact with, and in turn influences them. By 1922 jazz bands based on King Oliver were noted in Shanghai, Lagos and Bombay. Trotsky was even reported to have been welcomed on board the Battleship Potemkin by a jazz band. So America is not the only place from which great music comes. Salif Keita, for example, records in Paris with musicians who are thoroughly conversant with the jazz tradition. This music is not a different species, but a different breed of the same animal. The real question is whether or not black America remains the main centre of innovation in the world of music. So far no national capital has produced a music of the harmonic and rhythmic complexity, or continuing rapid evolution, of the jazz musicians of America.

Another of Charlie's misunderstandings is his idea that classical music was brought into jazz by middle class blacks. Classical music so dominated musical education that whether or not a musician was formally trained, they would see music in terms of harmonic structures invented by the classical composers. Gospel and military music both have the same overall approach, while the music lessons that working class blacks could afford would be given by teachers conversant with classical music. All the popular songs published up to the 1940s quite openly stole harmonic structures and melodies from composers who were safely dead and out of copyright. Classical music, the musical representative of the revolutionary bourgeoisie, dominated music education throughout European and American societies. In music as in other areas of social life, the culture of the bourgeoisie predominates. Underemphasising this detracts from the outstanding achievement of jazz music in effectively becoming the art music of the 20th century, not in isolation from the classical tradition, but out of it. As the music has progressed, it has grown further away from its classical roots.

Although Charlie has provided a concise account of jazz development, both the way he sets out the problem and his conclusions reproduce the same mistakes that previous critics have made. Instead of looking at the way the jazz tradition actually develops as a musical expression of deep social processes in various musical forms, he identifies jazz with its development up to a particular point in history. Thus every new development in jazz has been greeted by a chorus of critical voices proclaiming the death of the music. Currently critics brought up on the avant garde decry Wynton Marsalis for his 'traditionalism' and contemporary fusion for its 'commercialism' and the whole of jazz for its 'cold professionalism and technical proficiency'. Charlie's article resonates with a deep pessimism for the present, a depiction of a previous golden age and a retreat into Third Worldism.

Charlie's main problem is that he sees race as the only motor in the history of jazz's development. But jazz was not the product of the ghettos in general but of professional musicians in particular, contemptuously dismissed first as dance band musicians and more recently as session men. Secondly, slavery, segregation and the racism they produced are an integral feature of capitalist development and therefore cannot be separated from it. This analysis does not stop the moment a person picks up a musical instrument. Indeed, the history of jazz illustrates these relations clearly, and in the process shows the enormous achievement of jazz musicians in general and black musicians in particular.

Charlie, following Hobsbawm, shows how segregation ironically allowed black musicians a space to develop the jazz tradition without the levels of interference suffered by other working classes. However, this was not without the interference of capital itself, which does not have a skin colour. The dilution of the music for audience acceptance was not essentially racial, but the continuing attempts of capital in various forms to produce a cultural product which suits its purpose. Berry Gordy of Motown was not the first black capitalist to try to dilute the music. His relative failure reflected the high levels of struggle in the ghettos and the confidence this gave musicians in the studios. Benny Goodman was not somebody outside jazz who stole the music like some thief in the night, but was a respected musician inside the music who got caught up in the struggles round the integration of entertainment, fought out through copyright law and royalty payments.

Charlie completely ignores the role of jazz in the struggle for integration. This varies from the daily integration of after hours clubs and bars to the use of jazz as a conscious focus for integration. This is true for the 'diluter' Benny Goodman, who helped organise the first integrated band at Carnegie Hall in 1936 and later for Norman Granz, a real diluter, who used Jazz at the Philharmonic tours to desegregate audiences in the deep south. At a higher level, musicians from classical and jazz backgrounds organised against a segregated union. In California, for example, Charles Mingus was a key figure in a three-year campaign which started with a fundraising concert by an integrated symphony orchestra. The major symphony orchestras themselves did not desegregate until the early 1960s. Stravinsky insisted on using the black musician Richard Davis, a well respected modern jazz player, to play on a recording session of his music. Ron Carter, a key figure in 1960s jazz, joined him on the session, thus breaking the colour bar in American classical music.

The real contradiction in jazz is, how can a music which so expresses the potentiality of our class, and with an influence way beyond music, be so isolated from its class of origin, even in the black ghettos? As Ruby Braff explained years ago, jazz is 'a poor man's music which only the rich can afford'. The explanation is no mystery once the most basic ideas of Marxism are applied.

The specialised division of labour creates deep divisions within the working class, which isolate groups of workers from each other and is the material basis for sectionalism. Marx noted in *Theories of Surplus Value* how cultural production was separated from consumption even in live performance. He pointed out that 'an actor's relation to the public is that of an artist, but to his employer he is a productive labourer.'[4]

Through specialisation and the laws of private property and so on, capital has to create the conditions in which the vast majority of workers are dependent on the culture industries for their entertainment. This means that there will be continuous struggles both inside and outside the entertainment industries round the production and consumption of culture. As in other areas of social life, capital imposes capitalist relations of production on culture, but in so doing creates a specialised sector of the proletariat. The skills of cultural production are not removed from the working class, but concentrated in a specialised sector of it. People working in the entertainment industries will necessarily be isolated from the class as a whole, unless they develop an organic, and ultimately conscious, relationship with it. Thus capitalism creates a unique society, in which the majority of people are unable to make music, and many suffer from a non-existent medical complaint, tone deafness.

While musicians face the same struggles as other workers, may live in the same area as other workers etc, they will have sectional interests and attitudes, and develop all sorts of contradictory ideas, like other workers. This shows the material basis for the difference between the bourgeoisie and the proletariat in the cultural arena. As Trotsky says so eloquently, the bourgeois artists '...lived and still live, in a bourgeois milieu; breathing the air of bourgeois salons, they received hypodermic inspirations from their class. This nourishes the subconscious processes of their creativity.'[5]

The proletariat, in marked contrast, does not have such a cultural milieu. In music not only is the mass of the proletariat musically 'extremely backward' for all the reasons Trotsky pointed out in regard to literature, but those of its members who specialise in making music are structurally isolated from the class as a whole.

Jazz, a product of the particular conditions of American capitalism, illustrates these processes to the extreme. Hence its importance in the debates around culture and its ability to enlighten our politics. Jazz is the product of the most advanced capitalist relations of the production of music, in the biggest capitalist economy in the history of world capitalism, operating still under the most intense conditions of exploitation and racial oppression. Its isolation shows the importance of artists seeking a genuine expression of proletarian experience seeing the need to build organic links with the working class. The failure to do so, as the history of jazz so clearly shows, is not only that the majority of people miss out on good music, or that the liberating message of jazz is mediated by capital, or even that so many musicians have lived unnecessarily short lives. Much worse, the innovations and ideas which express the spirituality of our class, expanding our imaginations' horizons and stimulating the intellect, are turned into the opposite. The ruling class take the structures of the music and use them for their own purposes. Even in such a seemingly esoteric world as jazz music, the basic concerns of our politics remain: the enormous creativity and intellectual capacity of our class in its self activity, and the limitations of that activity, without the conscious knowledge that it is the basis for a socialist society.

Notes

1. These include multi-time playing, the use of alternate scales as a harmonic base, the use of out melodies and their acceptance to the human ear as well as new structures. As with all major changes in jazz, these affect rhythm section players the most, since they directly affect how the musicians relate to each other and the way in which 'swing' is articulated.
2. A detailed examination of the interrelationship between jazz development and black militancy is beyond the scope of this reply. The development of a small jazz academia, a concession to the 1960s uprising, and the expansion of the festival circuit, made jazz less dependent on the specialist clubs and record labels. This may have removed the music further from the ghettos, but it also isolated it from the extreme pessimism of the militant black movement. If you take the view that fusion/funk was a jazz form, then the music never left the ghetto in the first place.
3. D Rosenthal, 'Jazz in the Ghetto: 1950-1970', in *Popular Music* (1987), vol 7.
4. K Marx, *Theories of Surplus Value*, vol 1, p411.
5. L Trotsky, *Trotsky on Literature and Art*, p77.

2. DAVE HARKER

Charlie Hore's article deserves both to be welcomed, as a serious attempt at taking his kind of fun seriously, but also criticised, for not applying classical Marxist methods of analysis to his subject. True, Charlie has come to add a question mark to the title of his Marxism 93 lecture, 'Jazz: a People's Music'; and yet, strangely, he gives us no definition of 'jazz', of 'a people' or even of 'music'! Does the fact that music is played by black musicians make what they play 'black music'; and if so, precisely how? Then again, what, if anything, do the 'people' have to do with 'the nation', let alone the working class; and if we push this idea as far as Charlie does, aren't we in danger of making unnecessary concessions to black nationalism and separatism, as the US Communist Party did in the 1930s,[1] and as Finkelstein (from whose book Charlie took his own title) did in 1948: 'The Negro people are in a sense a group within America, a nation within a nation'.[2]

Are blacks a class, and are *all* the 'oppressed' to be found within the urban working class, or even in the working class as a whole? And why, in any case, is 'jazz' fundamentally 'American'[3]—by which, I take it, Charlie means the US? Was there really something there which could properly be termed 'the black American experience'[4], somehow monolithic and non-contradictory; and what sense does it make to write of a 'black culture' as a whole way of life when, as Trotsky reminded us, no oppressed class or group can hope to control many of the key cultural resources and institutions it needs?[5] (That said, we are still in need of a concept which accurately grasps the specificity of the cultural practices and products made and used by working class people.)

Then there are other questions we can fairly ask of this article, to do with historical factors and theoretical issues. If, as Charlie rightly insists at one point, 'jazz' was 'neither European nor African',[6] *exactly how* did such music appear in Chicago or New York, and from what precise musical and related cultural resources was it made? Did 'it' travel up from the Mississippi Delta, maintaining its alleged purity intact; or was it mainly a spontaneous creation of the recently migrating Northern urban poor? The article seems to postulate—though, of course, it doesn't name—the idea of some 'golden age' of 'jazz', containing some undefined *essence,* which then got 'watered down'[7], co-opted, commoditised or (in Frank Kofsky's revealing phrases) bleached out and whitened in later years?[8] Was there ever really an 'authentic' historical period or 'moment', which produced music that was an 'expression' of some unmediated, transhistorical and universal 'alienation'—a music, which, in turn, can be held to be one of the means to 'overcome' oppression? Can music ever do that, or is it really a question of how music, music fans and musicians relate to the wider *struggle?*

I hope by this point that the reader will accept that these questions and criticisms are not just nit picking, or churlishness, but relate to the problems we find when we try to analyse cultural products and practices from a classical Marxist perspective. One key problem for Charlie's article is the nature of the secondary literature in the field, which is both pretty dated and, amongst writers on the political left, of a certain kind. So the article leans rather heavily on *The Jazz Scene*, written under the pseudonym of Francis Newton and published in 1959 by Eric Hobsbawm, a writer we tend to find particularly unhelpful as a historian of this century, and also on Sidney Finkelstein's *Jazz: A People's Music*, first published in 1948, and dedicated to 'the people of the new nation' of Israel, with nary a mention of the Palestinians that 'new nation' displaced.

Of course, Hobsbawm was to some extent defying the prevailing Moscow line on 'jazz' by producing his book at all, and he gives us revealing asides on the romanticism of the likes of A L Lloyd and 'Ewan MacColl' (Jimmy Miller)[9]; but his book generally toes the Stalinist cultural line, as does Finkelstein's, for all its covert reliance on the cultural pessimism of Theodor Adorno[10], and its uncritical praise for the composer Ralph Vaughan-Williams[11], someone 'proud to be described as a bourgeois'![12] Charlie's other chief authority, Frank Kofsky, while not a thoroughgoing Stalinist—he dedicated *Black Nationalism and the Revolution in Music* to both Malcolm X and John Coltrane—shared Hobsbawm and Finkelstein's habitual masculinism, could be oblivious to the sexism of black musicians,[13] and clearly had serious illusions in the Cuban regime.[14] These are not very promising sources for a classical Marxist analysis; and, moreover, as Charlie notes in passing,[15] people like Hobsbawm took a position on other popular musical styles which was, well, unembarrassedly elitist.

Now, this is not at all to convict the article by association—but it is to suggest that what we take from such dubious sources needs to be evaluated very carefully indeed, and this is particularly true of what passes for theory in the works of the likes of Hobsbawm, Finkelstein and Kofsky.

Take just one example. Whenever these writers have a problem in explaining the complex connections between economic, political and cultural factors, they reach for their *mirrors*.[16] Actions, events, music even, 'reflect' something else; and when, as in Kofsky, the vulgar reflectionism seems too crude even for him, we simply get moved upmarket to *prisms*, which are said to 'refract'[17] whatever it is that can't be connected to this vulgar materialist perspective. Marx believed the matter was rather more complicated than that: he thought the term 'correspond'[18] encapsulated the complex and contradictory relations between what he called 'base' and 'superstructure'; yet Charlie carries over the bad habits of his sources, seeing mirrors everywhere, 'reflecting' reality in what seems to be an unmediated and mechanical fashion. Mirrors reverse images, and all you tend to see in them is yourself. Surely there are enough problems with using Marx's suggestive metaphor without inviting ridicule on this point?[19]

That said, it is also true that Charlie's article recognises some of the pitfalls of adapting to the Stalinist critique of 'jazz', including the refusal to accept Hobsbawm's smug elitism about rock and roll. For example, the article recognises that some 'Africanist' writers tend to be pulled towards a static, ahistorical essentialism about the music[20], as they adapt to the general politics of black nationalism or black separatism; but there is little evidence of a serious engagement with the important article by Philip Tagg,[21] which raises problems with analyses which regard 'Black music, Afro-American music and European music' as monolithic, static and self-enclosed entities. For example, Charlie repeats the old idea that 'blue notes' came only from Africa,[22] whereas Tagg is able to show that such sounds can be found in Scandinavia and Britain, as well as West Sudan, and in the white made music of the Appalachians in the US itself.[23] Tagg also criticises the idea that 'call-and-response', 'rhythm' and 'improvisation' have been or are unproblematically 'black' or 'white', and ponders long and hard about the implicit 'reverse racism' which seems to underpin many statements to the contrary.[24] In addition, the Hore article hints, quite correctly, that every single so-called stylistic or generic name for bodies of popular music has come under scrutiny in the past ten years, on suspicion of being conceptually soggy.[25] So, just as 'folksong' has been shown to have been a thoroughly *bourgeois* concept (taken over in the UK by Stalinists, and given a left populist inflexion, while retaining the nationalistic, reactionary and largely ahistorical content of the term),[26] so there are currently serious debates about what, precisely, is 'American' about 'the blues', where the 'punk-ness' is in punk music, and what is necessarily Liverpudlian about the 'Mersey Sound'. Much of this work has been prompted by the awareness of the general problem of *mediation* of 'popular' and working class cultural practices and products; and while Charlie's article mentions this difficulty, and the analogous problems of the commoditisation of 'jazz' by the capitalist music business, he doesn't really develop his analysis even so far as to explain what he terms the 'decline' of jazz' after 1945.

It is true that most of what we know about the cultural activities of working class people has come to us through the heads and hands of people who were (and are) usually white, male, heterosexual and overwhelmingly petit bourgeois or even bourgeois. The same is true of 'jazz'. Louis Armstrong, for example, is spoken *for* by Hobsbawm as 'not just a trumpeter: he is the voice of his people speaking on a horn'.[27] It is as though Hobsbawm, Finkelstein, Kofsky and, now, Hore offer to go back, so to speak, and grasp this golden age's *essence*, behind the back of bourgeois ideology and mediation! But how *did* that 'it', that 'jazz', remain uncontaminated on its travels, in what seems to be represented as a kind of social Darwinian progression across the United States of America; and how did those urban ghettos (so important to Charlie's thesis) remain hermetically sealed from the baneful influence of 'white' made music, even before bands came to be desegregated? How, after all, can you segregate a radio audience? And how do we know that 'jazz' was a majority taste, even in that ghetto—after all, Louis Armstrong was not known for his uncritical praise of 'bebop', as Charlie notes![28] Besides, could not the ability of black artists to make it in the white owned music industry— 'Thank God for Elvis Presley', Little Richard proclaimed[29]—be a key factor in the 'decline of jazz' from the mid-1950s? And why not make records for a black owned record business like Motown, if that label was best placed to exploit the commoditisation of black made music for a predominantly white audience? Isn't there something odd about the lament for the 'decline of jazz', through a phase which Hobsbawm openly admits was one in which 'a people's music' was made by *professionals* for a *tiny* percentage of the record buying public—and a largely white, male, college educated minority at that?[30] And is Charlie's article in danger of suggesting that we should be nostalgic for the cultural products coming out of older forms of *oppression*? Though the comparison is cruel, Hobsbawm saw fit to compare the sentimental idealisers of 'traditional jazz' of the 1950s with those people who 'regret that we cannot hear our Handel exactly as Handel meant us to because, unfortunately, we no longer castrate boy singers'.[31] The dangers are obvious; but at least Hobsbawm understood, as Charlie and Kofsky do not, that 'jazz by itself is not politically conscious or revolutionary'. Music—any music—cannot set us free.

So where does this take us? It seems obvious to me that, if we want our tradition to be taken seriously by people close to our politics and practice, then we have to accept there is a lot of work to be done in developing a distinctive and coherent position. It does us no credit to pretend that we should treat black artists as 'honorary workers', since many of them were decidedly lumpen proletarian in origin, and those who found a regular paying audience rapidly made the transition to bohemian, petit bourgeois or even bourgeois status. (This is in no way to devalue the *music*, naturally.) Similarly, whereas someone like Finkelstein may well have wanted 'jazz' to *become* 'A People's Music',[32] it was not, is not, and may never be working class music in any meaningful sense. To say anything else is to make concessions to left populism, popular frontism, and even outright Zhdanovism, against which Trotsky railed:

> *A revolutionary party is neither able nor willing to take upon itself the task of 'leading' and even less of commanding art, either before or after the conquest of power. Such a pretension could only enter the head of a bureaucracy—ignorant and impudent, intoxicated with its totalitarian power—which has become the antithesis of the proletarian revolution. Art, like science, not only does not seek orders but by its very essence cannot tolerate them.*[33]

Neither, outside the rhetoric of windy Stalinists, does the idea of 'a people' have any connection with the theory and practice of class struggle, or of a revolutionary party rooted in the working class.

That said, I want to acknowledge Charlie's initiative in risking showing us his enthusiasms and in trying to understand them, and I hope his article gets the feedback it deserves.

Notes

1 M Naison, *Communists in Harlem during the Depression* (New York, 1985), throughout.
2 S Finkelstein, *Jazz: A People's Music* (London, Jazz Book Club, 1964), p20. This book was originally published in New York in 1948.
3 C Hore, 'Jazz: a people's music?', *International Socialism* 61 (Winter 1993), p92.
4 Ibid, p91.
5 Trotsky, *Literature and Revolution* (London, Redwords, 1990), pp213-242.
6 C Hore, op cit, p94.
7 Ibid, p94. One of Hore's chief sources, 'Francis Newton' (aka Eric Hobsbawm), tended to use similar metaphors—see, for example, *The Jazz Scene* (London, Jazz Book Club, 1960), p13.
8 F Kofsky, *Black Nationalism and the Revolution in Music* (New York, Pathfinder, 1988), p32. This book was originally published in 1970.
9 Hobsbawm, op cit, pp42, 43n.
10 For example, Finkelstein, op cit, pp13, 28, 150, 159, 245, 249.
11 Ibid, pp264, 266.

12	R Vaughan Williams, *National Music and Other Essays* (London, Oxford University Press, 1963), p63. For Vaughan Williams' attitude to the 'Teutonic idiom and Negroid emetics', see pp47-8.
13	F Kofsky, op cit, p25n.
14	Ibid, p141.
15	C Hore, op cit, p103. For Hobsbawm on the 'infantilism' of rock and roll, see *The Jazz Scene*, op cit, p32.
16	For example, E Hobsbawm, op cit, pp18, 54 (twice), 76, 82, 90, 148, 166, 186, 243, 250, 259, 265, 269, 276.
17	F Kofsky, op cit, p163n.
18	*MECW*, vol 29, p263. See also F Jakubowski, *Ideology and Superstructure in Historical Materialism* (London, Pluto Press, 1990), throughout.
19	For a critique of various abuses of Marx's metaphor, see T Eagleton, *Marxism and Literary Criticism* (London, 1977), p49. It is true that some long standing Socialist Workers Party contributors to *International Socialism* do recognise the problem with this habit, as John Molyneux does in *International Socialism* 61, p63, but within nine lines he takes out his 'mirror' once more!
20	C Hore, op cit, p107, n4.
21	P Tagg, 'Black Music, Afro-American Music and European Music', *Popular Music* (Cambridge University Press, October 1989), vol 8, no 3, pp285-298.
22	C Hore, op cit, p94.
23	P Tagg, op cit, p288.
24	Ibid, pp289-90.
25	C Hore, op cit, p92.
26	D Harker, *Fakesong: the Manufacture of British 'Folksong', 1700 to the Present Day* (Milton Keynes, Open University Press, 1985), throughout. In another work in that series, P Oliver's *Black Music in Britain: Essays on the Afro-Asian Contribution to Popular Music* (Open University Press, 1990), pp5ff, 174, this highly respected authority on 'blues' also questions the conceptual and historical status of 'black music'.
27	E Hobsbawm, op cit, p121.
28	C Hore, op cit, p98.
29	*The Rolling Stone Interviews* (New York, 1971), vol 1, p371.
30	E Hobsbawm, op cit, pp146, 163, 239, 240, 242.
31	Ibid, p137.
32	Compare Hore at Marxism 93, on 'jazz' as the 'beginnings of a global culture'. This is not unlike the enthusiastic vegetarian several of us had to argue with some years ago, when she told us unreconstructed carnivores that 'after the revolution, we'll *all* give up meat'!
33	L Trotsky, *Culture and Socialism Manifesto* (London, 1975), p29. For the wit and wisdom of A A Zhdanov, see his *On Literature, Music and Philosophy* (London, Lawrence and Wishart, 1950), especially pp15, 38, 42, 54.

3. MATT KELLY

Charlie's piece on jazz was certainly valuable, and this reply is intended to be in the same spirit of debate. I am particularly concerned to comment on how the Marxist method may be used to address cultural matters—musical ones specifically—and certain aspects of historical interpretation in the history of music.

Despite his claims, Charlie's article does not discuss jazz in 'America', but rather in the US. This becomes an increasingly relevant point for Marxists attempting to define the way in which culture arises in specific historical circumstances. There was, after all, in both Southern America and the Caribbean islands, a very considerable (and in its own way particular) interaction between cultural forms exported from Europe, the influence of indigenous forms and the influence of various cultural forms from Africa brought by slaves. And indeed, there has been subsequent interaction throughout the 20th century across Europe, the Caribbean, South America and Africa—not a thing to ignore when we look at a form of music which arose in, among other places, New Orleans.

But further, there is the whole knotty problem (on the whole side-stepped by Charlie, but probably worth at least a mention) of what constitutes 'black' culture. Should it be defined purely in terms of US black culture; how is that differentiated class from class, urban from rural, north from south, east from west and period from period? Is there any reason to assume that cultural forms exist in anything other than contradictory, mixed forms, rather than pure ones?

The debate around what is specific about 'black music' has centred on musical features of blues and jazz, and the presence or absence of these features in music from different places on the globe. The most commonly discussed are: the use of blue notes; the use of call and response structures; the use of polyrhythm and the use of improvisation. Now the extent to which any of these is exclusive to music in which some element of 'African' origin can be traced is by no means clear.[1] It may well be the case that the *particular* kind of improvisation, call and response and so on found in jazz and/or blues is different from those found in European (or, say, Middle Eastern) music. This is certainly a matter requiring further thought and research. What is most pertinent here is the question of whether these aspects of music are particular to jazz.

To clarify this, we really need to search back to the origins of 'jazz'. We need to consider the history of the various musical styles which arose in the various parts of the US in the years between the civil war and the First World War. We know something about the kinds of music that flourished in the US in this period, though the further back we go, the less clear the picture becomes. Paul Oliver's researches have given some picture of some of the music which had arisen. He charts the rise of minstrel songs, ragtime, jazz, ballads, blues and gospel occurring between 1893-1914. 'The concentrated period of innovation was a mere decade: 1897-1907.'[2] His account of this, while tentative (and attempting to avoid the dangers of a mechanical explanation), suggests that it cannot be mere coincidence that these new styles arose at a time when the end of slavery was closely followed by post-war segregation, which was coming to be enacted and imposed in all its despicable oppressiveness.

So, while this remains an area crying out for continuing research, what is already clear is that, although at certain times jazz musicians claimed 'the blues' as an important antecedent to jazz, the various kinds of music that later became known as jazz and blues arose in broadly the same period in different places in the US. There is no clear evidence to identify jazz as 'based' on the blues—indeed, if anything, the blues was the *last* to develop of these new musical styles. Later the early jazz and blues recordings, both primarily for black audiences, were made during the same period, and whatever had given rise to the various styles of music played by black musicians, those styles interacted very strongly during this period of recording.

This starts out as a matter of historical detail, perhaps. But the consequences of this argument are that the claims made exclusively for jazz need to be clarified. It was the case, in fact, that a range of different musical styles arose in a specific historical period. Charlie seems to have set out to place jazz in the context of its historical development as one among a range of musical styles in the US but then moves on to make explicitly distinct claims for jazz alone. He acknowledges that the distinctions between the styles are by no means clear cut. But then he makes special claims for jazz as *the* black music of the urban working class. But if it is the case that minstrel songs, ballads, ragtime, various forms of what became known as blues, and various forms of what became known as jazz arose at the same time with their own particular mixtures of European, US, Caribbean, indigenous and African origins, would we not expect to find aspects of these other musical features in all these kinds of music? There is certainly a story to be told here about the rise of new musical styles, primarily played by black musicians for black, mostly working class, audiences.

This brings me to my third point, which is about the slight historical confusions underlying some of Charlie's account. Charlie argues, 'From the 1930s onwards the developments of radio, jukeboxes, televisions and cheap audio equipment...broke that separation [between black audiences and white audiences] down.' Elsewhere in the article there are further figures that are used to address the same matter, but they still cloud the issue. Let me try to clarify. It is true that in 1926 there were 'only' some 15 million homes with radios. It is also true that the home consumption of recorded music became relatively unimportant in the years after the 1929 crash. But 1925 was the *end* of the first phase of recording history, and the start of the second: electronic recording. The value of US recorded music sales peaked in *1921* at $106 million, and tailed off gradually until 1929 when they nose-dived (only $6 million in 1933).[3]

Ultimately, this partly depends on what you choose to emphasise, but my suggestion is as follows. It is best to characterise the rise of jazz, blues and the other musical styles as having taken place precisely at the same time as the development of the technology which led to recorded music, cinema and radio. It took the economic impetus provided by the First World War to ensure the US saw full development of radio, electronic recording, sound films and so on. So ultimately I'm carrying out a more thoroughgoing critique of Hobsbawm's idea than Charlie allows himself: although live performance remains of importance for most forms of music, jazz (and indeed blues) is primarily music of the technological age.[4]

Indeed, Hobsbawm's account has an element of the 'golden age' about it—a golden age when culture was not 'corrupted' by technology. Now, where do such arguments have their political root, and what is their consequence?

Writing about popular music is a particularly hard task at the best of times. There are few examples to follow. Many of those which do exist fall into the tradition more usefully identified as Stalinism than as Marxism. This is indeed a problem lying behind Charlie's title. He uses (a number of times) the phrase 'the people's music' to refer to jazz or, elsewhere, to rock'n'roll or soul. But nowhere in the article does he identify the origin of this phrase or discuss its meaning. I am assuming it is drawn from Sidney Finkelstein's book title, *Jazz—a People's Music*. What did it mean originally? How does Charlie rework it?

Unfortunately, there are problems with the word 'people' in this context. It was a fudge (not clarified by Charlie) which stems from the ideas about class, nationality and the popular front pushed by Stalin and his pals in the 1940s. We find, for example in Zhdanov, Stalin's cultural axeman, such spurious internationalism as, 'it is impossible to be an internationalist in music or in anything else unless one loves and respects one's own people. All the experience of the USSR testifies to that.'[5] (This sentence is also quoted approvingly by Finkelstein in his 1952 book, *How Music Expresses Ideas*, p105). That is the kind of context in which we find the word 'people', and it lurks behind the title of Finkelstein's book. It blurs questions of class. Charlie rightly identifies some traces of a similar brand of ideas in Hobsbawm's writing.

We need to start from a Marxist position (not a Stalinist one) on class and nation before we can move into the question of national identity and struggles against national oppression. In a useful quotation from Trotsky, Charlie raises the idea that 'Marxism alone can explain how and why a given tendency in art has originated in a given period of history'. It seems to me that, by and large, Trotsky was not suggesting that this had already been done, but rather that it was a task that as yet awaited attention. I have yet to read an effective account from a bourgeois or Marxist theorist of the process of musical style change: it's *hard*. So there are (and I'm trying to be helpful here) a number of theoretical areas which usefully could be addressed.

i) Trotsky's point about explaining how and why styles arise etc—can Marxism actually do this? Let's find out!

ii) Over much of today's writing on popular music falls the shadow of 1940s-50s Stalinist writing. We haven't, by and large, any body of writing (journalistic, scholarly, practical, theoretical or otherwise) which can combat or replace this as things stand. Perhaps our comrades feel (as I do from time to time) that other things should come first; but continued chipping away by writers from our tradition would do no harm at all. Why not aim at hegemony on the left in such areas?

iii) There are areas in which we should intervene as cultural critics. Charlie rightly identifies that this should take off from the bits of decent Marxist writers who comment on culture, in however fragmented a way: Marx and Engels, Lenin and Trotsky, Gramsci (but not Gramscians),

Benjamin, Lukacs... The current hegemonic forces of cultural studies and popular music studies come out of Althusser via Stuart Hall via Gramscianism, and hence little is said about what could loosely be termed 'what is to be done'. But I'm hopeful that the theoretical understanding and the depth of cultural knowledge exists in and around our tradition to put this right.

iv) To do this, we need to clarify another issue: how do we learn from cultural history? Not an easy question, and one which Charlie has clearly felt a need to try and answer. I hope his attempt provides the starting point for a new stream of valuable contributions.

Notes

1   These four areas are explored (and our 'commonsense' assumptions about them are called into question) in P Tagg (1989), 'Open Letter: Black Music, Afro-American Music and European Music', *Popular Music*, vol 8, no 3, pp285-298.
2   P Oliver, 'The First Revolution in Black Popular Music', paper given at Paris Conference of International Association for the Study of Popular Music (1989).
3   D Harker, *One for the Money* (London, 1980), p223.
4   I suspect Charlie's emphasis gives more apparent support for the idea that bebop was the key period of jazz development. But this seems to be pushing unnecessarily for a mechanical correspondence between 'culture' and 'society'.
5   A A Zhdanov (1948), 'On Music', speech at a conference of Soviet Music Workers, reprinted in *On Literature, Music and Philosophy* (Moscow, 1950), p63.

Bookwatch: South Africa—the struggle continues

CHARLIE KIMBER

The defeat of apartheid in South Africa was one of the greatest achievements of the working class movement in decades. It was gained by the militant struggles of black workers which forced the white regime to the negotiating table. Those struggles were a challenge to racist stereotypes and equally to the idea that the methods of strikes and demonstrations are outdated and ineffective. The African National Congress's victory in the elections in April this year has opened a new chapter in the struggle. South African workers no longer face the institutionalised racism of apartheid. Instead they confront the 'normal' racism that capitalism has created throughout the world, and the poverty, bad housing, unemployment and low wages that the bosses' system imposes.

Millions of black people voted for the ANC because they believed it would deliver on its election slogan of 'Peace, jobs and freedom'. They have found very swiftly that, although they have won political rights, other more fundamental changes will require a fight using the same methods that were used to topple apartheid.

In the first three months after the election there was an explosion of struggle. Car workers, shop workers, traffic policemen, print workers, postal workers, court officials, health workers, municipal staff and dozens of other groups launched powerful strikes. Big demonstrations paraded through all the major cities. The strikers and protesters found that very little had changed. The police were still brutal and anti working class. They still used rubber bullets, teargas and dogs to break up pickets. Hundreds of trade unionists were arrested for daring to argue for solidarity outside strikebound workplaces.

A deeply challenging period has opened in South Africa and practically every day real activity demonstrates more truths about the nature of the state, the roots of racism and the power of the working class more forcefully than most of the millions of words that have been written about that struggle.

But to really understand what is happening now there are some books which are very useful. Looking at the history of South Africa and how apartheid developed shows that it is capitalism which has been the enemy of the black majority and where the power lies to defeat capitalism. Anyone inspired by the present battles will be interested in the working class and the trade unions—their history and their politics. The unions have been the crucial factor in the modern period. The central core of the battle against apartheid was the black working class. The state could torture and murder activists, it could infiltrate and repress community organisations, it could murder the guerillas sent to challenge its military might. But it could not destroy the unions or blunt their economic power.

Where the unions came from and how they were built are the subjects for several good books. Look at Dennis MacShane's *Power!*,[1] Steve Friedman's *Building Tomorrow Today*[2] and Jeremy Baskin's *Striking Back, a history of COSATU*,[3] all of which have lots of useful information. Baskin leaves out some things and distorts others where the union leaders were opposed by the rank and file, but it is still a very helpful background. Friedman is right to say that the union movement has 'given powerless people a chance to yield power for the first time in their lives'.[4] The modern union movement was born after a wave of strikes in 1973 centred on the area around Durban. Despite immense repression it grew, slowly, during the 1970s so that by the end of the decade it clearly posed a real potential threat to apartheid's rulers. They responded by calling for a professor to investigate the unions. His plan was an attempt to co-opt workers before their strength was too great:

> The unions' potential strength meant they must be controlled—their present weakness means this should be done soon. It would, the report argued, be far healthier to allow the unions to register at an early stage. This would counter polarisation, ensure a more orderly process of bargaining and expose African unions more directly to South Africa's trade union traditions and the ensuing institutions thus inculcating a sense of responsibility to the free market.[5]

Rarely can a ruling class have been more wrong. As Baskin shows, the unions exploded from small organisations to major players during the 1980s. In 1982 they were able to hold their first political strike of the modern era—a half hour stoppage involving 100,000 workers in protest at the death in police custody of organiser Neil Aggett. By the mid-1980s their involvement in wider political issues meant that other groups felt confident to appeal to their strength. In 1984 a student organisation said:

The boycott weapon is not strong enough against our common enemy, the bosses and the government. Workers, we need your support and strength in the trade unions. We students are ready to help you struggle against the bosses in any way we can. But today we need your support.[6]

This involvement in political issues did not mean that the unions simply did what the nationalist organisations told them to. From the start the majority of people who built the unions argued for the need to do more than act simply as a prop to the ANC. They had seen what happened in Zimbabwe where a white minority regime was overthrown but workers still faced poverty and the repressive anti-union laws used by the previous government. When miners' union leader Cyril Ramaphosa opened the founding conference of the COSATU trade union federation he had to reflect that feeling:

If workers are to lead the struggle for liberation we have to win the confidence of other sections of society. But if we are to get into alliances with other progressive organisations, it must be on terms that are favourable to us as workers. When we do plunge into political activity we must make sure that the unions under COSATU have a strong shop floor base not only to take on the employers but the state as well. In the next few days we will be putting our heads together not only to make sure we reach Pretoria but to make a better life for us workers in this country. What we have to make clear is that a giant has risen and will confront all that stand in its way.[7]

Of course while nodding towards these sentiments the majority of union leaders have always argued for a tight alliance with the ANC. The second conference of COSATU adopted the ANC's Freedom Charter which was very far from being a socialist document. Most of the individual unions took the same path.

After the release of Nelson Mandela and the unbanning of the anti-apartheid organisations in 1990 the ANC saw many strikes and protests as 'destabilising' and unhelpful in coming to a negotiated settlement with the representatives of the National Party. The union leaders were vital in helping to argue for this line—although they also had to reflect the concerns of their members and were sometimes forced to call action even when the ANC was hesitant to do so.

It is the same situation today. The union leaders both urge faster and more fundamental change while doing their best to curtail the frequency and scale of open battle against the employers and the state. It is on this terrain and around these issues that the most important struggles will take place in the coming period. Again Baskin's book is a useful starting point. He writes:

> The union movement is used to being labelled a disruptive force, and blamed for inflation, unemployment and a variety of other ills. Union leaders are accustomed to being called 'communists', 'terrorists' and 'agitators'. In the past unions have dismissed these charges, secure in the belief that they represented the interests of the great a majority of the population. The unions can expect to be accused of disruption even in the post-apartheid era. The charges will be packaged differently: There will be less talk of 'communists' and more of 'sabotaging national reconstruction'. The unions will have to take these allegations seriously, especially since they come from a popularly elected government. COSATU is attempting to face this challenge by developing a comprehensive programme for union involvement in social and economic reconstruction.[8]

The first two thirds of Baskin's analysis has proved spot on. It took Nelson Mandela just a few weeks to turn from praising the unions as crucial in the defeat of apartheid to castigating militants precisely for failing to make the shift from 'resistance to nation building'. The last third of Baskin's prediction has turned out quite differently. Certainly the trade union leaders have secured an input into the plans for reconstruction. Former general secretary of COSATU Jay Naidoo is a minister in the cabinet, charged with overseeing the implementation of the Reconstruction and Development Plan. Other ex-leaders of trade unions have found similar positions.

But the real concerns of the majority of workers have been ignored in favour of seeking alliances with domestic and international capital. Nelson Mandela has rammed home the message that 'scaring off foreign investors' is the greatest danger at present and that there is nothing worse than strikes to upset international capitalists. The first budget saw the ANC renege on its promise to remove VAT from basic goods. It also cut the major element of business taxation and left the rich almost untouched. There is much talk of housing expansion, but in practice the homeless still have only their shacks and the squatters face repression at least as vicious as during the apartheid era.

South Africa is now an explosive mix of heightened expectations, people who have felt their power and their ability to change society during the defeat of apartheid, and a strong trade union movement. But the trade union leaders will, just like their counterparts in the rest of the world, seek to limit the struggles to the boundaries imposed by capitalism and the market. Perhaps some of the most useful reading that anyone could do about South Africa at the moment would be to look at some of the classic Marxist accounts of reformism and the trade unions. One South African trade unionist I know recently described Cliff and Gluckstein's *Marxism and the Trade Union Struggle*[9] as 'the best book to understand what's going on now even though it's mainly about another country 70 years ago'.

How does the union movement fit into the wider history of South Africa and what forces have emerged on the left? For a very basic introduction to the country's history look at something like *Apartheid: the Facts*[10] or *The Apartheid Handbook*.[11] These are just beginnings but give you a sense of the inhuman nature of racism in South Africa. Much of their material is also, thankfully, out of date. The 'homelands', the forced removals and the laws assigning people to racial groups have been banished to the museum of capitalism's atrocities. But we should not forget.

For a fuller treatment there are three 'classic' histories. They are J J and R E Simons's *Class and Colour in South Africa 1850-1950*,[12] E Le Roux's *Time Longer than Rope*[13] and Tom Lodge's *Black Politics in South Africa since 1945*.[14] I think Lodge's is the best account of the later period. Simons's is more centred on the working class than Le Roux—but all of them are well worth a look.

At the centre of these histories is the ANC, and the authors, although very sympathetic to the ANC's political perspectives, cannot help but show some of its deficiencies. Simons and Simons make clear how timid the early ANC was:

> *The leaders of Congress were intellectuals and trade unionists, but the trade unionists were too weak to set the pace. The clergyman, lawyers, writers, teachers, clerks and chiefs who founded Congress or who decided its policies were constitutionalists who aspired to political equality within the framework of parliamentary government. Until the 1950s Congress was a radical liberal movement which never envisaged anything so far-reaching as the socialisation of the land, mines, factories and banks.*[15]

The ANC was radicalised by the struggles of the 1950s—the bus boycotts of Evaton and Alexandra in the mid-1950s, the campaign against the destruction of Sophiatown, the women's struggles and the beginnings of intervention in trade unions. These battles increased the pressure from below from a new generation of activists for a less deferential organisation. One indication of that was the adoption of the Freedom Charter in 1955 which promised, in very general terms, to provide fundamental reform in the interests of workers and the oppressed. But Lodge makes it clear that the ANC's shift, although real, was limited:

> *In 1955, despite its increasing sensitivity to the preoccupations of the least privileged, and despite the increasing strength of its links with worker organisations, the ANC was not a movement strongly oriented towards the working*

class. The endorsement of the Freedom Charter reflected the changing character of the movement's leadership: in contrast to the previous decade it was younger, less affluent and more likely to be drawn from a legal, trade union or non-professional background than the politicians of the 1940s. But despite a more radical leadership the ANC was often slow and ineffective in its efforts to resist fresh infringements on existing freedoms and rights.[16]

This period also saw the emergence of an alternative reformist tradition to the ANC—the Africanist movement. They differed from the ANC leaders on two points—the role of whites and the relationship between leadership and spontaneity. Africanists believed that whites were allowed too great a role in the ANC, and they used as evidence the clauses in the Freedom Charter which guaranteed the rights and status of all 'national groups'. Without a clear statement of black leadership, they claimed, the psychological subservience of blacks would remain. Secondly, the Africanists claimed, the crucial role of an organisation was not to lead or direct the masses but simply to 'show the light' and let the masses find their own way. The Africanists, who split from the ANC to form the Pan-Africanist Congress in 1958, could often sound radical or even revolutionary. But in practice they have followed a very similar path to the ANC. If anything they have been less centred on the working class and its organisations.

For a detailed and interesting account of the battles before and during the Second World War, see Baruch Hirson's *Yours for the Union, Class and Community Struggles in South Africa 1930-47*.[17] It gives a real sense of the fledgling attempts at union organisation and why they ultimately failed in this period despite heroic efforts. The 1960s were a low point of the South African struggle. After the banning of the ANC and the Communist Party and the arrest of many leading activists, the movement went into a deep lull. It seemed virtually impossible to hit back against such a well organised and ruthless opponent.

The Soweto rebellion of 16 June 1976, coming after the revival of the unions, showed that it was possible to fight. Two good books are Baruch Hirson's *Year of Fire, Year of Ash. The Soweto Revolt*[18] and Denis Herbstein's *White Man We Want To Talk To You*.[19] Hirson writes about the roots of the revolt in the growing anger among the pupils who were pushed though the school system that apartheid had developed. His is also one of the few books that looks in some detail at the Black Consciousness movement—although he still overplays the role of the ANC. Much of the impetus behind the Soweto revolt came from new organisations that had emerged during the doldrums of the 1960s: 'Its leaders spoke of black awareness and of black identity and this was a language that appealed particularly to students and intellectuals.'[20]

Herbstein's is a more journalistic account but what it lacks in theory it more than makes up for by conveying well the spirit of struggle. Despite the repression that followed the uprising Herbstein was far sighted enough to write that, 'After the 16 June 1976, only the most ostrich-like whites can still say that time is on their side. For the nationwide uprising constituted the first step on the long haul to black rule.'[21] Nobody could read these accounts of great struggle without gaining a profound respect for the fighting power of the black workers and township residents who fought so courageously. They also prove that there is no tyranny which cannot be opposed and ultimately defeated if we use our strength.

One of the great debates on the South African left has been the precise nature of the relationship between capitalism and apartheid. The political implication was whether to form alliances with 'progressive' capitalists to destroy what was seen as a monstrously aberrant form of capitalism, or to centre on the struggles of workers against both apartheid and the bosses' system. The Marxist tradition has held that apartheid was not simply a monstrous system of racism. It had its own logic for a capitalist class which was seeking the best method to exploit South Africa's natural resources and its black workers. The full apartheid state was not established until after the 1948 election, but racial oppression has been a dominant feature in South Africa since the Dutch arrived in 1652.

There are a whole series of books and articles which were written in the 1970s to show that apartheid was indeed a product of capitalism rather than simply an irrational horror which could be cured by supporting a 'nice' capitalism. For those who want to delve deeper into South African history, these are interesting works although some of them are far from easy and assume quite a lot of knowledge.

Michael Williams's article 'An analysis of South African capitalism'[22] and Martin Legassick's 'Capital accumulation and violence'[23] might be in your local college library. They are now quite old but still exciting polemical writing. They insisted that the main struggle inside South Africa is between capital and labour and that this struggle would be the one that determined what happened in the future.

In the same vein a series of books showed that capitalism was the main feature of South African society from the late 19th century and that the traditional African societies had been destroyed. Look at Jeff Guy's *The Destruction of the Zulu Kingdom*[24] and Duncan Innes's *Anglo American and the Rise of South African Capitalism*.[25]

The modern forms of racial discrimination emerged with the discovery of diamonds and gold and the need to recruit a vast black workforce to labour for very low wages in the hellish conditions of the mines. To drive African peasants from their land required decades of war, cruel laws and naked repression. It is process very well described in

Vic Allen's *The History of Black Mineworkers in South Africa*.[26] The strength of the book is its stress on the resistance by black people. In the early days of the 1860s and 1870s they simply walked away from the mine sites if they were not paid enough or if conditions became intolerable. To force them to work the employers and the state imposed taxes which had to be paid in cash, destroyed the agriculture which provided Africans with their basic needs and crushed independent African rulers.

Even this was not easy. Colonial rule was resisted fiercely and with some temporary successes. Far from melting away before the power of the Boers and the British, Africans frequently fought them to a standstill. The 'commonsense' notion that workers have no means of life except by working for a capitalist boss was imposed by a minimum of 20 years of war and by immense bloodshed. Vic Allen shows how resistance then continued in a new form in the strikes of 1913, 1918, 1920 and 1946 and discusses why the union was defeated.

A much, much more detailed study of part of this process is found in Noel Mostert's much praised *Frontiers*.[27] It is a huge book which if it had been half as long would have been twice as good. It tells the history of the Xhosa people of the Eastern Cape who were defeated only after a century of war. No less than nine separate campaigns were necessary to subdue the Xhosas. Mostert has dredged up every possible detail and some of it is engrossing. But too often the meandering sentences lead nowhere—or into a semi mystical evocation of the 'African spirit'. You could not read this book without finding some fascinating insights. But it is far from a priority.

Allen's book is a much better introduction and so is Eddie Webster's *Cast in a Racial Mould*[28] which looks at how the South African working class—black and white—was created. For a vivid account of conditions at the mines and the struggle to build unions, see Laurie Flynn's *Studded with Diamonds and Paved with Gold*.[29]

One of the most brutal and violent players in South Africa has been Chief Buthelezi's conservative Inkatha organisation. It has posed, fraudulently, as the defender of Zulu speakers' interests while butchering those among the majority of Zulus who dare to support the ANC or left forces. It has worked with the apartheid government to unleash a terrible township war and still has considerable power after its fixed win in the KwaZulu-Natal region in the recent elections. L Vail's *The Creation of Tribalism in South Africa*[30] shows that the divisions which Buthelezi and the old government played upon are not rooted in centuries of ethnic conflict but were deliberately encouraged and deepened as instruments of policy to divide and rule the oppressed and exploited. As Baskin says:

> *To describe the Natal violence as 'black on black' is accurate only at the most superficial level. It ignores the role of the police and the army. It avoids detailing what is being fought for, and what is being opposed. Ultimately it is a deeply racist explanation implying that innate and savage violent tendencies among black people have caused the conflict.*[31]

Mzala's *Gatsha Buthelezi, Chief with a Double Agenda*[32] is good on the brutalities of Inkatha and the way Buthelezi has worked with apartheid. But it underestimates the way the ANC failed to confront, and even encouraged, Buthelezi at the start of his career. This failure and the constant compromises since have allowed Buthelezi to survive when all the other 'homeland' leaders were deposed. One of the greatest and potentially most dangerous compromises with murderers was to agree a crooked election result which gave Inkatha the majority in Natal, and allowed them several cabinet ministers. All the history of South Africa shows that cuddling closer to reactionary forces simply provokes more killing. When local ANC leaders objected to the deal in Natal they were told to shut up rather than encouraged to step up their struggles.

For the history and politics of the South African Communist Party, which was and remains a very significant player on the left and now boasts a clutch of cabinet ministers, see Simon Phillips's 'The South African Communist Party and the South African Working Class'[33] in an earlier edition of this journal.

It will come as no surprise that I think the most useful way to understand South Africa is to read Alex Callinicos's books and articles. Reading *South Africa between Reform and Revolution*,[34] a collection of writings over a decade, you can find particular stresses which were wrong in terms of immediate detail but the whole analysis is brilliantly sustained by its stress in three areas.

Firstly Alex always insisted on the need to centre the struggle on the working class. Their struggles were the only force which could guarantee the smashing of apartheid and their further victories are now required to bring genuine liberation. Secondly, the method of using mass struggle but focusing on negotiation and accommodation with the white state in order to remove apartheid has brought about significant change at the top but cannot offer a transformation for the black masses in their economic and social position. Alex wrote six years ago that if the ANC did come to power:

> *The African petty bourgeoisie would have a strong interest in ensuring that South African capitalism were as competitive as possible in the international arena, and in maintaining the flow of foreign exchange generated by gold exports. This would require appealing to 'discipline' and 'sacrifice' on the part of the working class, and if that were not forthcoming, attacking the*

workers' movement, as the Mugabe regime did in Zimbabwe in the early 1980s.[35]

Thirdly Alex has shown that it is perfectly possible both to argue for unconditional support for the ANC's struggles against apartheid and also to insist on going much further than the ANC's bourgeois politics and the need to build a genuinely revolutionary socialist workers' party:

> *The hope that socialism and nationalism can be reconciled under the ANC banner amounts to nothing less than an attempt to wish away the class struggle and the structural contradictions underpinning it. The nature of post-apartheid South Africa will indeed...depend on the 'actual correlation of class forces' at the time... But a 'favourable correlation' itself presupposes the political independence of the working class, which requires organisational expression in the shape of a revolutionary socialist party.*[36]

Alex's *Between Apartheid and Capitalism*[37] carries interviews with six leading figures on the South African left and in the trade union movement. It shows all the arguments that were current before the end of apartheid and remain relevant today. His short introduction sets out why President de Klerk was driven to seek a political settlement with the ANC. It exposes the government and Inkatha's responsibility for the political violence which saw thousands of people shot or hacked to death during the period of 'peaceful change' after 1990. The interviews are not only about South Africa but also take up the fundamental questions facing socialists after the fall of the Berlin Wall. Is some sort of market capitalism the only way forward? In the long term can capital and labour coexist amicably so that industry expands and the welfare of the masses improves? What do we mean by socialism and how can it be achieved? Devan Pillay, the editor of *Work in Progress*, says:

> *You can't talk about insurrection. Insurrection, I've come to believe, is a very dangerous concept in our time. It's loose and it's irresponsible. The left project is all about equipping ourselves theoretically and moving slowly and strategically in various arenas of struggle.*[38]

Fortunately the workers, students and soldiers who launched an insurrection to destroy the Bophuthatswana 'homeland' before the 1994 elections, gain the right to vote and show a glimpse of what a revolution could be like, had a rather different vision of 'arenas of struggle'. Communist Party central committee member Jeremy Cronin admits, 'Although the October Revolution hasn't worked out as expected at all and reassessment is required, maybe there are other trajectories from October 1917 which we are still living out here in South Africa'.[39]

Alex insists throughout on the need for a socialist party, for evolution and for no reliance on other class forces. He bases himself on the tradition of 'militant abstentionism' by which he means workers' history of 'combining the development of strong workplace organisation with a refusal to take any responsibility for the management of South African capitalism'.[40]

One of those Alex interviews is Neville Alexander, a well known Marxist intellectual who has produced interesting work. After his release from imprisonment on Robben Island he wrote *One Azania, One Nation*[41] on the national question and followed it with *Sow the Wind*[42] and other works including *The Language Question in South Africa*.[43] His latest collection, *Some are more Equal than Others*[44] sums up his and the Workers Organisation for Socialist Action's position on current questions. These are undoubtedly interesting books which are well worth reading. They are an attempt to find an alternative to the ANC's version of national liberation and the Communist Party's vision of socialism. But they are marked by a failure to come to terms with what sort of society the Soviet Union was and the relationship between reform and revolution. Alexander virtually ignores the importance of the ANC's defeat of the National Party at the polls and has consistently argued that a military takeover is likely in the near future.

How can you find out about the struggles that are happening today and the contemporary debates on the left? *Socialist Worker* and *Socialist Review* carry frequent reports and analysis. *The Socialist*, the monthly paper of the International Socialists South Africa, the SWP's sister organisation, is also very useful. *The Weekly Mail* is a left liberal South African paper available on subscription. *Work in Progress* is a monthly magazine which carries lots of useful information about the trade union battles and the arguments about how to relate to the ANC and what sort of socialist party is necessary. *South African Labour Bulletin* is also good and gives a real flavour of the people and the discussions in trade union circles.

Finally, to jump media for a second, there are several films which are very good at conveying something of the reality of life under apartheid and the courage of those who battled against it. *Mapantsula* gives at least a glimpse of how life is really lived in the townships like Soweto and how the atmosphere of struggle drew in even the most unlikely people. There are heroes and villains, the cowards and the courageous, political people and people who care only about the next bottle of beer—and the film is all the more realistic for it. *A Life Apart* looks at the life and struggles of Ruth First, a Communist Party member. It is about both the viciousness of apartheid and also the nature of political commitment.

Cry Freedom is about the life and death of Steve Biko. Some critics accused the film of overplaying the role of Biko's white friend Donald Woods. But that is to miss the genuine power of the film and its total condemnation of apartheid. I was convinced of its strength during an afternoon showing in a near deserted cinema in Llanelli. Two 70 year olds who had originally entered to shelter from the rain were mesmerised almost from the first frames. At the end one turned to the other and said, 'Look at what they did to that poor black man. It's no wonder they fight, is it? I do hope they manage to win one day and get their own back.' Well, they did—and we all won with them. And they are still fighting.

Notes

1. D MacShane, *Power!* (Nottingham, 1984).
2. S Friedman, *Building Tomorrow Today* (Johannesburg, 1987).
3. J Baskin, *Striking Back, a history of COSATU* (Verso, 1991).
4. S Friedman, op cit, p6.
5. Ibid, p156.
6. J Baskin, op cit, p44.
7. Ibid, p54.
8. Ibid, p465.
9. T Cliff and D Gluckstein, *Marxism and the Trade Union Struggle* (Bookmarks, 1986).
10. International Defence and Aid Fund, *Apartheid: the Facts* (London, 1990).
11. R Ormond, *The Apartheid Handbook* (Penguin, 1988).
12. J J and R E Simons, *Class and Colour in South Africa 1850-1950* (Harmondsworth, 1969).
13. E Le Roux, *Time Longer than Rope* (Madison, 1972).
14. T Lodge, *Black Politics in South Africa since 1945* (Longman, 1983).
15. J J Simons and R E Simons op cit, p621.
16. T Lodge, op cit, p174.
17. B Hirson, *Yours for the Union* (Zed, 1989).
18. B Hirson, *Year of Fire, Year of Ash* (London, 1979).
19. D Herbstein, *White Man We Want to Talk to You* (Harmondsworth, 1978).
20. B Hirson, op cit, 1979, p7.
21. D Herbstein, op cit, p229.
22. M Williams, 'An analysis of South African capitalism', in *Bulletin of the Conference of Socialist Economists*, 4:1.
23. M Legassick, 'Capital Accumulation and Violence' in *Economy and Society* 3:3.
24. J Guy, *The Destruction of the Zulu Kingdom* (London, 1979).
25. D Innes, *Anglo American and the Rise of South African Capitalism* (Johannesburg, 1982).
26. V Allen, *The History of Black Mineworkers in South Africa*, vol 1 (The Moor Press, 1992).
27. N Mostert, *Frontiers* (Pimlico, 1993).
28. E Webster, *Cast in a Racial Mould* (Johannesburg, 1985).
29. L Flynn, *Studded with Diamonds and Paved with Gold* (Bloomsbury, 1992).
30. L Vail, *The Creation of Tribalism in South Africa* (London, 1989).
31. J Baskin op cit, p342.
32. Mzala, *Gatsha Buthelezi, Chief with a Double Agenda* (London, 1988).

33 S Phillips, 'The South African Communist Party and the South African Working Class', in *International Socialism* 51.
34 A Callinicos, *South Africa Between Reform and Revolution* (Bookmarks, 1988).
35 Ibid, p193.
36 Ibid, p194.
37 A Callinicos, *Between Apartheid and Capitalism* (Bookmarks, 1992).
38 Ibid, p59.
39 Ibid, p78.
40 Ibid, p152.
41 No Sizwe (N Alexander), *One Azania, One Nation* (London, 1979).
42 N Alexander, *Sow the Wind* (Johannesburg, 1985).
43 N Alexander, *The Language Question in South Africa* (Cape Town, 1989).
44 N Alexander, *Some are More Equal than Others* (Cape Town, 1993).

The Socialist Workers Party is one of an international grouping of socialist organisations:

AUSTRALIA: International Socialists, GPO Box 1473N, Melbourne 3001
BELGIUM: Socialisme International, Rue Lovinfosse 60, 4030 Grivengée, Belgium
BRITAIN: Socialist Workers Party, PO Box 82, London E3
CANADA: International Socialists, PO Box 339, Station E, Toronto, Ontario M6H 4E3
CYPRUS: Ergatiki Demokratia, PO Box 7280, Nicosia
DENMARK: Internationale Socialister, Postboks 642, 2200 København N, Denmark
FRANCE: Socialisme International, BP 189, 75926 Paris Cedex 19
GERMANY: Sozialistische Arbeitergruppe, Postfach 180367, 60084 Frankfurt 1
GREECE: Organosi Sosialisliki Epanastasi, c/o Workers Solidarity, PO Box 8161, Athens 100 10, Greece
HOLLAND: International Socialists, PO Box 9720, 3506 GR Utrecht
IRELAND: Socialist Workers Movement, PO Box 1648, Dublin 8
NEW ZEALAND:
International Socialist Organization, PO Box 6157, Dunedin, New Zealand
NORWAY: Internasjonale Socialisterr, Postboks 5370, Majorstua, 0304 Oslo 3
POLAND: Solidarność Socjalistyczna, PO Box 12, 01-900 Warszawa 118
SOUTH AFRICA:
International Socialists of South Africa, PO Box 18530, Hillbrow 2038, Johannesberg
UNITED STATES:
International Socialist Organization, PO Box 16085, Chicago, Illinois 60616
ZIMBABWE:
International Socialists, PO Box 6758, Harare

The following issues of *International Socialism* (second series) are available price £3.00 (including postage) from IS Journal, PO Box 82, London E3 3LH.

International Socialism 2:63 Summer 1994
Alex Callinicos: Crisis and class struggle in Europe today ★ Duncan Blackie: The United Nations and the politics of imperialism ★ Brian Manning: The English Revolution and the transition from feudalism to capitalism ★ Lee Sustar: The roots of multi-racial labour unity in the United States ★ Peter Linebaugh: Days of villainy: a reply to two critics ★ Dave Sherry: Trotsky's last, greatest struggle ★ Peter Morgan: Geronimo and the end of the Indian wars ★ Dave Beecham: Ignazio Silone and *Fontamara* ★ Chris Bambery: Bookwatch: understanding fascism ★

International Socialism 2:62 Spring 1994
Sharon Smith: Mistaken identity—or can identity politics liberate the oppressed? ★ Iain Ferguson: Containing the crisis—crime and the Tories ★ John Newsinger: Orwell and the Spanish Revolution ★ Chris Harman: Change at the first millenium ★ Adrian Budd: Nation and empire—Labour's foreign policy 1945-51 ★ Gareth Jenkins: Novel questions ★ Judy Cox: Blake's revolution ★ Derek Howl: Bookwatch: the Russian Revolution ★

International Socialism 2:61 Winter 1994
Lindsey German: Before the flood? ★ John Molyneux: The 'politically correct' controversy ★ David McNally: E P Thompson—class struggle and historical materialism ★ Charlie Hore: Jazz—a people's music ★ Donny Gluckstein: Revolution and the challenge of labour ★ Charlie Kimber: Bookwatch: the Labour Party in decline ★

International Socialism 2:60 Autumn 1993
Chris Bambery: Euro-fascism: the lessons of the past and present tasks ★ Chris Harman: Where is capitalism going? (part 2) ★ Mike Gonzalez: Chile and the struggle for workers' power ★ Phil Marshall: Bookwatch: Islamic activism in the Middle East ★

International Socialism 2:59 Summer 1993
Ann Rogers: Back to the workhouse ★ Kevin Corr and Andy Brown: The labour aristocracy and the roots of reformism ★ Brian Manning: God, Hill and Marx ★ Henry Maitles: Cutting the wire: a criticial appraisal of Primo Levi ★ Hazel Croft: Bookwatch: women and work ★

International Socialism 2:58 Spring 1993
Chris Harman: Where is capitalism going? (part one) ★ Ruth Brown and Peter Morgan: Politics and the class struggle today: a roundtable discussion ★ Richard Greeman: The return of Comrade Tulayev: Victor Serge and the tragic vision of Stalinism ★ Norah Carlin: A new English revolution ★ John Charlton: Building a new world ★ Colin Barker: A reply to Dave McNally ★

International Socialism 2:57 Winter 1992
Lindsey German: Can there be a revolution in Britain? ★ Mike Haynes: Columbus, the Americas and the rise of capitalism ★ Mike Gonzalez: The myths of Columbus: a history ★ Paul Foot: Poetry and revolution ★ Alex Callinicos: Rhetoric which cannot conceal a bankrupt theory: a reply to Ernest Mandel ★ Charlie Kimber: Capitalism, cruelty and conquest ★ David McNulty: Comments on Colin Barker's review of Thompson's *Customs in Common* ★

International Socialism 2:56 Autumn 1992
Chris Harman: The Return of the National Question ★ Dave Treece: Why the Earth Summit failed ★ Mike Gonzalez: Can Castro survive? ★ Lee Humber and John Rees: The good old cause—an interview with Christopher Hill ★ Ernest Mandel: The Impasse of Schematic Dogmatism ★

International Socialism 2:55 Summer 1992
Alex Callinicos: Race and class ★ Lee Sustar: Racism and class struggle in the American Civil War era ★ Lindsey German and Peter Morgan: Prospects for socialists—an interview with Tony Cliff ★ Robert Service: Did Lenin lead to Stalin? ★ Samuel Farber: In defence of democratic revolutionary socialism ★ David Finkel: Defending 'October' or sectarian dogmatism? ★ Robin Blackburn: Reply to John Rees ★ John Rees: Dedicated followers of fashion ★ Colin Barker: In praise of custom ★ Sheila McGregor: Revolutionary witness ★

International Socialism 2:54 Spring 1992
Sharon Smith: Twilight of the American dream ★ Mike Haynes: Class and crisis—the transition in eastern Europe ★ Costas Kossis: A miracle without end? Japanese capitalism and the world economy ★ Alex Callinicos: Capitalism and the state system: A reply to Nigel Harris ★ Steven

Rose: Do animals have rights? ★ John Charlton: Crime and class in the 18th century ★ John Rees: Revolution, reform and working class culture ★ Chris Harman: Blood simple ★

International Socialism 2:52 Autumn 1991
John Rees: In defence of October ★ Ian Taylor and Julie Waterson: The political crisis in Greece—an interview with Maria Styllou and Panos Garganas ★ Paul McGarr: Mozart, overture to revolution ★ Lee Humber: Class, class consciousness and the English Revolution ★ Derek Howl: The legacy of Hal Draper ★

International Socialism 2:51 Summer 1991
Chris Harman: The state and capitalism today ★ Alex Callinicos: The end of nationalism? ★ Sharon Smith: Feminists for a strong state? ★ Colin Sparks and Sue Cockerill: Goodbye to the Swedish miracle ★ Simon Phillips: The South African Communist Party and the South African working class ★ John Brown: Class conflict and the crisis of feudalism ★

International Socialism 2:49 Winter 1990
Chris Bambery: The decline of the Western Communist Parties ★ Ernest Mandel: A theory which has not withstood the test of time ★ Chris Harman: Criticism which does not withstand the test of logic ★ Derek Howl: The law of value in the USSR ★ Terry Eagleton: Shakespeare and the class struggle ★ Lionel Sims: Rape and pre-state societies ★ Sheila McGregor: A reply to Lionel Sims ★

International Socialism 2:48 Autumn 1990
Lindsey German: The last days of Thatcher ★ John Rees: The new imperialism ★ Neil Davidson and Donny Gluckstein: Nationalism and the class struggle in Scotland ★ Paul McGarr: Order out of chaos ★

International Socialism 2:46 Winter 1989
Chris Harman: The storm breaks ★ Alex Callinicos: Can South Africa be reformed? ★ John Saville: Britain, the Marshall Plan and the Cold War ★ Sue Clegg: Against the stream ★ John Rees: The rising bourgeoisie ★

International Socialism 2:45 Autumn 1989
Sheila McGregor: Rape, pornography and capitalism ★ Boris Kagarlitsky: The market instead of democracy? ★ Chris Harman: From feudalism to capitalism ★ plus Mike Gonzalez and Sabby Sagall discuss Central America ★

International Socialism 2:44 Autumn 1989
Charlie Hore: China: Tiananmen Square and after ★ Sue Clegg: Thatcher and the welfare state ★ John Molyneux: *Animal Farm* revisited ★ David Finkel: After Arias, is the revolution over? ★ John Rose: Jews in Poland ★

International Socialism 2:43 Summer 1989 (Reprint—special price £4.50)
Marxism and the Great French Revolution by Paul McGarr and Alex Callinicos

International Socialism 2:42 Spring 1989
Chris Harman: The myth of market socialism ★ Norah Carlin: Roots of gay oppression ★ Duncan Blackie: Revolution in science ★ International Socialism Index ★

International Socialism 2:41 Winter 1988
Polish socialists speak out: Solidarity at the Crossroads ★ Mike Haynes: Nightmares of the market ★ Jack Robertson: Socialists and the unions ★ Andy Strouthous: Are the unions in decline? ★ Richard Bradbury: What is Post-Structuralism? ★ Colin Sparks: George Bernard Shaw ★

International Socialism 2:39 Summer 1988
Chris Harman and Andy Zebrowski: Glasnost, before the storm ★ Chanie Rosenberg: Labour and the fight against fascism ★ Mike Gonzalez: Central America after the Peace Plan ★ Ian Birchall: Raymond Williams ★ Alex Callinicos: Reply to John Rees ★

International Socialism 2:35 Summer 1987
Pete Green: Capitalism and the Thatcher years ★ Alex Callinicos: Imperialism, capitalism and the state today ★ Ian Birchall: Five years of *New Socialist* ★ Callinicos and Wood debate 'Looking for alternatives to reformism' ★ David Widgery replies on 'Beating Time' ★

International Socialism 2:31 Winter 1985
Alex Callinicos: Marxism and revolution in South Africa ★ Tony Cliff: The tragedy of A J Cook ★ Nigel Harris: What to do with London? The strategies of the GLC ★

International Socialism 2:30 Autumn 1985
Gareth Jenkins: Where is the Labour Party heading? ★ David McNally: Debt, inflation and the rate of profit ★ Ian Birchall: The terminal crisis in the British Communist Party ★ replies on Women's oppression and *Marxism Today* ★

International Socialism 2:29 Summer 1985
Special issue on the class struggle and the left in the aftermath of the miners' defeat ★ Tony Cliff: Patterns of mass strike ★ Chris Harman: 1984 and the shape of things to come ★ Alex Callinicos: The politics of *Marxism Today* ★

International Socialism 2:26 Spring 1985
Pete Green: Contradictions of the American boom ★ Colin Sparks: Labour and imperialism ★ Chris Bambery: Marx and Engels and the unions ★ Sue Cockerill: The municipal road to socialism ★ Norah Carlin: Is the family part of the superstructure? ★ Kieran Allen: James Connolly and the 1916 rebellion ★

International Socialism 2:25 Autumn 1984
John Newsinger: Jim Larkin, Syndicalism and the 1913 Dublin Lockout ★ Pete Binns: Revolution and state capitalism in the Third World ★ Colin Sparks: Towards a police state? ★ Dave Lyddon: Demystifying the downturn ★ John Molyneux: Do working class men benefit from women's oppression? ★

International Socialism 2:18 Winter 1983
Donny Gluckstein: Workers' councils in Western Europe ★ Jane Ure Smith: The early Communist press in Britain ★ John Newsinger: The Bolivian Revolution ★ Andy Durgan: Largo Caballero and Spanish socialism ★ M Barker and A Beezer: Scarman and the language of racism ★

International Socialism 2:14 Winter 1981
Chris Harman: The riots of 1981 ★ Dave Beecham: Class struggle under the Tories ★ Tony Cliff: Alexandra Kollontai ★ L James and A Paczuska: Socialism needs feminism ★ reply to Cliff on Zetkin ★ Feminists In the labour movement ★

International Socialism 2:13 Summer 1981
Chris Harman: The crisis last time ★ Tony Cliff: Clara Zetkin ★ Ian Birchall: Left Social Democracy In the French Popular Front ★ Pete Green: Alternative Economic Strategy ★ Tim Potter: The death of Eurocommunism ★

International Socialism 2:12 Spring 1981
Jonathan Neale: The Afghan tragedy ★ Lindsey German: Theories of patriarchy ★ Ray Challinor: McDouall and Physical Force Chartism ★ S Freeman & B Vandesteeg: Unproductive labour ★ Alex Callinicos: Wage labour and capitalism ★ Italian fascism ★ Marx's theory of history ★ Cabral ★

International Socialism 2:11 Winter 1980
Rip Bulkeley et al: CND In the 50s ★ Marx's theory of crisis and its critics ★ Andy Durgan: Revolutionary anarchism in Spain ★ Alex Callinicos: Politics or abstract thought ★ Fascism in Europe ★ Marilyn Monroe ★